T0301592

The State and Transnational Corporations

NEW HORIZONS IN INTERNATIONAL BUSINESS

General Editor: Peter J. Buckley
Professor of Managerial Economics
Management Centre, University of Bradford

This series is aimed at the frontiers of international business research. Each volume tackles key problem areas in international political economy. The study of international business is important not least because it gives researchers the opportunity to innovate in theory, technique, empirical investigation and interpretation. The area is fruitful for interdisciplinary and comparative research. This series is established as a central forum for the presentation of new ideas in international business.

New Directions in International Business
Research Priorities for the 1990s
Edited by Peter J. Buckley

Europe and the Multinationals
Issues and Responses for the 1990s
Edited by Stephen Young and James Hamill

Multinational Enterprises in the World Economy
Essays in Honour of John Dunning
Edited by Peter J. Buckley and Mark Casson

Multinational Investment in Modern Europe
Strategic Interaction in the Integrated Community
Edited by John Cantwell

The Growth and Evolution of Multinational Enterprise
Patterns of Geographical and Industrial Diversification
R.D. Pearce

Multinational Enterprise and Public Policy
A Study of the Industrial Countries
A.E. Safarian

Transnational Corporations in Southeast Asia
An Institutional Approach to Industrial Organization
Hans Jansson

European Integration and Competitiveness
Acquisitions and Alliances in Industry
Edited by Frédérique Sachwald

The State and Transnational Corporations
A Nework Approach to Industrial Policy in India
Hans Jansson, M. Saqib and D. Deo Sharma

Competitive and Cooperative Macromanagement
The Challenges of Structural Interdependence
Gavin Boyd

The State and Transnational Corporations

A Network Approach to Industrial Policy in India

Hans Jansson
Professor
Institute of Economic Research
School of Economics and Management
Lund University
Sweden

M. Saqib
ICRIER; New Delhi
India

D. Deo Sharma
Dr.
University of Uppsala
Sweden

Edward Elgar
Aldershot, UK • Brookfield, US

© Hans Jansson, M. Saqib and D. Deo Sharma 1995

All rights reserved. No part of this publication may be reproduced, stored in a retrieval system or transmitted in any form or by any means, electronic, mechanical or photo-copying, recording, or otherwise without the prior permission of the publisher.

Published by
Edward Elgar Publishing Limited
Gower House
Croft Road
Aldershot
Hants GU11 3HR
UK

Edward Elgar Publishing Company
Old Post Road
Brookfield
Vermont 05036
US

British Library Cataloguing in Publication Data
Jansson, Hans
    State and Transnational Corporations: Network Approach to
    Industrial Policy in India. – (New Horizons in International
    Business Series)
    I. Title II. Series
    338.88854

Library of Congress Cataloguing in Publication Data
Jansson, Hans.
    The state and transnational corporations: a network approach to
industrial policy in India / Hans Jansson, M. Saqib, D. Deo Sharma.
    264p. 23cm. — (New horizons in international business)
        1. International business enterprises—Government policy—India.
    2. Industrial policy—India. I. Saqib, M., 1956– . II. Sharma, Dharma Deo.
    III. Title. IV. Series.
    HD2900.J36   1995
    338.8'8854—dc20   95–5519
                                                              CIP

ISBN 1 85898 255 3

Printed and bound in Great Britain by
Hartnolls Limited, Bodmin, Cornwall

Contents

List of Figures

List of Tables

Preface

Within recent years many excellent treatises on transnational corporations (TNCs), their benefits and costs, and their international competitiveness have appeared. Questions of the strategies and structures of TNCs in different countries and environments have been discussed. Little attention has been directed, however, at the important topic of the strategic interaction between TNCs and the governments of the host countries. In courses in international business we have taught, as well as in research we have carried out on TNCs, we have become increasingly conscious of this lack. A prevailing view in the literature has been that TNCs tend to adopt their strategies towards governments of less industrialized countries without interacting with these governments or with other political bodies appreciably. Similarly, TNCs are often regarded as being economic entities alone, their political behaviour being overlooked. In addition, the occurrence of conflicts between TNCs and the governments in question is frequently emphasized, their relationship being viewed as that of a zero-sum game in which the parties are continually on a collision course.

Our research on TNCs pointed to the fallacies of the literature in these respects and to the relationship between TNCs and national governments being largely one of a non-zero-sum game. We noted frequent interaction on a wide variety of issues such as those of economic development, taxation, research and development, exports and imports, and the formulation and implementation of industrial policy. We found neither the national governments nor the TNCs to be monolithic bodies that determine and implement policies in an ivory tower. Indeed, interaction between them, with the exchange of views and information as well as consideration of the needs and interests of the other party, would seem to be necessary for the formulation and implementation of governmental policy in this area to be successful.

This book concerns the mutual benefits to TNCs and to the host governments of close network-type relationships between the two being established. An increasing number of governments of developing countries are attracting direct foreign investment in order to gain access to the technology, know-how and management skills of TNCs. This has led to important changes in the strategic environment of TNCs, a matter likewise dealt with here.

The book provides an account of our research on relationships between TNCs and the host governments. It also covers a wide variety of interrelated topics of both a strategic and an operational nature, such as the reasons TNCs have for seeking to interact closely with the host governments, which persons in the management of a TNC are most likely to communicate directly or indirectly with governmental decision makers, how frequently this occurs, and what media are employed. The manner in which managers from the head offices of TNCs interact with foreign subsidiaries and with the governments involved is also considered. Questions of how the local subsidiaries are integrated into the overall group, partly in terms of strategy towards the local government and partly in terms of business operations, are likewise dealt with. In addition, the political and administrative organization of governmental networks is examined. To increase the value of the book for managers, strategic implications for TNCs of the research we have carried out are taken up.

The research involved was conducted in India between 1986 and 1989. Its immediate aim was to study how the liberalization of industrial policy there that started in 1984/85 influenced strategies of TNCs towards the Indian government. The background to these matters is described in a separate appendix on the liberalization of the Indian economy.

The book presents, among other things, the main account to date of an international research project involving researchers from the Department of Business Administration of Lund University, Sweden, the Department of Business Studies of Uppsala University, Sweden, and the Indian Council for Research on International Economic Relations located in India (ICRIER). The major researchers have been Professor Hans Jansson of Lund University, Professor Deo Sharma of Uppsala University, and M.Sc. M. Saqib of ICRIER.

Looking back at how the book evolved, we note the luck and the pleasure we had in being able to work closely with practitioners, who in many different ways have contributed to the final product. Of great importance has also been the kind cooperation of the corporations and government studied. We are greatly indebted to the persons we interviewed at affiliates of Swedish and German transnational corporations and at various ministries in India, who shared their knowledge and experience with us during the two main rounds of interviews we conducted during the period 1986 to 1990. We wish to express our deep gratitude to these persons, without whose both direct and indirect help the completion of the study reported would not have been possible, as well as to the organizations to which they belonged. Due to an agreement of confidentiality made with the persons interviewed, neither the executives involved nor their companies, unfortunately, can be named. The authors benefited much from contacts with various universities and research institutions, particular the 'home' ones mentioned above. Our thanks to all of you!

We also wish to thank the Swedish Agency for Research Co-operation with Developing Countries (SAREC) that so generously financed the entire research project on which the book is based. We gratefully acknowledge as well a grant from the Foundation for the Advancement of Economic Research of Lund University (Stiftelsen för främjande av ekonomisk forskning), which made finalization of the book possible. We express our sincere appreciation also to Maj-Britt Johansson at the Department of Business Administration of Lund University for her very professional typing and editing of the book.

Hans Jansson
M. Saqib
D. Deo Sharma
March 1995

1. Strategies in Government–TNC Networks

The flow of financial resources in the shape of either foreign direct investment (FDI) or portfolio investment is a growing feature of international economic exchange, transformation and integration. During the last few decades these flows have accelerated due to increasing liberalization and privatization throughout the world. During the 1980s the lion's share of FDI went to the US and Britain. The latest figures show that for 1989 and 1990 the inflow of FDI to the developed countries was US $152 billion, while it was US $32 billion to the developing countries. However, this pattern has been reversed in the 1990s and the stock of FDI in the developing nations has started to move up, while the inflow to the developed countries has decreased. Thus, in all these years the share of the developing countries has been relatively small, but important. The annual average of FDI to developing nations declined from US $13 billion in 1978-1982 to less that US $10 billion in 1983-86 (Ellis, 1990, p. 5). In 1967 developing nations as a whole accounted for around 31% of the total FDI in the world. This declined to around 23% in 1986 (US Department of Commerce, 1988). These figures, however, hide significant differences between nations. In China and India, for example, FDI is responsible for a relatively small proportion of invested capital. In Singapore, on the other hand, over 60% of the invested capital in the manufacturing sector comes from transnational corporations (TNCs). The stock of FDI among the developing countries is thus unevenly distributed. Indeed, there is a concentration of these flows to a limited number of countries, with the lion's share going to the economies in Asia. For example, between 1986-1990 the developing countries on an average received US $26 billion of FDI a year. Of this sum, US $14 billion went to the countries in East Asia. Nations in Latin America received US $9 billion and those in Africa a mere US $3 billion (Economist, 1992).

The increase in the inflow of FDI to the developing countries since 1990 is on account of several factors. One reason seems to be the increasing realization on the part of the governments of these nations

1

that relationships with TNCs are vital and beneficial to economic progress and that TNCs own and control huge amounts of valuable financial, commercial and technical resources. A growing emphasis on liberalization and privatization has contributed to this trend.

As a consequence of this realization, several countries have liberalised their foreign investment laws to welcome FDI. Indeed, this is a worldwide trend, visible in developed as well as developing countries. Even the newly re-born republics in Eastern Europe have realized the value of FDI and introduced liberalized laws. In the last 2-3 years alone, altogether 34 nations, rich or poor, have liberalized their FDI laws (World Investment Report, 1993). All in all, 82 big changes have been introduced, 80 of these rules have made FDI less restrictive. Twenty one countries, among them India and Egypt, liberalized their ownership rules in 1991. Another 16 countries substantially loosened their approval procedures. Still others offered more, or newer incentives to attract FDI. In 1992 several other bold changes were introduced. India, for example, opened up its stock market to foreign investment, as well as allowed TNCs to operate in a number of new industrial fields; for instance, in the energy sector. Indonesia started its reform process much earlier. Legislation was introduced to allow the inflow of foreign capital in its banking and financial sectors. Similarly, many other nations eased their rules concerning transfer of profits and/or capital. Even communist countries, like China and Vietnam liberalized their economic policies and procedures to attract FDI. There are rumours that even North Korea is planning policy measures to attract TNCs.

Still the quantum of foreign private capital and FDI by TNCs to less developed countries (LDCs) has remained below expected levels. Why? One reason seems to be that national governments are unable to implement their liberalized policies towards FDI and TNCs (Jansson & Sharma, 1993).

HOST GOVERNMENT–TNC INTERACTION

The figures above symbolise a growing integration and interdependence between respective nation states and the TNCs. Nation states are attracted by the TNCs as they need the financial, technical and commercial resources controlled by TNCs to improve their economy and national welfare.

There are three important reasons why nation states welcome

TNCs. First, industrial growth demands investment of capital resources either from domestic or international sources. Not all nations
are in a position to procure from the domestic market all the financial
resources they need to undertake industrialization. TNCs as a group
command vast sums of financial resources which can be utilized for
productive purposes. The total stock of FDI was estimated to be over
US $1 trillion in 1988. For developing countries a fraction of these
vast sums make a huge difference and increase in their capital stock.
The stock of FDI in countries such as China has risen steadily, which
may be offing in countries like Indonesia and India. In China the
annual inflow of FDI in 1991 was US $4.8 billion. In India, the net
inflow of FDI in 1992 jumped to around one billion dollars, a significant improvement from previous years.

Secondly, TNCs command vast commercial resources, distribution
channels and experience. They own or control subsidiaries throughout
the world, which can be used to export products and services. In 1991
there were more than 35,000 TNCs, with over 150,000 foreign affiliates (IMF Survey, 1992, p. 228). The above figures, however,
understate the resources controlled by TNCs. In addition to wholly or
majority owned subsidiaries, these TNCs exert influence on a much
larger share of commercial resources through different types of alliances and cooperative agreements such as licensing, management
contracts franchising and sub-contracting. Indeed, in some industries
cooperative means constitute the dominant mechanism to operate
abroad, for example in the hotel industry. This is all the more important, as a growing proportion of international trade is internalized
within TNCs. Goods and services are traded within the same concern
or firm. The total volume of this trade is estimated to be 25% of the
total world trade (ibid., p. 229).

A recent study on Swedish industry shows that in 1991, 46% of the
Swedish exports to countries within the European Union went
through the subsidiaries of Swedish firms (DI, 1992, 30 Sept., p. 8).
Four years ago the corresponding figure was merely 30%. The same
study shows a similar trend for imports into Sweden. This is especially true for manufactured products. Thus, nations that want to
increase exports increasingly come in contact with TNCs. A
consequence of this is that nation states, especially those favouring
export-oriented growth, are in no position to unilaterally impose
conditions on TNCs. Their governments must prudently adopt policies to make possible a workable relationship with TNCs. Thus, for
nations interested in achieving economic integration with the rest of

the world economy, a link with TNCs is a necessity. This can be the fastest route to international integration.

Thirdly, TNCs own a vast pool of technical resources. These firms invest huge sums of money in technical development, which can be used to improve productivity and product quality. These resources are transferred to other countries, including developing countries, in a variety of ways. One is the traditional FDI consisting of a package of financial, administrative, marketing, and technical resources. In several other cases all or parts of these resources are transferred abroad through alternative mechanisms such as pure sales of technology, management contracts or other alternative routes. Thus, the total value of commercial resources that TNCs control and can contribute to a country is significantly more than the one depicted by the published figures.

Lastly, an efficient and modern industrial base is built only when domestic firms are exposed to the full force of competition in the national and international market (Porter, 1990; Stopford & Strange, 1991, p. 12). Competition in the domestic market is a pre-condition for the effectiveness of domestic firms. In this respect, TNCs play an important role by providing competition to domestic firms, thereby forcing them to be outward-looking. TNCs also further technical progress by both introducing new and efficient technology directly or indirectly, by imposing quality standards and demands on their suppliers. A supplier relationship with TNCs exposes local firms to the international environment, facilitates learning and achieving quality standards applied in the international market.

TNCs in their turn, are also dependent on host governments. Firstly, governments supply industrial infrastructure like electricity and water, as well as guarantee essential law and order. Secondly, where the availability of a particular raw material is essential for the survival of a TNC, a host government with access to or control over a critical resource such as oil would certainly hold the advantage. TNCs in that case must interact with such host governments and accommodate their wishes. Similarly, some countries have a large population and a vast attractive domestic market, over which national governments exercise a certain degree of control.

The economic growth rate in a number of developing countries is higher than those in industrialized countries, which are the traditional markets for TNCs. For example, in Asia with a huge population of three billion people the economic growth rate is twice as high as in the industrialized nations. TNCs cannot overlook these markets.

CHANGING ATTITUDES

The attitudes and the policies of national governments towards TNCs have gradually changed. During the 1950s, the 1960s and the 1970s many national governments perceived TNCs as a threat to their decision making power and sovereignty. Certain nation states even tried to keep TNCs away from the domestic market.

Since the mid-1970s, but more especially from the beginning of the 1980s, there has been a radical departure from such more or less hostile attitudes to either friendliness or accommodation. This radical about-turn is not entirely due to a change of heart and feelings with regard to the TNCs. Occasionally these changes have been enforced or imposed upon the nation states by international or multinational agencies such as the World Bank. Nevertheless, it is fair to state that relationships between the nation states and TNCs have been radically transformed, as a consequence of which the share of FDI in the gross domestic capital formation has risen.

Three factors can be identified behind these changes. First, TNCs have become better citizens of the host countries by being more willing to identify themselves with the needs and feelings of these nations (Ellis, 1990, p. 3). National and international agencies have made efforts to codify the rules of conduct and behaviour for TNCs in host countries (Kline, 1985, pp. 76-85). Although the rules are not binding on TNCs and are more in the nature of recommendations, they have influenced the behaviour of TNCs. The increasing tendency to accommodate the wishes of the nation states has resulted in co-operative and other forms of non-financial international alliances.

Second, developing countries and TNCs have a better understanding of each other. Nation states have developed or acquired skills to deal with TNCs resulting, inter alia, in a more confident outlook. Some countries have become more powerful as their economies have grown and they have started to produce a much wider spectrum of products and services.

Third, for many countries partnerships with TNCs have proved to be more beneficial than earlier thought. The contribution of financial, technical and economical skills, lacking in the host countries, is highly valued. In countries such as Brazil and Mexico this situation has arisen due to the debt problem, the governments have had difficulties in raising hard currency loans from the international market. It has been realized that FDI can act as a catalyst to economic development by earning hard currency and developing or broadening the export base. For TNCs this has provided a better opportunity as well as flexibility to allocate resources to improve their competitive advantage.

These are many examples where failure of nationalization and government takeovers resulted in the supply of massive subsidies. On the other hand, countries like Singapore, which welcomed FDI and offered incentives improved their economic lot and achieved spectacular growth. The evidence of changing attitudes is seen in the growing emphasis on and demand for privatization of state-owned enterprises. From Mexico, Brazil, and Argentina in Latin-America to Pakistan, India, Sri Lanka, and Indonesia in Asia, the demand for privatizing state-owned enterprises is being increasingly raised. As a result within a limited period of two years Pakistan sold off 57 state owned enterprises and India opened the energy sector to FDI (Far Eastern Economic Review, 1992). A similar demand is evident in many African nations.

It is therefore seen that fundamental economic and political changes in the international arena have in recent years led a number of nations to modify their policies towards FDI and TNCs. These changes have concurrently implied more active contacts and interaction between TNCs and host country governments.

THE POLITICAL BEHAVIOUR OF TNCs

The above discussion illustrates that TNCs and governments are necessarily involved in an interactive relationship for TNCs to act politically. A good citizenship can be achieved by adapting to various demands of local environment, chiefly government. But these demands can also be influenced by TNCs. The political behaviour of TNCs is complex, given the complexity of the means or strategies available to accommodate or influence governments – liaisoning, lobbying, both legal and otherwise. There is a large grey area between the official enunciation of public policies and actual practice. In addition it is not clear what is meant by being a good 'citizen' or being legitimate in the eyes of government. This affords TNCs considerable scope for political behaviour. This behaviour is founded upon the relationships established between TNCs and the government ministries, local bodies and decision makers. The manner in which these relationships are established and the strength of the relationships varies, and is partially dependent on the means used by TNCs. This also contradicts the common assumption that governments are exogenous actors in the field of business. In fact governments are active players in the business area, employing perhaps, different means. Hence in dealing with political entities such as governments, TNCs cannot rely merely on economic means but must also employ non-economic means. Indeed, in a number of situations the reliance on non-economic or political means is preponderant. This is different from the dominant approach to explain the behaviour of TNCs as stated by Boddewyn (1988, p. 344).

> Still, they contrast with the economic and managerial paradigms used in most analysis of Multinational Enterprises (MNEs), which tends to take narrow and more autonomous views of the economic system and of the organisations and individuals that participate in its functioning.

Thus, economics and politics are interdependent and interactive. This means that economic criteria are not the sole or not even the most dominant criteria in decision making. In addition, economic rivalry is not the only type of competition, since TNCs also compete for political influence and government contacts. The political behaviour of TNCs is directed towards a number of non-economic agents in society such as government of the host country, local community groups, and private interest groups.

We are concerned here with the strategies employed by TNCs in dealing with the government of the host country. Governments are often the chief decision makers and readily distribute 'favours'. In exchange, the benefactors may seek favours for themselves or their group. There is every reason to believe that TNCs would try to 'internalize' or even 'monopolise' governments. Thus, through interaction with decision makers in the government, TNCs can, and do, create entry barriers for competitors, making these processes an endogenous part of their strategic behaviour. The critical issue, therefore, is how this is achieved and how open or covert are these political processes.

A number of significant questions arise:

What determines the political behaviour of TNCs? On which occasions and how do TNCs adapt to or influence governments? What are the main objectives. Which strategic issues are involved? What strategies do TNCs employ in order to achieve a successful and fruitful interaction with host country governments? What kind of exchange relationship exists between TNCs and host governments? How do TNCs manage their relationship with host country governments? At what organisational levels within TNCs do their personnel interact with the host governments and their decision makers? How is the political behaviour controlled or organized by the TNCs? Is it controlled centrally from the head office of the TNCs or is it decentralized?

STRATEGIES TOWARDS GOVERNMENTS

As will be discussed in the following pages there is a paucity of theoretical and analytical framework to analyse the strategies of TNCs towards host governments. A suitable theoretical framework would encompass the political dimensions. The political nature of the host government must be recognized in addition to the economic aspects of Government–TNC interaction and integrated in the theory. This is the primary purpose of our endeavour – to develop a theoretical framework to analyse TNC–host government interaction and the strategies that TNCs pursue towards host governments.

The issue of TNCs–government interaction is not limited to the developing countries alone, or countries adopting the import substitution or inward looking policy. It is relevant to all nation states that deal with TNCs one way or another.

TNCs' strategies towards government aim at adapting to or influencing government policies at two different levels:

1. Policy formulation.
2. Policy implementation.

This conflicts with the prevailing view in most current literature on the subject that TNCs and governments are independent on each other. Governments are supposed to formulate and implement policies without being influenced by TNCs, while TNCs do not deliberately influence government policies. Moreover, bureaucracy implements these policies in an impartial, objective manner (Boddewyn, 1988). It is assumed that government officials and policy makers formulate and implement policies in an impartial manner irrespective of their personal choice, preferences and values. This is obviously an erroneous assumption as other earlier research shows that in several cases performance requirements are requested by TNCs in exchange for monopoly in the domestic market (Bales, 1990, pp. 61-62). Performance requirements are subject to project-to-project base negotiations between TNCs and the host country government, although host governments can waive the imposition of requirements. TNCs and governments can also bargain about which performance requirements to impose and which not. Or, one requirement could act as a substitute for the other. In all these cases interaction with the host government is important within a government–TNC network. Interactions are also strengthened by the fact that government officials possess wide powers to interpret laws and make exceptions. Governments do influence the network strategy of the TNC as also the manner in which policies are formulated and implemented.

It could be observed from the above discussion that TNCs' strategies towards governments cannot be studied from the perspective of the TNCs alone. Government must also be included, since the strategic behaviour of TNCs in the political arena cannot be fully studied without considering how the main political organizations behave, in this case the political and administrative parts of a government. To know how TNCs act towards governments, the effect on TNCs of how industrial policies are executed have to be studied. What differences are there between the behaviour of the political and administrative parts of a government? What does this mean for the orientation and implementation of company strategy? How does a government build its contacts with the TNCs in order to implement particular policies, especially when sophisticated technologies are involved? And which authorities are responsible for the contacts on the government side? Moreover, do the frequency and the pattern of the contacts between the government ministries and the TNCs change with changes in industrial policy? And indeed, how important are such contacts and relationships to obtain official clearance for the proposals put forward to the government by the TNCs?

The focus on the government-transnational corporation network (GTN) implies that policy implementation is emphasized and not policy formation in contrast to earlier research on TNC–government relationships that focus on policy formulation. The paucity of research on why industrial policies fail due to faulty implementation is obvious from a reading of the literature on industrial policies and their implementation.

Public policies, in their turn, influence TNCs' strategies. The policies formulated and implemented by host governments must be acceptable to and considered legitimate by TNCs for the latter to invest in a country. This is true, irrespective of whether the policy adopted by the government is inward-looking or outward-looking. Several countries of the latter type have failed to attract FDI because of faulty implementation of policies. On the other hand countries like China have been successful in attracting TNCs.

A NETWORK APPROACH

The management of relationships and contacts with governments is a vital and strategic issue for all firms, more so for TNCs that, in their foreign operations, come in contact with a number of host governments. This implies, among other things, contacts and interaction with a variety of cultures, traditions, values, norms, laws, rules, and regulations. Managing these is important as TNCs are criticized, should they fail to abide by host country laws, rules and regulations. In the past the existence of such institutions has been depicted as 'interference' by the host country government in the operations of TNCs. The word 'interference' embodies a negative connotation.

To illustrate the complexity of contacts that are established with governments, an example is chosen from India, to depict the decision process within government for the grant of permit to import technology. As is well known, controls over TNCs are traditionally very tight in India. Figure 1.1 shows how an application for importing technology is routed through different administrative units within the Indian Government. From the standpoint of the TNC this figure shows the most important 'contact or influence points', where it could be important to establish relationships.

The application is presented at the Secretariat of Industrial Approvals at the Ministry of Industry (SIA). This is mainly a registering and co-ordination body that distributes various copies of the application to concerned units, inter alia, different units within the Ministry of Industry. The most important is the Directorate General of Technical Development (DGTD). This is a separate organization within this ministry which is the principal technical advisory organization of the Government of India on matters relating to industrial development of the country. Its functions are three fold: advisory, developmental and regulatory. The main areas covered are scrutiny of applications for industrial license/registration, proposals for foreign collaboration (mainly import of technology) and import of capital goods. A critical unit is the Technology Development Division (TDD), which coordinates matters relating to development of industrial technology, acquisition of technology, its absorption, adaptation

Figure 1.1   Foreign collaboration application procedure

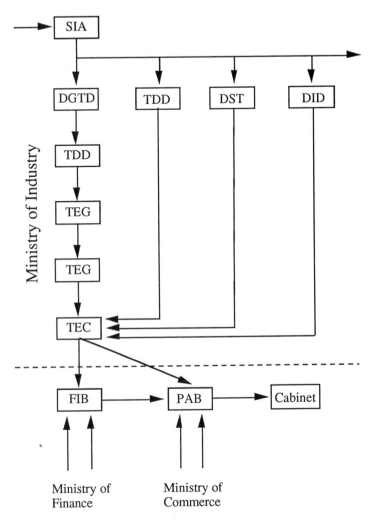

SIA   = Secretariat of Industrials Approvals
DGTD = Directorate General of Technical Development
TDD   = Technology Development Division
TEG   = Technology Evaluation Group
TEC   = Technology Evaluation Committee
DST   = Department of Science and Technology
NRDC = National Research and Development Council
DID   = Department of Industrial Development
FIB   = Foreign Investment Board
PAB   = Project Approval Board

and improvement, technology forecasting, research and development, entrepreneurial guidance, etc. Another important body within the DGTD is the Technology Evaluation Group (TEG). If the proposal is cleared by the group, it is mostly approved by the DGTD. It then passes on to inter-departmental groups within the Ministry of Industry such as Technology Evaluation Committee (TEC), which has members from DGTD, Department of Science and Technology (DST), National Research and Development Council (NRDC), and Department of Industrial Development (DID). TDD also serves as a secretarial to the TEC, whose main objective is to ensure that different disciplines of technical expertise from the above mentioned units interact and evaluate the need for import of technology. The Committee advises the Foreign Investment Board (FIB) and Project Approval Board (PAB). Projects of a certain size are referred to the FIB, where officials mainly from DGTD meet with officials from the Ministry of Finance to deal with the matter. Larger projects go on to the PAB, where more representatives participate. For large projects the Cabinet is also involved. This means that the administrative process is joined by the political process, whereas the matter becomes very complicated or even delicate.

The procedure illustrated above is the official one that is followed according to set guidelines and rules, as per the mandates given to the various government units on how to decide on a proposal for technical collaboration. This official procedure does not function by itself, which means that government does not operate on its own to clear different license applications. Along the way there are a lot of contacts between the government units and the TNCs. Such contacts take place regularly and in such a manner as to establish stable linkages between the Government and the TNCs. There is an arm's length network, that can even change the sequence of formal procedure illustrated above.

TNCs operate within government–TNC networks in certain ways, following specific strategies. Such a network strategy varies considerably among TNCs due to factors internal to companies such as type of global organization or type of industry and products sold. Host country characteristics such as the type of industrial policy, its formulation and implementation, also influence how TNCs act. These factors also influence how strategies and operations are organized within TNCs, for example how well their various units are integrated throughout the world, or if they are centralized or decentralized.

Policy implementation is very much dependent upon how interfaces between TNCs and governments are organized in the form of a network of relationships, where this main network is defined as the Government–TNC Network. In order to explain how this specified key network works, it is related to two other main networks, that is the relations among different units in Government (the Government Network) and the different units within the TNCs (the TNC Network).

Governments are hierarchies with a number of departments and units separated through delegation of authority and responsibility. To succeed in government contacts, TNCs must establish linkages in the 'right' departments, with the 'right' people, and at the 'right' level. An important research issue is, then, at what level in the host country governments do TNCs maintain relationships and why? How frequent are these contacts? What contact media is used and why? How are networks established? What do they look like?

PREVIOUS RESEARCH

Over the years research on transnational corporations has yielded differing insights. It has been emphasized that TNCs face differing legal, social, and economic environment in different parts of the world (Kindleberger, 1969; Vernon, 1971; Dunning, 1988, 1993; Rugman, 1986). Moreover, it takes time and resources to learn about the host country in order to become international (Johanson & Wiedersheim-Paul 1975; Johanson & Vahlne, 1977; Cavusgil, 1980).

The previous research on TNCs has predominantly, if not exclusively, been based on economic factors. Researchers have tried to explain the behaviour of TNCs and FDI based on three factors; firm specific advantage, location specific advantage and internalization advantage (Dunning, 1988, 1993). However, the same authors have also recognized the importance of non-economic factors, such as the host (and even the home) government, in what TNCs do and how they do it (Dunning, 1988, ch. 12). In the research on TNC and FDI, researchers have stated that the various types of advantages that TNCs or nations enjoy are conditioned and affected by the actions and policies adopted by national governments. These factors are often treated as externally determined or beyond the reach of TNCs. These are held to be exogenous to a single firm (Boddewyn, 1988, p. 344).

How TNCs relate to the nation state in less developed countries is thus a relatively well researched area, for example the impact of

TNCs on host countries (transfer of technology, balance of payments, resource usage, taxation etc.). Reactions of governments in the form of national controls over FDI have been investigated (see e.g. Dunning, 1993; Lall, 1978; Robock & Simmonds, 1989). In the past, several researchers have also investigated the relationships between national governments and TNCs. Among the more macro-oriented frameworks the 'sovereignty at bay' and 'dependency' models are well-known (see e.g. Brewer, 1992). The analysis according to the former model is based on the premise that the relationships between TNCs and governments are inherently antagonistic due to conflicting goals (Vernon, 1971). This is a zero sum game: what TNCs win, nation states lose. Moreover, the bargaining power of one vis-a-vis the other changes over time. TNCs in developing countries may enjoy a superior bargaining power in the beginning of their relationship with the government. But, as they invest money and deepen their involvement in the nation, the bargaining power tilts in favour of the host states. On the whole, however, TNCs are in a stronger position compared with national governments (Brewer, 1992, p. 297). Moreover, the very nature of the involvement of TNCs leads to an infringement upon the sovereignty of host governments.

The marxist inspired 'dependencia' theory is another important school of thought, which is concerned with the dependence on TNCs of national governments. TNCs are viewed as long arms of Western industrial states, more powerful than host developing countries which are in a weak bargaining position and therefore dependent upon the TNCs (Barnet & Muller, 1974; Muller, 1975). In this literature the mutual interdependence between TNCs and governments is overlooked; dependence is depicted one sided, with LDCs seen to be dependent on or even dominated by the TNCs.

Large parts of the political risk literature is also relevant, particularly the micro-oriented literature that takes up organizational responses to the risks (Robock & Simmonds, 1989; Brewer, 1992; Miller, 1992). Another important contribution relevant to the present work is the attempt to integrate TNCs' political behaviour and economic behaviour as expressed in the electic paradigm (Boddewyn, 1988). Two main theories on how TNCs act towards governments are also relevant. The first focuses on bargaining processes, for example on how the bargaining position with the government is improved, mainly when TNCs enter a country (Behrman & Grosse, 1990; Lecraw & Morrison, 1991; Grosse & Aramburo, 1989; Gladwin & Walter, 1980; Poynter, 1985). The other theory views government–

business relations as part of TNCs' international strategies (Mahini & Wells, 1986; Doz, 1986; Encarnation & Vachani, 1985; Prahalad & Doz, 1987; Pinelo, 1973). However, few researchers have posited TNC–government relations as a strategic management issue. The only major work in this area is Mahini (1988), while Austin (1990) has devoted part of one chapter to these 'operational issues', as he calls them.

This neglected area of international management towards governments is the focus of this book, particularly since the research referred to above on international strategy and government strategy is mostly biased towards a strategic focus based on Porter (1979, 1985).[1] Moreover, this strategy literature is largely normative in kind.

Mahini (1988) makes a distinction between three major relationship strategies towards government. At one extreme is the structured mode, where the TNC has a strong policy approach towards government. This strategy is similar to the planned strategy, which is a 'realised deliberate strategy' as defined by Mintzberg & Waters (1985) in their well-known classification of strategy types. At the other end is the diffuse mode, where problems involving government are solved on an ad hoc basis, which then, is a typical emergent strategy, most closely resembling the unconnected or imposed strategies according to the grouping by Mintzberg and Waters. Mahini's third major strategy is called the assertive mode, which finds a place inbetween the polar strategies mentioned above. This is partly a deliberate and partly an emergent strategy with a strong similarity with the umbrella or process strategies, where the TNC creates certain boundaries, within which it acts. In this book this assertive mode will primarily be developed more.

Mahini (1988) has also studied, from the same strategic management perspective and the standpoint of the group as a whole, the organization of the strategy and process of TNC–government relationship. Our focus is on TNC–government relations, from the standpoint of the subsidiary into which organizational issues concerning the group as a whole are integrated. We study, for example, how the control of government linkages is divided between different group units and how the group reporting system works. Our premise is that the government in the TNC–government relationship is not a monolith. Organizational issues are therefore penetrated more thoroughly than in Mahini's book.

Weaknesses of Previous Research

Earlier research on TNCs–government relationships suffers from a few deficiencies. First, like much of the research in the field of international business, it is a mere extension of the domestic theories into the world scene (Boddewyn, 1988, p. 359). Secondly, as pointed out earlier, policy making by host governments is considered to be independently established by sovereign states exogenous to firm behaviour. Host governments are seen to be sovereign states that formulate independent policies. From these independently established positions, bargaining that is both sincere and honest results (Doz, 1986; Poynter, 1985). There is no room for either opportunism, misleading information or misuse of office. The effect of counter actions by domestic and foreign firms in influencing the decision makers either at the policy formulation stage or during its implementation is not considered. As observed by Boddewyn (1988, p. 345-346), however, host governments are not so sovereign:

> Instead, governments are the target of political activities designed to generate firm-specific advantages and to internalize governmental decisions-makers, thereby revealing and explaining the existence of 'political market'.

Thirdly, we have already stated that the starting point of previous research is the ideal type bureaucracy, where government officials are assumed to carry out the task assigned to them according to the rules and regulations, irrespective of personal values, preferences, and convictions. Both host and home states are considered to be impersonal entities, independent of the people or group of people engaged in these processes (Boddewyn, 1988, p. 345). Evidently, this description does not suit the real world, in which personal feelings likes and dislikes, friendships, misrepresentation, and corrupt practices exist. Although, the international press is full of stories that describe collusion between bureaucracies and domestic and international firms, in the available literature, these practices are either not touched upon or treated as 'sin, mistakes and unfair practices' and covered under the single heading of 'market imperfections'. In reality, however, these practices are widespread rather than an occasional error.

Except for LDCs, previous research on TNCs have largely neglected the above important research topics. In part this could be due to the fact that most of the research on TNCs concern operations in the Western market economies. It is presumed that such contacts are less vital these economies as TNCs are free to manage their business operations. It is believed that governments are objective and natural and apply the same laws in the same manner to all firms. There is no specific need to cultivate relationships with the government. There is, nevertheless, a growing realization that host country governments are a vital player even in the Western economies (Steiner & Steiner, 1988).

The main difference between earlier attempts to study government-TNCs relations and the present book lies in the theoretical approach. The development and use of a network theory for this strategic field implies a much more systematic approach, which is more analytical than earlier more descriptive works. In conclusion, then, most important aspects of how TNCs act, plan to act, should act or how such activities are organized have been taken up earlier, but they have not been systematically researched.

The dominance of the specific strategic management perspective mentioned above in previous research is unfortunate, since the literature becomes rather monotonous and superficial from a theoretical viewpoint and inadequately covers the main issue: government relationships. As will be developed below the government side is too special to allow such mechanistic transferrals of strategic business theories to it.

Thus, the importance of TNC–government relationships have been realized, but inadequately explored systematically. Knowledge concerning TNCs–government relationships is insufficient, being mainly anecdotal. Difficulties in collecting data is probably a major reason. Few writers on TNCs have penetrated these issues, although the importance of the same is evident and well recognized by both theoreticians as well as practitioners.

THEORETICAL FRAMEWORK AND METHODOLOGY

The advantages of using a network approach were strengthened by the need to focus on various interfaces. As was argued above the study of TNCs' strategies towards government necessitates an inclusion of both parties and their interaction. Furthermore, a study of strategy at the organizational level means that the two main types of organizations are broken down into major parts. Such a disaggregated view of the government is also useful for the type of policy studied.[2] This network approach will also give new insights into how industrial policies are implemented. But since there were no ready network models that could be used directly to analyze these problems from such an approach the main task was to develop a network theory for this field of inquiry. How this was done will be described in appendix 1. In Chapter 2, the main result of this endeavour is presented – a network theory that is valid for the three main types of networks studied.

The network theory was developed for this area. The nodes of the network consist of organizations and the linkages between TNCs and government agencies are classified according to three dimensions: purpose, type and structure. Networks are thus studied at the organizational level and not at the individual level. Organizations are joined by a variety of links which communicate by exchanging information and socialize by exchanging sentiments, which together create influence.

Since very different organizations are studied, it is essential to find constructs that can separate main types of networks. We thereby make a distinction between arms-length and hierarchical networks. Arm's-length relations facilitate concerted action on the part of autonomous organizations in situations, where there is no formal authority within the network to impose coordination. The network is hierarchical, where such a formal controlling authority is directly present within the network. The Government–TNC Network (GTN) is defined as an arm's-length transorganizational network, where coordination is mandated from outside by a formal authority. These non-market relations are thus governed by rules and objectives determined by the external organization. The TNCs represent a hierarchical network.

Legitimacy is an important concept of the network theory. It is assumed that the reasons behind the behaviour of the parties within networks and which represent their main objectives are concerned with establishing legitimacy. The quest for legitimacy is the main objective behind the government-relations strategy.

Because of the complexities involved in network research, method and theory are inseparable (see further, appendix 1). A dual utilization of theory and method is achieved through comparative case studies. The cumulative nature of knowledge is emphasized, where formal theories, for example inter-organizational theories, help to develop substantive theory, which in turn, through an empirical process, helps to extend or generate modified formal theories. Both types of theories then become grounded in data. Cases – Swedish and German TNCs in India – were compared and inferences drawn from them through qualitative and quantitative analysis. A preliminary theoretical framework was first developed by doing a few broad case studies. In a second stage this framework was developed further through a re-examination of these cases and the inclusion of several more cases.

INDUSTRIAL POLICY

Industrial policy is defined in many ways. Normally it is a general term used to encompass the diverse economic, fiscal, and monetary measures enacted in order to further the industrial development of a nation. The scope of industrial policy varies, to cover all or only a restricted segment of the industry. It has obvious ideological implications. In India, for example, it has been identified with a socialistic policy of central planning, nationalization, and state ownership of industry. In spite of recent liberalization, the impact of the free-market ideology is low. From a position in-between these two extremes, industrial policy could be seen as a voluntaristic measure and not something imposed by the bureaucracy (Johnson, 1984). It is seen to be active and encourage cooperation and partnerships between enterprises and the state. This is a pragmatic approach to industrial policy of the East Asian type, chiefly Japanese style.

Industrial policy could thus be coercive or incentive based. The content and shape of the industrial policy of a country is contingent upon the prevailing industrial structure and business climate in the country, existing and missing institutions, and the aims or the ambitions of the nation (Johnson, 1985).

At a broad level the industrial policy of nations can be classified into two categories: inward-looking or import-substitution policy and outward-looking or export-oriented policy. In the former case the control and the incentive system applied by national governments are oriented towards domestic firms and markets and protection is given to domestic producers against foreign competition. Import tariffs are very high. At the same time TNCs are controlled through a licensing regime that regulates which TNCs should be allowed entry into the country and which should be barred (Stopford and Strange, 1991). There is also a policy to improve the export performance of the non-traditional sector and manufacturing through an incentive system (ibid, p.11). China, India and Argentina are examples of countries with an inward-looking policy. For example, in India the effective rate of tariff protection during the year 1990 was 150%.

Countries that are totally outward-looking and encourage production for exports are, for example, the four small 'dragons': Korea, Taiwan, Hongkong, and Singapore. They favour production for the international market rather than for the domestic market. This, however, does not imply that import tariffs or export incentives are low. Rather the balance between the two is in favour of exports so that import tariffs are more that balanced by export incentives (ibid.).

In between these two extremes lie a variety of other alternatives like being moderately outward-looking or moderately inward-looking.

The above two policy regimes apply a mixture of policy measures to hinder or attract TNCs. The inward-looking regimes have designed legislation imposing demands or 'performance requirements' on TNCs. On the other hand, the outward-looking regimes have relied more on incentive schemes to attract TNCs. Such incentives have also been offered by inward-looking countries, but rather in order to offset some of the negative consequences of their restrictive policy measures (Bales, 1990, p. 61). Table 1.1 supplies a sample of these measures.

Table 1.1   Incentives and performance requirements

PERFORMANCE REQUIREMENTS	INCENTIVE SCHEMES
1. local content requirements	1. tax holidays
2. export performance requirements	2. outright grants
3. trade balance requirement	3. tariff protection
4. technology transfer and licensing requirements	4. export subsidies
5. exchange and remittance restrictions	
6. domestic sales requirements	
7. local equity requirements	
8. product mandating requirements	
9. manufacturing requirements and limitations	
10. limiting the scope of FDI to restricted industrial fields or product sectors	

Source: Wallace (1990, p. 8) and others.

It may be stated that, barring a few exceptions, the outward-looking countries have relied more heavily on positive controls such as incentive schemes than on performance requirements. Inward-looking nations, on the other hand, have emphasised negative controls such as performance requirements.

POLICY IMPLEMENTATION

Industrial policy is both a package of measures as well as a sequence of measures, where the success of the policy depends upon the effectiveness of the entire package. The measures can be separated into macro and micro level variables (Sarathy & Samuel, 1987). Examples of the former type include exchange rate policy, the cost of capital, and tax structure. Our focus here is on micro-level variables.

Policy changes and modifications introduced by the government would have a profound effect on TNC–government relationships. For example, liberalization of industrial policies might be desired in order to attract more foreign investment, or because liberalization is expected to positively influence domestic industry through introduction of new and better technology, know-how, and competition in the market. It may be expected to force indigenous companies to modernize and become more effective as well as more productive. This would also improve the competitive position of the domestic industry in international markets.

To know how policy measures such as liberalization affect strategies towards government, it is necessary to study the degree to which liberalization has been achieved. The questions which arise are: How has liberalization come about? Have all the intended procedural simplifications been made? Is there any resistance from highly institutionalized set-ups like the 'iron triangle' (see below)?

In this process, contacts with officials and government departments involved in decision making become necessary. Newer contacts are continually established in what becomes a lengthy procedure as was illustrated in Figure 1.1.

Foreign investment laws in many LDCs are not enforced in an objective way. Officials might be influenced through their TNC contacts to bend the rules to favour certain firms. Policy guidelines themselves often provide the decision making officials with opportunities to interpret laws at their discretion. Hence it becomes important for TNCs to seek and nurture contacts with officials and decision makers in the ministries at various levels. Firms are required to develop and then maintain relationships with the concerned authorities. Evidently, which contacts and relationships are developed and nurtured and how this is achieved depends upon a number of factors. It is easy to see that informal ties with decision makers are important. Indeed we must keep in mind that relationships between the TNCs and government do not always follow official channels.

Implementation of industrial policies is an organized activity. Objectives are stated, rules and procedures worked out and organizations built up. So far, studies have been limited to the administration of policies within Government and have not considered the parties towards which the actions are directed, namely TNCs. Most of the so-called implementation research falls into this category. However we have seen that TNCs must know and understand the government in order to be able to interact with the latter.

The government perspective and TNC perspective are thus combined in this study. Therefore it will focus on the organization of the implementation of industrial policies with an transorganizational focus on Government and TNCs.

The implementation of industrial policy through the TNC–government network is mainly focused in this study. This approach to research on industrial policy is another main contribution of this project. It is in the tradition of the research on Government–Industry Relations (GIR) (e.g. Wilkes & Wright, 1987). But this study is more analytical than descriptive, as it builds on a more elaborate theoretical base. In addition the focus is on the organizational level and not on the more common industry level.[3]

THE CASE COUNTRY STUDY

Industrial policy implementation was studied in India between 1984 and 1990. Therefore, this period is mainly covered in the book, but where a follow-up of more recent developments in Indian industrial policy is given in Appendix 2.

India was selected for research for three major reasons. First, the country has a modern industrial base with a vast potential for FDI, and is an interesting market for TNCs. India is large in area and population, is well endowed with natural resources and is among the largest industrial nations. It ranks among the top ten according to certain estimates. There is a well-established engineering industry.

The middle class is large and rapidly growing. It is estimated to be anywhere between 150-200 million, increasing at an annual rate of 20 million. This huge Indian middle-class provides a market which is bigger than the domestic market of any single European country. The economic and political situation in the country is comparatively stable. Nevertheless, the amount of FDI is small. This FDI is not due to an unattractive market, but because Indian laws traditionally do not encourage FDI and the process of entry in the Indian market is resource demanding, lengthy, and cumbersome.

Second and perhaps more important, India is an example of a country where it is imperative for TNCs to develop and maintain relationships with the government. In the heavily regulated environment such as is found in the country it is hard for TNCs to do anything without a permit from government. Since Independence Indian government has pursued a policy of self-reliance, import-substitution and active intervention in industrial development. Business operations of TNCs in a number of fields is either totally banned or restricted (for example, consumer goods industry). TNCs must seek permission from the Indian government in every sphere before entry into the Indian market, the employment of expatriates, capacity expansion, change in product composition, introduction of new technology, royalty payments, imports, exports and so on.

TNCs must continuously justify their operations and presence in the country. In general they are banned from holding more than 40% of the equity shares in an Indian firm. As a rule any alteration in the business operations of TNCs results in contacts and interaction with the government. Indian laws provide wide opportunities, and also delegate power to the government officials, to interpret the laws and enforce implementation. It is generally accepted that it is through interaction and contacts with the government that TNCs can consolidate their position in the country. Managing contacts with the government is a strategic issue and often the function of higher level functionaries.

Since Independence Indian government has practised an active and interventionistic industrial policy, which is a mixture of incentives and coercive measures. They have been guided by the long-term economic goals of the government pronounced through the various Five Year Plans, frequently without consideration for where India's comparative advantage lies (Banerjee, 1975, p. 98). The industrial policy resolutions outlined the following objectives: the allocation of investment according to plan priorities; the prevention of private monopolies; balanced regional development; and the protection and encouragement of small scale industries. All the basic and strategic industries were reserved for the public sector. Seventeen Industries were exclusively reserved for the public sector. In 12 industries the state was granted the dominant control (Government of India, Second Five Year Plan, 1956, p. 43).

The development of domestic industries through a policy of import substitution has been emphasized. The underlying emphasis has been on self-reliance, mainly to save on foreign exchange and to protect domestic industry (Banerjee, 1975, pp. 76, 98). Import restrictions have been rigid and tariffs high. The major criteria used in issuing import licenses has been the domestic availability of items. The import substitution policy has encouraged the establishment and development of investment goods and heavy industries.

In addition, to further restrict the flow of foreign exchange, the activities of the large Indian business houses in general and TNCs in particular have also been controlled. Foreign firms are, in principle, barred from a number of business areas. With the implementation, in 1973 of the Foreign Exchange Regulation Act (FERA),[4] TNCs were either forced to dilute their equity share holding or leave the country.[5] A consequence of these measures was that foreign investment in the Indian industry dwindled and competition suffered. The growth rate of the Indian industry and economy slowed down.

Liberalization

The third reason for choosing India as a case study is that from about mid-1980s, there has been a definite change in the hitherto regulated environment. There has been growing realization that the industrial policy in general, and foreign investment policy in particular, needed modifications and changes. The detrimental effects of the restrictions imposed on the large Indian firms and foreign firms were apparent. Efforts have been made to remove some of the severe irritants, particularly after 1984. Tax rates have been slashed and a number of restrictions imposed on the expansion of firms have been either removed or relaxed. This has provided an excellent opportunity to study how government relationships, strategies and processes have changed with changes in industrial policy and their implementation.

Liberalization has not, by any means, been total. It can be characterized as 'controlled liberalization', 'controlled and directed competition' or as 'selective deregulation' (Financial Times, 1986). After all it is hard to change a highly entrenched system that has been in place for many years. An 'iron triangle' consisting of the political system, the bureaucracy and big business has been institutionalized over the years (Myrdal, 1968) and there is always some interest group that has something to loose from a change in policy.

The official view is to free the economy without losing the direction. Liberalization in its present context is not the same as absence of planning. It would be fair to say that in recent years the thrust of the liberalization efforts has been on procedural simplification rather than altering the law per se. The licensing procedures have been simplified and the paper work reduced. A time limit of 90 days is put within which the licenses are issued. In a few cases efforts have been made to evolve a single window clearance, that is, all the permissions and licensing are issued simultaneously.

The policy liberalization measures introduced, in particular since 1984, can be classified into three categories, namely;

1. procedural simplifications, 2. efficiency improvement, and 3. modernization. (Bhagavan, 1988)

Procedural simplifications have consisted mainly of a relaxation of limits on capacity creation and expansion. Import laws have been liberalized and the import restrictions on capital goods, raw materials and intermediate goods have been relaxed. The tariff structure has been rationalized, and better export incentives introduced.

The aim is to improve efficiency through competition. FERA and the MRTP companies are now allowed to expand and diversify production. A number of exclusive preserves of the public sector, notably telecommunications, electronics and so forth have been opened to competition.

A number of macro policies have been introduced; such as, devaluation of the rupee, reduction of taxes and easing restrictions on raising money in the stock market.

If desired results are to be achieved, these must induce TNCs to consider India a commercially viable investment area. However, foreign investment laws in India have remained cumbersome. Most investment propositions, import matters and technology issues are scrutinized by the government. Such official clearances take time and are resource consuming and frustrating. The FERA and MRTP[6] laws are still valid for most foreign investments. Bureaucratic barriers remain tight. Thus, it would be fair to state that the removal of some of the most serious restrictions on investments and operations of

firms have been done without changing the framework of the industrial and the foreign investment policies.

The moves to liberalise economy and industry produced results.
Exports as well as imports have increased rather sharply. So did the
number of foreign collaboration agreements and the amount of
foreign investment. However, this surge is from a low base and the
annual new foreign investment into India is still small, around US
$600 millions. The growth rate during the 7th five year plan was
better than those in the previous plans. It was around 5.25% over the
entire 7th plan period. The industrial sector did significantly better.
During the 1980s the average industrial growth rate was around 8%
and since 1985 the average growth rate has been around 8.9%.
(Business India, 1990).

The License Procedures Studied

Licensing has been a major instrument in allocating resources to
achieve the aims formulated by the Government of India. Licensing
has been used to direct resources into priority areas, and to protect
Indian firms from external competition. It has been used to protect
the interest of the small scale industrial sector against that of the large
firms.

Four different licensing areas have been studied, namely, production licenses, licenses for import of raw material and components,
licenses for import of capital goods, and licenses for foreign collaboration to import technology and skills. In each of these four areas
TNCs are required to seek permission from the government. The
procedures to seek licenses are long and complicated.

Industrial licensing has been used to promote growth of priority
areas of the Indian economy, while decentralizing plant location to
backward regions and attempting a measure of resource conservation
through adherence to a physical balance between domestic supply and
demand. Through such capacity licensing, the government has
attempted to control the total amount of domestic capacity, as well as
the allocation of that capacity among sectors, firms and location.

Technology and foreign investment licensing through regulating
capital goods import and foreign collaborations have been used to
save foreign exchange, avoid multiple imports of the same technology, and stimulate domestic production of capital goods. Firms must
as a result seek government clearances to purchase technology outright, to enter into a technical agreement, that is, to licence a product

or process technology, to accept a foreign equity partner, to employ foreign consultants or technicians, or to import capital goods that are not under the 'Open General License' (OGL) import category. This is illustrated in Figure 1.1.

Import of raw materials, components and consumables are also, in many instances, subject to approval by the Government of India, through the means of 'supplementary licenses'.

THE COMPANY CASES

Thirteen TNCs from two West European countries have been studied. They were selected because of their similarities regarding certain aspects, such as, type of group, industry, and experience of managing government relations. But also for their dissimilarities concerning other aspects, mainly for those characteristics that imply a variation in how government policies influence the conduct and performance of the TNCs. All the TNCs included in the research are large, belong to the engineering industry, and operate world-wide. They have production in India from before 1980 and are responsible at the time of the study for more than half of the investment from the respective country, in India. Experience in managing relationships is essential to be able to detect the pattern of TNCs–government interaction and contacts and how they are managed. During these years the firms have applied for and been granted a large number of licenses from the government of India. TNCs who have been in the Indian market for a shorter time period have not yet developed these contact patterns.

OUTLINE OF THE BOOK

The more general network theory developed in the project is presented in Chapter 2, while the research methodology is given in Appendix 1. The network theory will be used throughout the book to analyze various aspects of TNCs' strategies towards government: in Chapter 3 the objectives and strategic issues involved in the GTN, in Chapter 4 the operational characteristics of the GTN, in Chapter 5 the respective political and administrative parts of the government, in Chapter 6 the control and organization of strategies towards government, and in Chapter 7 in building a normative-oriented strategy model for how to act towards governments. Appendix 2 analyzes the more recent changes in industrial policy implementation that have taken place after the study reported in this book was finished, that is between 1991 and 1994.

SUMMARY AND CONCLUSIONS

Host governments play an important part to induce or obstruct the operations of Transnational Corporations in their respective countries. Governments with liberal economic policies favour and encourage foreign direct investment. Those following the import substitution policies, on the other hand, are selective and interventionist in their approach. In these countries governments through bureaucracy is active as a negotiating partner and seek assurances from Transnational Corporations (TNCs) on various issues, e.g. technology imports, exports, local content, development of local suppliers, etc. In addition, in more or less all the countries government at various levels are frequently the largest buyers and consume a rather significant part of the GNP. In other cases the same are important as suppliers of basic infrastructure facilities. Consequently, in import substitution economies in particular, and also in host countries in general, it is important to manage relationships with governments. This is important for all business firms but for TNCs in particular as these are more easily identified and levelled as foreigners. TNCs are also more readily a target of attack and discrimination.

There are, then, important issues that concern the development and management of relationships between TNCs and governments: Why do TNCs develop and maintain relationships with host country governments? How are they managed? And who is responsible in the TNCs for the management of these relationships?

TNC–Government contacts are mainly shaped by a quest for legitimacy in the administrative and the political segments of the Indian environment. TNCs establish and nurture contacts at those levels in the government which can best further their purpose.

To further analyze strategic issues in Government–TNC relationships, a network theory is developed, which was accomplished through the use of a research methodology based on a network approach to reality.

NOTES

1. This is no surprise, since the common denominator for most of these researchers is that they come from Harvard Business School.
2. Other research shows that a disaggregated view of government is preferred for the type of industrial policy issues studied in the project:

    There are also level of analysis issues concerning government actors. In distribution issues, governments are usually characterized as individual executive agencies or legislative entities that parcel out political goods to firms. In regulation issues, government administrative and legislative entities are more appropriately characterized as members of coalitions – with some governmental actors on one side of the issue and other on the opposite side. A disaggregated view of the government as multiple actors reflecting varying interests of multiple constituencies is therefore appropriate. (Brewer, 1992, p. 306, note 7)
3. In this context another objective of this research project is to develop the government-policy model sketched in Caves (1982).

    The government-policy model seems to hold a good deal of explanatory force. This fit is rather obvious for socialist interventionist governments openly disinclined to accept market allocations of resources. Another lies in the preference of some governments for using informal suasion on economic agents rather than laying down clear rules – a logical compromise when the policy goal in question is controversial or is in conflict with more general policies or precepts. Still another support for the government-policy model lies in the practice of some hosts to capture surplus from the MNE not as revenue but in the form of policy commitments – exports, training or promotion of nationals, etc. These policy commitments imply (via the excess-burden theorem) that the government finds itself short of instruments to respond to some discrepancies between market and shadow prices. Finally, the model may explain some nations' decisions to regulate MNE's entry, especially when the regulation aims not to enforce explicit policies (such as inclusion of local partners) but rather to give government officials an opportunity to bargain with incoming MNEs to favor whatever preferences the government may currently hold.

    Requiring local minority shareholding or participation, however, is hard to explain, because it neither maximizes the incomes of nationals nor mitigates foreign control. Perhaps governments believe that it sensitizes the subsidiary to informal suasion, thus serving the government-policy interest. In short, the policy of national equity participation seems more consistent with the political-behaviour models than with the straight maximization of national income.

    This whole research can thus be seen as a further development of this government-policy model.
4. Under this act foreign firms are, in principle, barred from a number of business areas, notably services and consumer goods industries. The foreign equity participation is limited, except in a few cases, to less than 40%.
5. Some TNCs preferred to leave the country, the most well-known cases being Coca Cola and IBM. For an analysis of the IBM case, see Negandhi & Palia (1988).
6. The Monopolies and Restrictive Trade Practices (MRTP) Act was put into effect in 1970 with the objectives: (a) to curb the concentration of economic power; (b) to prevent practices that restrict competition; (c) to control unfair trade practices. Companies subject to the MRTP Act on the basis of size, dominance or 'interconnection', and must register with the Department of Company Affairs

(DCA) in addition to the normal industrial licensing requirements. The DCA must clear all proposals by MRTP firms to enter, expand, relocate, merge etc.

2. The Transorganizational Network Theory

The relationship between TNCs and the state is a popular subject but has almost never been systematically studied. We have undertaken the study using a network approach to relationships and a network theory to analyze linkages.

Networks are viewed as consisting of nodes connected by relationships or linkages. The basic unit of the network is the linkage, constituting the building block of networks. The organization of such linkages forms the core of our study. A linkage, event or process is deemed to be organized if it exhibits regular patterns and structures.[1] In what we consider is a more basic network approach compared to most other research on organizational networks, organizational boundaries are closely studied. Given this broader definition of a network, the theory is in many ways similar to transaction cost theory.[2] However, while the institutional economic theory only relates transactions to their economic context (the economic institution), network analysis is broader in the sense that it does not discriminate between different kinds of relations and societal contexts. It transcends such borders.

The basic node of the network consists of subunits of larger organizations. The theory focuses on the structural properties of networks within which individuals are embedded. The definition of interorganizational networks is broad and includes relations between organizations that lack formal authority over one another as well as relations between organizations, where there is such a formal authority. The first type is defined as an arm's-length network and the second type is called a hierarchical network.

NETWORK ORGANIZATIONS

There are different organizational patterns of linkages. The main distinction is between intra- and interorganizational structures of linkages, which is founded on how independent the connected

31

organizations are. Relations between separate organizations are inter-organizational, while intra-organizational relations take place within each separate organization.

The focus of our network approach is not entirely on the network around a particular organization or on how it assists this organization to achieve its goals, that is the organization set (Aldrich & Whetten, 1981). Nor do we view the network only as a whole, where the function of the individual components is to serve the interest of the whole. Rather our networks combine both perspectives. Organizations within the network have both their own interests and are part of a larger collective with a right to carry out work on behalf of the whole network.

> This dualistic quality of network analysis — its capacity to illuminate entire social structures and to comprehend particular elements within the structure — probably accounts for its rapidly increasing popularity among social theorists and researchers who have found the individualistic tradition wanting as a framework for understanding social phenomena. (Knoke & Kuklinski, 1982, p. 10)

This holds true for organizational networks. Organizations both influence and are influenced by the network, as has been highlighted by Scott:

> The focus is on the joint control over the collectivity by constituent bodies and agents, all exercising rights and fulfilling obligations, their joint activities constituting the choices and actions of the collectivity as a corporate body. (Scott, 1983, p. 166)

DIFFERENT FORMS OF TRANSORGANIZATIONAL NETWORKS

Organizational networks are structures for coordinating organizational activity. These organizations are populated by persons, who represent formal organizational processes (prescribed), such as interaction between departments and organizations, and informal processes (emergent) such as coalitions and cliques. Transorganizational networks are, then, clusters of people joined by a variety of links which exchange goods and services, communicate by exchanging information and socialize by exchanging sentiments, all of which together create influence.

Type of organizational network structure varies with how collective action is governed, for example, if linkages between organizations take place within hierarchies or through markets. In the latter case, the ideal-type neoclassical market is not seen as a network. Interorganizational networks do not exist here, since there is no administrative coupling of units, organizations being linked only through relatively short term exchanges of goods. Units here are discrete, formally autonomous actors acting only on price information, with no boundary interpenetration.[3] Coordination takes place through an 'invisible hand'. Linkages are defined so as to exclude interorganizational relations. The same thing may be said of classical bureaucracy, where the boundary inclusion of the linkages is total and only intraorganizational relations are present. This type of administrative coordination is defined as a network in our study. Units in such a 'bureaucracy' network are highly interdependent and organized under a single, unitary administrative hierarchy. This extreme network is defined as a prescribed hierarchical network.[4] Between these two extreme cases lie various intra- and interorganizational networks that exhibit varying degrees of boundary interpenetration.[5] Some are loosely connected, market-like autonomous organizations where entry into and exit from the network is fairly easy. Networks characterized by opposite traits more resemble or are hierarchies.[6] This means that the boundary line between intra- and interorganizational relations is revoked, and a network linkage being viewed as a more basic relationship between units inside and outside a specific organization. Therefore, the concept transorganizational linkage is utilized to denote both these types of relations. This quest for a more basic organizational theory has been undertaken by researchers using the 'loosely coupled systems' concept. The basic problem is the same:

> Loose coupling has proven to be a durable concept precisely because it allows organizational analysts to explain the simultaneous existence of rationality and indeterminancy without specializing these two logics in distinct locations. Loose coupling suggests that any location in an organization (top, middle, or bottom) contains interdependent elements that vary in the number and strength of their interdependencies. The fact that these elements are linked and preserve some degree of determinancy is captured by the word coupled in the phrase loosely coupled. The fact that these elements are also subject to spontaneous changes and preserve some degree of independence and indeterminance is captured by the modifying word loosely. The resulting image is a system that is simultaneously open and closed, indeterminate and rational, spontaneous and deliberate ... Thus, the concept of loose coupling allows theorists to posit that any system, in any organizational location, can act on both a technical level, which is closed to outside forces (coupling produces stability), and an institutional level, which is open to outside forces (looseness produces flexibility). (Orton & Weick, 1990, pp. 204-205)

The organizational networks studied in this project are also subject to such a characterization and therefore this is an important base for the transorganizational network theory developed in this research project. We proceed further from such basic concepts towards a more specific theory.[7]

We make a distinction between arms-length and hierarchical networks. Arms-length relations are formed to facilitate concerted action on the part of autonomous organizations in situations where there is no formal authority to impose coordination. Where such a formal authority is directly present within the network controlling it, it results in a hierarchical network. The chief example of the latter form is the TNC. In the former, an example of which is the subsidiary-government network, on the other hand, coordination is mandated by a formal authority not present within the network. This arm's-length network gets a comparatively high degree of boundary interpenetration through mandates from this formal authority. This network consists of non-market relations that are governed by rules and objectives determined by the external organization. (This was illustrated in Chapter 1 (Figure 1.1) that shows how an application for importing technology is routed through different administrative units within the Indian government.)

The organization of networks provides opportunities for joint decision making and action. The degree of collective orientation is a critical factor in this context: the degree to which organizations are committed to a unified division of labour, to common goals, values, definitions of the situation and ranking of priorities and to a single leadership segment, the height of entry and exit barriers. (Schnelberg 1986, pp. 13-15). It is seen that the collective orientation is higher in a hierarchical network than in an arm's-length network.

THE NETWORK THEORY

The transorganizational network theory is summarized in Figure 2.1. We make a distinction between four different elements in assessing networks and their environments: instrumental, social, normative, and historical. There are also two levels of network environments: societal and world-system contexts.[8] Networks consist of relational connections among organizations expressed as flows or linkages.[9] Instrumental factors are concerned with the tasks or purposes of the network or of its environment. Social factors express the social

Figure 2.1   The transorganizational network theory

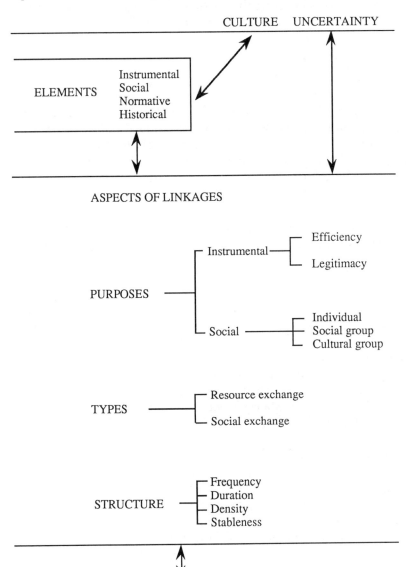

aspects of networks, which may or may not be instrumental. Normative elements comprise of rules and cognitive belief systems relevant to the network and its environment. Historical factors take into account past conditions relevant for understanding the present and the future of these networks.

Culture

Values, norms and rules both at the societal level and at group or organization level are influenced by the national culture of the country. Efficiency, for instance, is a main expression of a rational system. It is an accepted norm in many Western societies and a 'natural' part of their culture. But this may not be true of a developing economy in the East. Culture is thus an important normative factor at the societal level, which determines organizational patterns found at the network level. As an institutional factor or a dimension of society it significantly influences networks.

Uncertainty

Individual organizations attain their objectives by participating in various networks. This leads to dependency on other networks and subjects an organization to the manipulations and influence of other organizations outside its sphere of control. This creates uncertainty, inter alia, concerning the organization's capacity to acquire reliable and adequate resources to attain its goals, for instance to keep up its competitive position. Management of this uncertainty, without loss of organizational autonomy, is a chief concern for individual units within a network.[10]

A common strategy for reducing uncertainties associated with interdependency in cases where merger is impossible, is that of partial incorporation. Linkages can provide the tied organizations with vehicles for negotiation and agreement, opportunities for communication and the potential for coopting external influences (Schnelberg, 1986, p. 26). We discuss below how networks with different organizational characteristics are formed when organizations use these vehicles to reduce uncertainty.

Historical Elements

A network at any point of time is a cross-section of elements that are residues of diverse past processes. Our Indian study is concerned with the changes in network structures during a five year period which has witnessed the liberalization of industrial policy. The reasons for including the time dimension in network studies are well stated by Scott (1983, p. 169):

> Both because different organizations and transorganizational networks are founded at differing times and under varying circumstances and because they may change in differing ways and at varying rates, it will be important to attend to time dimensions in examining the structure and composition of transorganizational fields.

Normative Elements

Along with instrumental and social factors, there are also normative constraints on the direction, spread, and substance of transorganizational relations. These normative elements are specified for the networks and for two levels of environment, one affecting the other. Transorganizational connections could, for example, have a public aspect and be accountable to an audience through some kind of public 'score' or legitimacy.

Normative contexts in networks are broadly characterized as follows. There is a distinction between competitive and cooperative networks. Another distinction is made between contingent and mandated cooperation. As discussed above, the latter concept is important to our study, since it covers the rules expressing industrial policy that have to be followed by TNCs.

Normative elements or meaning systems influence the collective goals or values of the network. The study of the coupling between the societal level and network level is a crucial feature of our work. It involves a close investigation of technically defined network procedures or actions to understand how they are based on and guided by values, which originate at the societal level.

We seek to develop further the following contention made by Meyer & Scott (1983, p. 140):

> Networks operate in institutional sectors characterized by the elaboration of rules and requirements to which individual organizations must conform if they are to receive support and legitimacy from the environment. Technical sectors are those within which a product or service is exchanged in a market such that organizations are rewarded for effective and efficient control of the work process.

There is enormous variation along these two dimensions with respect to different organizations. TNCs in India, for instance, operate simultaneously in technical sectors demanding efficiently produced outcomes and institutional sectors, e.g. government. In many cases institutionalized rules closely resemble technical rules. As noted by Meyer and Scott (1983, p. 160):

> Organizations are special-purpose collectivities created to achieve goals, to perform work. Their meaning, their legitimacy, and their potency come from appearing to be rational systems.

Legitimacy is thus a concept important to our research. As we shall see legitimacy or legitimation is a two-way process. From above it is a claim of validity for what one knows is justifiable. From below this claim is justified according to the valuations, norms and rules of a certain group. Depending upon the type of organization which makes such a claim, three kinds of legitimacy are distinguished: political, administrative, and business legitimacy. It is noticed that this means that the main types of organizations studied – political and administrative organizations together with TNCs – are involved in communication activities towards each other, claiming and giving legitimacy.

Linkages

Three aspects of linkages are studied: purpose, type and structure. The first concerns the purpose of exchange; the second, types of links that are established and what they contain; the third deals with the structural characteristics of these linkages. Organizations are connected for one of the two purposes: instrumental or social. Instrumentality is defined as purposive action, that is organizational units are assumed to make conscious, intentional decisions to establish linkages, for example, the exchange of products to increase profit or exchange of information, gifts and sentiments to create influence in order to get legitimacy.[11] In both these cases there could be differing norms behind the purposive action which might be voluntary or mandated.[12]

Social relations take place for three reasons: persons within two organizations may share a liking for each other, which is related to their individual attributes, as for example 'kindness'; or, because they belong to the same social group defined by kinship or occupation; or on account of the fact that they come from the same cultural or national group. In practice, however, it is difficult to compartmentalize these bases of social relations.

Types of linkages

Linkages have two kinds of contents: the exchange content and the normative content.

1. Exchange content comprises resources and sentiments. Exchange of resources is mainly related to how the instrumental factor is expressed as a linkage between organizations. There are two main types of flows, one constituting a material resources network and the other a communications network. In the former case material means and conditions are important, for example products, gifts, and money, and in the latter case cognitive aspects like information and ideas are important. Depending on the purpose of the linkage and its organization, different types of information can be exchanged: know-how, advice, directives or commands with varying results. Both these main types of flows are vital in the TNC network, while the government and TNC–government networks mainly are communications networks. Time seen as an opportunity cost or an actual cost is an important resource in the TNC–government network, e.g. time spent in filling out forms, preparing and processing applications.

2. Sentiments such as affection and liking are the expressive or emotional factor of the linkage and originates from the social element. Friendship and trust are main characteristics of the social exchange. Social exchange, in contrast to economic exchange, is signified by unspecified obligation as it involves the principle that one person does another a favour, and while there is a general expectation of some future return, its exact nature is not stipulated in advance (Blau, 1964, p. 93). Diffused future obligations are created and are not precisely specified as in economic exchange. Social exchange calls for trust in the discharge of such unspecified obligations.

There are also two types of normative contents: rules and values.[13] Transorganizational networks have different types of boundary penetration relations, where this project deals with networks that have more definite organizational boundaries, for example TNCs and governments, and with networks that have more indefinite boundaries, for example the TNC–government network.

Structural characteristics of linkages

Most network analyses highlight social relations, are rather technical and preoccupied with the form of the network. Network structure of linkages or the form of a network is, for instance, divided into overall network structure and clustering within networks. Different measures of structural properties are used like connectivity, clustering, density, etc.[14] We have not attempted this kind of elaborate quantitative analysis of organizational relations. Instead, a deep qualitative study of a limited network of organizations has been undertaken on the basis of such factors as breadth, frequency, density, duration and length of linkages.

Legitimacy

As observed above, legitimacy is related not only to the normative element of the transorganizational network, but also to the instrumental and social factors. Both main types of legitimacy – technical and institutional legitimacy – are also relevant, since TNCs in India operate simultaneously in technical sectors demanding efficiently produced outcomes and institutional sectors, e.g. government.

Hence, legitimacy can be achieved indirectly through the economic system by being efficient, or directly from government, for example, by demonstrating that the activities of the TNC in the country take place according to government rules and according to generally accepted societal values. While efficiency is performance based, legitimacy is judged on valuations. The basic idea behind the legitimacy concept, as it is used in this book, is that stable relations between rulers and ruled are not only based on coercion, utility, affection, or ideality. Actions are also constrained by legitimacy.[15] This general statement is here used in a transferred meaning and is supposed to be valid for the relations studied in this project, i.e. within governments and TNCs and between these two main types of organizations. For instance, legitimacy constrains the regulative acts of government towards the TNCs. Legitimacy is given to an organization or person by other organizations/persons from the actions of that organization or person. Such an acceptance is based on a test or assessment of these actions, where ideologies, valuations, and norms are the criteria. The actions themselves are tested or more precisely the reasons behind them and how justified they are. This definition of legitimacy corresponds to a definition of legitimation given by Cipriani (1987, p. 1) as

Among the various possible meanings of what has been defined as legitimation, two should be borne in mind as more pertinent to sociological analysis: the attribution of validity to a given situation, action, function or authority (from below);

But legitimation also has another meaning:

and (from above) the more or less motivated justification of what by itself would not be lawful or valid ... In fact, claim, demand, recognition, ratification, acceptance – all are social and individual actions which presuppose endowing what is going to be done with meaning ... By way of further distinction, legitimation in reality is said to be based on two 'couples' of behaviour; from above, as a claim of validity only for what one is convinced of, or, instead, as a cynical claim of validity for what one knows is not justifiable; and from below, as a well-founded recognition of the legitimacy of something or, contrarily, as a de facto acceptance, though without foundation, of the legitimacy of something. The attribution of a 'foundation' simply means that this does not exist and so must be 'constructed', and on this depends the whole scaffolding of a complex of guiding ideas which orient attitudes and behaviour. And since, in general, a foundation is something in common, to be shared, its own particular character represents its potential for diffusion and ability to provide the sense of belonging to a group as to a party, a community or a whole nation.

Legitimation is further precisely defined by Karlsson (1991, p. 116) as

an act of communication through which desired or implemented actions are made meaningful (our translation)

Karlsson (1991) adds that this act of creating meaning is strongly related to the valuations, norms, and rules of the group, to which the organization/individual that attributes validity to the actions belongs. To legitimate is thus to justify or rationalize.

To gain legitimacy or legitimation is thus a two-way process, where the main types of organizations studied – political and administrative organizations together with TNCs – are involved in communication activities towards each other, claiming and giving legitimacy. The three main types of legitimacy are represented in Figure 2.2, where they are compared to the efficiency and rationality concepts. Another legitimacy concept used in the book, procedural legitimacy is also taken up. These concepts and relations between them will be developed further below and in the coming chapters.

The quest for legitimacy is the main objective behind the government-relations strategy. How TNCs conform to the government's rules and norms as well as justify their existence in the host country is defined as business legitimacy. How TNCs do so would depend upon how the political system and executive bodies work. When the

Figure 2.2   Related legitimacy concepts compared to efficiency and rationality

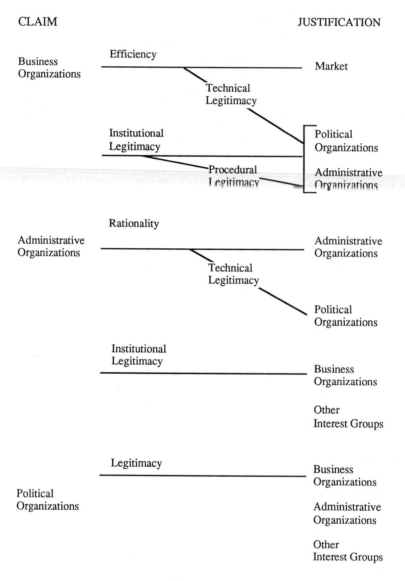

CLAIM   JUSTIFICATION

Business Organizations

Efficiency ──────────────────────────── Market

Technical Legitimacy

Institutional Legitimacy   Political Organizations

Procedural Legitimacy   Administrative Organizations

Administrative Organizations

Rationality ──────────────────────────── Administrative Organizations

Technical Legitimacy

Political Organizations

Institutional Legitimacy   Business Organizations

Other Interest Groups

Legitimacy   Business Organizations

Political Organizations

Administrative Organizations

Other Interest Groups

political system is creating legitimacy for itself with the citizens or with different interest groups or organizations, there is political legitimacy. Administrative legitimacy, on the other hand, is achieved by furthering the interests of the administrative units with the political system or with organizations such as TNCs.

Organizations, including TNCs, are open systems and depend upon resource exchanges with the environment to ensure survival. One important resource is legitimacy which is supplied by the environment to organizations in return for valued output (Pfeffer, 1978). By legitimacy is implied 'the process whereby an organization justifies to a peer or subordinate system its right to exist, that is, to continue to import, transform, and export energy, material, and information' (Maurer, 1971, p. 361). Without legitimacy organizations cease to exist (Selznick, 1948, 1965; Zucker, 1983; Singh, Tucker & House, 1986). The GTN reflects the desire of the TNCs to secure legitimacy in the host country. The contacts and the contact media used assign legitimacy to TNCs, which is the main purpose of the GTN.

Technical and institutional legitimacy

The environment facing an organization may be either technical or institutional (Scott & Meyer, 1983, pp. 129-153). The former includes those segments of the environment with which organizations exchange resources to effectively survive, namely consumers, suppliers and so on. The latter is the environment of rules, regulations and myth to which organizations must adhere in order to seek environmental support and resources. Indeed, a majority of organizations interact with both types of environments, although one type usually predominates.

TNCs interact with three types of environment, namely, commercial, political and administrative. The commercial environment includes financiers, suppliers and clients. In this segment TNCs gain technical legitimacy by being effective and competitive in production, distribution, and marketing. This is, however, not sufficient, especially in international operations, where TNCs need to show respect for national laws and be a good citizen by contributing to national development and economic welfare (Vernon, 1971).

The political environment includes, among others, political parties and farmers groups. These groups can influence industrial policy and laws which, in turn, affect the operations of TNCs. The administrative environment includes the executive bodies of the government, which apply laws, rules and regulations, that is the bureaucracy. Two dimensions are identified, namely, the purely legal dimension, and the procedural. The former concerns the laws and their interpretation.

The latter concerns the procedures and the channels that TNCs should pursue to secure licenses, and involves dealing with matters like how many copies of an application should be submitted, when and to whom. The political and the administrative environment contribute towards institutional legitimacy (Meyer & Rowan, 1977; Meyer & Scott, 1983, pp. 129-153).

Hence, host country governments evaluate TNCs not merely on commercial or technical basis, but also on contributions to industrial and technological development. TNCs need to reflect these public goals in their strategy and operations, and give evidence of achievement of them. Host country governments enact laws, rules and regulations to guide, direct, and regulate TNCs and their operations. As stated earlier these are more detailed and elaborate in countries which have to pursue import substitution policy.

The institutional legitimacy enjoyed by TNCs in the political and the administrative segments of the environment is not absolute. It is influenced, as it is, by a number of powerful sub-segments of the Indian society, which judge TNCs according to non-commercial criteria. TNCs would jeopardize the interest of the country by being monopolistic and powerful, thereby hurting the growth of domestic firms, or accelerating concentration of economic and political power in a few hands and in a few geographical areas.

Our view is, then, that TNC–government relationships are guided and shaped by a quest for institutional legitimacy. TNCs establish and nurture relationships with the host country governments to gain institutional legitimacy, which helps them to grow, prosper, and survive. We thus expect TNCs to engage in interaction and contacts with the host country governments to express commitment to the host society, its rules, regulations, and wishes.

MAIN TRANSORGANIZATIONAL PATTERNS

We discuss below a few critical theoretical concepts expressing transorganizational patterns of the entire GTN: for instance, tight or loose coupling and hierarchical or arm's-length networks.[16] It is worth repeating that the model, its constructs and relations, depicted in Figure 2.1 concerns entire networks. The transorganizational patterns therefore typify such whole networks.

As noted above, organizations are the nodes of the networks studied, and the linkages between these nodes are classified according to three dimensions: purpose, type and structure. Therefore, the transorganizational patterns express a certain combination of nodes, which in their turn are a result of a specific linkage structure. This structure contains certain types of linkages, which are based on specific purposes for establishing and maintaining these linkages. Our transorganizational network theory thus explains how these three linkage dimensions are connected, which is typified through the transorganizational patterns. Aspects of linkage structure are combined with types of linkages and the purposes and translated into main organizational patterns. Or inversely, these patterns contain these combinations of linkage aspects.

Stability

Stability or persistence is a key characteristic of transorganizational networks, as it is of a loosely coupled system. The ultimate predictor of network stability is the probability of a link failing, which depends on the duplication and multiplicity of linkages (Aldrich & Whetten, 1981, pp. 391-392). The classic paradoxes of flexibility versus stability, and efficiency versus effectiveness are also salient for networks. Similar dimensions analyzed here are, for instance, adaptations to a new industrial policy and other government measures as well as the responsiveness versus integration dimensions within the TNC network.

Degree of Coupling

A loosely coupled system has certain basic features that are valid for the organization networks of this project. One main determinant of the working of such a loosely coupled system concerns how its different parts are joined, that is if they are loosely or tightly coupled. As observed above, variation along this dimension is primarily determined by the degree of uncertainty. Under conditions of high uncertainty a tightly joined network may not be stable since any external influence could disrupt it. A shock quickly spreads to all parts of the network. This is not the case in a loosely coupled network. A hierarchical, loosely joined network composed of a number of sub-networks with only scattered links between elements, benefits from the advantages of loosely as well as tightly coupled networks. Each sub-network would in such a case be tightly joined within itself and thus sensitive to external influence. But relations between these hierarchies would be rather weak. Such a loosely joined hierarchical network would show short-run independence of sub-networks and long-run dependence in an aggregate way (Aldrich & Whetten, 1981). The adaptive advantages of this type of network are thus considerable in a complex, heterogeneous, and changing environment. But certain changes are also sealed off by being neutralized through buffering (Orton & Weick, 1990, pp. 213-214)

Network organization is depicted here as being loosely joined, hierarchically differentiated and adaptive in ways that preserve network structures (Aldrich & Whetten, 1981, p. 388). Such a linking of environment and network structures explains why some basic TNC network structures are more loosely coupled than others and why the GTN is more strongly structured in certain aspects than in others.

Emergent and Prescribed Networks

Networks are formed by the behaviour of individual organizations and are thus purposively constructed. This behaviour is constrained by an organization's position in a network structure, this structure, in its turn, being influenced by the constituents of the network as well as by parties outside the actual network. One example of a case where the influence from outside parties is strong is the mandated arm's-length network. Acting within a network thus constrains future behaviour of individual organizations. The extent to which individual organizations influence the formation of networks varies. In a mandated network this influence is restricted. In other arm's-length networks, the influence may be stronger, since it is up to an individual organization to determine whether it wants to participate in the network or not, for example, if a TNC should invest in a country and thereby tie itself up to various local parties. This type of inter-organizational network is usually emergent or formed from below and not a system prescribed by units within or outside the network. Thus, for emergent networks, the actual conduct of an individual organization within the network is emphasized. But as stated above, most networks are a combination of prescribed and emergent networks and are consequently both individually and structurally determined. It is thus important to combine individual organizational behaviour analysis with structural network considerations. This is especially important since we have to examine cases, where there is a large difference between prescribed and actual behaviour.

As discussed earlier in Chapter 1, if a TNC entirely acted according to the prescription from government or only followed the laws, rules and procedures stated in the guidelines, when applying for licenses, there would be no TNC–government network. TNCs and government would then share a limited connection. But this is far from the actual situation. As we shall subsequently see there are a lot of contacts between these parties. A GTN emerges from just such an interaction. Unplanned structures and behaviour patterns will always figure in such a network, since only a portion of the network structure is prescribed or planned.[17] This difference between prescription and action makes networks more emergent than they otherwise would be.

The interdependent nature of the prescribed and the emergent dimensions of networks find emphasis in our work.[18] An important assumption of this work is that the prescribed organization structures are the basis for and constrain emergent network structures. The emergent network organization thus changes with variations in formal or prescribed organization, for example mandated procedures for applications in the GTN or the formal organization in TNC networks and government networks. Due to the focus of this study, the opposite situation of emergent networks influencing prescribed networks is not so much researched. But in the literature there are examples of emergent networks that gradually are formalized into prescribed organizations during the period of formation.

Organization of the social linkage
The organization of the social linkage is a vital element of our study which distinguishes between coalitions and cliques. Coalitions are defined as temporary alliances of distinct parties for a limited instrumental purpose. Friendship mainly originates from this instrumentality. Coalitions are a deliberate creation for the purpose of increasing control over either a task (e.g. a decision) or an organization. They are often formed during times of unusual or non-routine task demands, as when a certain administrative decision is to be influenced.

Cliques are chiefly socially determined and more permanent than coalitions. Friendship is important. People keep together, because they like each other or belong to the same social group and do not primarily associate themselves for work reasons. Instrumental aspects are thus inferior to social reasons. The intimacy of such relations could vary from a more shallow liking of each other through being 'real friends' to a very deep emotional bonding. In coalitions, friendship is supposed to be more professionally determined and a consequence of the necessity to meet to solve common problems. Instrumental aspects predominate. Hence, social exchange varies from being rather calculative as in coalitions to various forms of emotional friendship as in cliques. Coalitions are hypothesized to be dominated by a professional trust among involved persons, who can be labelled business friends and not family friends. We thus assume a minor bias from more emotional influences on action.

Uncertainty and network formation

When uncertainty is low in a communications or information network, simpler integrating devices such as rules and procedures can adequately coordinate task requirements. Plans can be formulated and followed as blueprints for information, and influence flows. One example of the situation mentioned above would be if TNCs only needed to follow the official guidelines in their application for licenses. In such a highly formalized structure controlled by administrative rules, it is supposed that emergent or informal networks largely emerge to fulfil social affective needs which are not met by the prescribed roles. This would hold good for government bureaucracies.

In the hierarchical network of the transnational corporation, where the uncertainty is higher, more complex integrating devices such as liaison roles, teams and task forces are often used to coordinate work. Since the possibilities for planning are fewer, people are allowed to improvise and rely on 'unofficial' networks to coordinate and carry out their work. In that way there is a similarity with the GTN, as decision-making is more dependent on coalitions. In such task oriented coalitions the social linkage is subordinated to the more instrumentally oriented resource-exchange and influence linkages.

Cliques, on the other hand, are created by the inevitable conflict between collective task demands and individual needs, and tend to be non-task oriented and remain relatively stable and closed. Both cliques and coalitions are emergent networks that could be labelled 'flexible rigidities', since they are less stable, standardized and formalized than prescribed networks.

Hierarchical Networks

As all organizations studied in this book, the TNC is viewed as a transorganizational network consisting of exchange relationships among organizational units. This approach to the organization of the TNC has only recently started to be developed (Bartlett & Ghoshal, 1990; Forsgren & Pahlberg, 1991; Forsgren & Holm, 1992). One main advantage with a network approach, stressed by Bartlett & Ghoshal (1990), is that the contingency aspect of the TNC organization can be developed considerably by combining an internal network with its various external networks. This is a major departure from the earlier tradition of viewing the TNC as a unitary organization operating in highly simplified environments. Our study contributes to the new network approach through a detailed study of how one specific external network, the GTN, is connected to the internal group network. The emphasis is on how institutional environments influence the structure and behaviour of organizations (Meyer & Scott, 1983).

The network approach has been used to emphasise the importance of informal organization or the emergent network. Several studies, including our study, have demonstrated organizational variables or internal management process to change more often than formal structure (e.g. Bartlett & Ghoshal; 1989 Doz and Prahalad, 1981, Prahalad & Doz, 1987). But it is also seen that the prescribed organization structure continues to be an important control of subsidiary action. A corollary is then that both formal structure and internal management processes are important.

Further, a network approach which includes the external network, gives a more holistic view of TNC organization. By thus combining intra- and interorganizational networks, a neglected aspect in organizational studies of TNCs comes to light. (Bartlett & Ghoshal, 1990).

The other main hierarchical network of the study is the Government bureaucracy, which is a rationally structured hierarchy with well-defined authority and sanctioning patterns, objectives, rules and regulations. Such a vertically prescribed network with clear authority and responsibility lines is often hard to coordinate horizontally.

Arm's-Length Networks

Research on interorganizational networks, which are defined as arm's-length networks in our study, focuses on horizontal relations that facilitate some forms of coordinated activity and inhibit others (Schnelberg, 1986, p. 9).

In the mandated arm's-length subsidiary-government agency network the uncertainty is high. From the TNCs' point of view the license system does not function as prescribed (or expected from mandates and formal organization) which creates uncertainty. From the government's point of view it is hard to judge the operations of these technologically advanced TNCs. Suspicion or mistrust thus create uncertainty. It is, therefore, important to have relationships to solve common problems. There is a need for arm's-length coalitions, and not just cliques. This emergent network is chiefly controlled by implicit rules (customs) and trust, which makes the degree of formalization low. The social linkage is critical in such a network.

Prescribed arm's-length networks

The typical arm's-length network that we describe, consists of mandated interactions, which, as observed earlier, are prescribed constraints from outside the focused network. They involve laws or regulations, specifying areas or domain, information and other flows. The question is how the organization of this prescribed arm's-length network influences the organization of the TNC network or government network respectively. The TNC network, for example, is loosely joined in order to enable the local Indian subsidiary-government network to function properly. Compared to 'normal' arm's-length interactions, Aldrich (1976) found that mandated interactions tended to be more intense, favouring one organization, and associated with lower perceived cooperation (Hall et. al., 1977, p. 459), which seems to be valid for this study as well.

This vertical and mandated ingredient make these prescribed arm's-length networks resemble hierarchical networks.[19]

This mandated arm's-length networks is established from the top. Such top down formation of networks occurs where powerful organizations, for example, governments, have an interest in controlling and governing a larger set of organizations. This is precisely what industrial controls aim for. These controls are an institutional vehicle by which a core organization can negotiate with and regulate many and dispersed organizations. Formalities such as organization structure, rules, and procedures for getting licenses determine how trans-organizational decisions are made. To this formal part is added an informal part due to the fact that the decision process is not totally prescribed or mandated which leaves a certain discretion to individual organizations and decision makers. This top-down formation process resembles the formal hierarchical relations of the TNC network.

The more diverse the state bureaucracy, the more adapted it is to participating in and mediating a varied and dynamic set of transorganizational relations. This is typical of the all-encompassing Indian bureaucracy, which also has an interest in negotiating with, coordinating, controlling and otherwise governing these transorganizational linkages.

Emergent arm's-length networks

As discussed above, the formal network does not wholly prescribe every decision or action made, since there is also room for other decisions and actions through emergent networks, inter alia, to adapt informally to changing conditions. The reason why industrial policies are implemented in ways other than the ones intended can largely be explained by the fact that networks do not work as planned. Herein would be the difference between actual and prescribed networks.

In an emergent network, norms such as general expectations about behaviour may be negotiable to a certain extent. The legitimacy purpose, for instance, also seems to be more loosely defined and open to question. Ad hoc solutions and bases for interaction are invented, not prescribed. As a consequence, these networks are less clearly bounded. Links change as new tasks are confronted and non-prescribed, multiple bonds are established. Although these networks are emergent, they are purposively constructed by individual parties. Furthermore, they provide flexible and fluid conditions that help to shape future organizational decisions and already-established network links, including the more institutionalized existing network links. All such linkages may, therefore, be treated as exchangeable resources. Such an environment, that makes possible manipulation of relations in the interest of the organization, might be called 'an opportunist society'. In such a situation the skilful management of network links becomes a specialized concern for many kinds of brokers outside or inside the organization, as for example liaison managers and liaison officers.[20, 21]

SUMMARY AND CONCLUSIONS

We have attempted to place in perspective the manner in which industrial, or for that matter any, government policy is implemented. India's policy towards foreign investment has served as the example. Policy implementation has been viewed as the process of organizing an interface between the government and TNCs. Our perspective can be defined as the network approach wherein a network theory of transorganizational activity explains policy implementation.

Linkages between the organizational nodes are classified according to purpose, type and structure. There are two main intended purposes behind the organization of the network: instrumental and social reasons, which are inter-connected in the way that social purposes may support instrumental factors, thus becoming instrumental by themselves. But the social purpose is seen as a dimension of its own in this research and divided into three basic reasons for having linkages: a sharing among individuals of common attributes and belongingness to the same social or cultural group. The two main instrumentalities of networks, efficiency and legitimacy, are treated more extensively in most of the following chapters.

The purposes are connected to the types of linkages established in the network, i.e. exchange of resources and of sentiments. In addition to the instrumental and social aspects, normative and historical elements are included in the analysis of the networks. Dimensions of the structure of linkages or the linkage pattern, e.g. frequency, duration and density, informs about how the organizations within the network are connected to each other. By jointly analysing the purposes of linkages, types of linkages and their structural characteristics, a number of organizational properties of the entire network are derived, e.g. uncertainty, stability, degree of coupling, arm's length or hierarchical networks and emergent or prescribed networks.

The Government–TNC Network (GTN) is analyzed in the next two chapters according to this theory. Legitimacy is the main purpose behind this communication network, where social relations are an important type of linkage, mostly supporting the instrumental purpose of creating influence.

How a network is formated from above or from below depends on many things, for instance how powerful the central agency present is, the nature and level of organizational dependency, the number of organizations in the relevant population and the type of transactions requiring coordination. The size of the relevant organizations will also matter.[22]

NOTES

1.   This definition is inspired by Barney & Ouchi (1986). The basic problem when defining organizations is well analyzed by Orton & Weick (1990, pp. 216-218):
     Most definitions of organization consist of at least two components: (a) a source of order which consolidates, unifies, or coalesces diverse elements or fragments and (b) elements or fragments, which are consolidated, unified, or

coalesced by a source of order. When researchers define organizations as monolithic corporate actors, they overemphasize order and underemphasize elements; when researchers define organizations as mere aggregates of individuals, they overemphasize elements and underemphasize order.

2. One important difference is, however, that transaction cost theory is an economic theory and therefore of limited relevance for this research project which encompasses a broader array of organization issues, for example, political and administrative organizations. According to institutional organization theory, which is one basis of the project, economic theories belong to technical sectors, and could then be used to explain economic activities of TNCs, but not political activities in more institutionally developed sectors like government. Another major difference is that transaction cost theory is an economic institutional theory, while network theory is an organizational theory. Transaction cost theory explains economic structure based on traits of individuals, where structure is a consequence of personal properties (methodological individualism). Network theory, on the other hand, focuses on the structural properties of networks within which individuals are embedded. The focus is on organizational structures that have no meaning at the level of the individual actor. Network theory is thus a more useful general theory for this project. To join these two major types of theories it is necessary to either transform network theory into an institutional theory of economic organization or change transaction cost theory into an organizational theory. Neither is done in this project. For a further treatment of transaction cost theory as an organizational theory for international business, see Jansson (1994a, b).

3. Compare McNeil (1974), Williamson (1985), and Jansson (1992).

4. But as is evident from modern organization theory, few organizations can be analyzed according to such a simple and mechanistic formula. Control of today's organizations is far more complex. First, informal coordination of actions plays an important role, e.g. through social means. Tichy & Fombrun (1979), for instance, use network analysis for research on informal organization and how it relates to formal organization. Second, organizations cannot be studied in isolation from their environment. Controlling interdependencies become much more complex in an uncertain world. Organizations adapt to various contingencies by differentiating their activities in parts and integrating them. This implies that there is no best organization theory in general, only partial theories. Third, goal conflicts are common and there is no consensus around goals. As shown in Jansson (1994a), the development of organization theory of the TNC to a large degree parallels the development of the organization theory in general. Coordination mechanisms used by Galbraith & Nathanson (1978) and others, for instance, are also found in many organizational studies of TNCs. Similarly, the main issue is how to manage the contradictory forces of connection (coupling) and autonomy (loosely coupled) or global integration and local responsiveness as these forces are usually termed in literature on the organization of the TNC.

5. Compare Schnelberg (1986, pp. 4-7).

6. The theory of organizational networks used in this research project is founded on later developments of organization theory along these lines. Accordingly, institutional organization theory is viewed as an extrapolation of contingency theory. The environment or the society is divided into different sectors, for example, highly institutionalized sectors such as politics and low institutional sectors like private industry. Organization theories are particular to each main sector, between which the trade-off is low (see for example Scott & Meyer, 1983; Perrow, 1984). Even for such more or less idiosyncratic theories there is a need for relating them to each other and to the environment. This role is here played by the transorganizational network theory. It goes beyond these theories, to

common building blocks of organizations, inter alia, abolishing the boundary between intra- and interorganizational studies.

7.   Although it is a good base, the preliminary model of loose coupling theory developed by Orton & Weick (1990) is too general for the purpose of this project. Primarily the concepts used to characterize loosely coupled organizations are valid for specifying basic qualities of the organizational networks studied in the project, i.e. persistence, buffering, adaptability, satisfaction and effectiveness.

8.   Compare Scott (1983, p. 163).

9.   We do not totally dissolve organizational boundaries and select individuals as the basic theoretical unit. The reasons for this are discussed in a separate appendix on network methodology.

10. Based on Schnelberg (1986, p. 25).

11. Oliver (1990) distinguishes the following six reasons for establishing interorganizational relationships: necessity, asymmetry, reciprocity, efficiency, stability, and legitimacy. As emphasized by Oliver few attempts have been made to integrate and study multiple determinants, especially in empirical research. Most research stresses one or two of the reasons. The present work makes a contribution by integrating four of these determinants: necessity, stability, efficiency and legitimacy. Necessity, which occurs when an organization establishes linkages to meet necessary legal or regulatory requirements, i.e. mandated interactions, is subordinated to legitimacy. We find that when there are such demands from the government, there is also a need to create legitimacy with the regulatory agencies. A TNC may also experience a need to establish its credibility in such a new market before it can earn any profits. Hence, mandated and voluntary relationships are both established to gain legitimacy. As emphasized by Oliver (1990, p. 245) IOR studies based on efficiency are rare, particularly when efficiency is defined as a goal, as is done in this study, and not as an outcome of action. Stability is not defined as a reason in itself, but as a characteristic of the networks established for reasons of efficiency and/or legitimacy. Asymmetry, which refers to the potential to exercise power and control over another organization, is connected to theories of political economy (e.g. Benson, 1975) and resource dependence (Pfeffer, 1978; Pfeffer & Salancik, 1978). Since these theories are not included in the research project, we have not developed this aspect. The reciprocity determinant, which stresses cooperation and harmony, does not form part of our study.

12. Different norms are developed at the network level depending upon type of network. For instance, there are fundamental differences between three basic networks: the political network, the administrative network and the TNC network.

13. In the available literature on the subject, there are other classifications of relations according to content, e.g. types of boundary penetrations, types of decisions made by higher and lower units within the field, authority/power relations (mandated) and types of inter-level controls that are exercised, e.g. structural, process or outcome (Knoke & Kuklinski, 1982; Mitchell, 1979; Scott, 1983).

14. See for example Tichy & Fombrun (1979).

15. This definition is based on Karlsson (1991, chapter 4).

16. Concepts of organization drawn from resource-dependence theory will be of limited use, for example, resource concentration, formalization, intensity, reciprocity, symmetry, standardization (Benson, 1975; Pfeffer & Salancik, 1978, Aldrich, 1979); commitment and centrality of power (Emerson & Cook, 1984). In most of these studies, power and social control figure centrally as both a cause and consequence of network structure. This is not our perspective.

17. Compare Mintzberg & Waters (1985) and Mintzberg (1987) for a similar terminology.

18. This dependence is studied by Tichy & Fombrun (1979, pp. 923-931). They found that structural linkage characteristics complied with the theory of mechan-

istic organization and organic organization. A network approach with a network method or technique was used. The approach is that of the sociologist or anthropologist, starting with the individual and building the analysis up from that level. The pattern then emerges from the data. The large differences between these structures, for example, regarding structuring of activities, concentration of authority and content of communication, can also be transferred to transorganizational structures of our project.

19.   Voluntary interaction, but standardized through some form of formal agreement, also belongs to this prescribed category. Exchanges occur in the development of the formal agreement, but interactions subsequent to the agreement are guided by it. This is particularly valid for action networks.

20.   Compare Anderson & Carlos (1976, pp. 29-33).

21.   Another type of emergent networks has been studied in this project, viz. the action network or the lobbying group. This is a network that is consciously and deliberately created by a group of organizations as a means to enhance their capacities for coordinated collective action. Another type of emergent network, that has not been investigated here, is an exclusively voluntary exchange, typical of the social network (e.g. Granovetter, 1973, 1982; Mitchell, 1979; Emerson & Cook, 1984; Tichy & Fombrun, 1979). Translated to an organization network, this situation becomes more of a bottom-up process of network formation of the arm's-length type. It can emerge in a piecemeal way as an unintentional by-product of organizations' individual efforts to manage their environment. In either of these two cases, the emergence of centralized networks would be relatively unlikely as no organization has sufficient power to impose a set of transorganizational relations on other organizations or otherwise circumscribe the autonomy of these organizations.

22.   See Schnelberg (1986, p. 28).

3. Main Objectives and Strategic Issues

In Chapter One we stated that TNCs' strategies toward government aim at adapting to or influencing policy formation and implementation of policies. The different policy measures applied by government either to attract or to restrain firms in general were discussed. It was pointed out that some governments rely more on incentives, others more on restrictions.

Adaptations to policy implementation and the influence that TNCs exert on it are part of a conscious strategic process, particularly since competitive advantages could be gained through the process. By such acts TNCs gain access to vital resources, namely, preferential access to various kinds of licenses to operate in a country, to enter an industry or part thereof, to receive incentives of various types (export incentives, incentives to locate a plant in a particular area and so on).

An important issue which merits investigation is, then, for what reasons do TNCs interact with the government? We analyse here why TNCs need to maintain relationships or contacts with the host government in India. How important are these relationships for the TNC and which are the main objectives underlying them as manifested in a Government–TNC Network? Which are the main strategic issues involved? Are there any differences in objectives and strategic issues dependent upon the nationality of the TNCs?

Through their contacts with government, TNCs both cooperate for common causes as well as compete with one another. In the former case TNCs within an industry could cooperate to see that the policy favours their industry so that resources are made available to them. Indeed, firms do this because firms belonging to one industry compete with firms belonging to another industry for financial and other resources. In this respect all the firms in a nation show a degree of pooled dependence (Thompson, 1967). Firms within the same industry could also compete for resources. In this respect government relations are competitive as domestic firms compete against TNCs, local producers against importers and so on.

At the policy formulation as well as implementation stage, it is important for firms to keep in mind both these situations. In the first situation, firms in a particular industry or a number of industries engage in cooperative strategies and form cooperative organizations (industrial associations, for example) to plead for government favour. This may involve lobbying with the government. In the second situation, on the other hand, the firms keep in contact with the government independently. Each firm maintains its own contacts and develops its own network of relations in the hierarchical bureaucracy. Evidently, an active and durable interaction with the government can not be achieved without the active participation of the parties (TNCs as well as government bodies). TNCs engage in interaction with governments to seek favours or to minimize disfavours, where TNCs must prove to the bureaucracy that their activities are advantageous to the nation and in conformity with the rules and regulations of the society. TNCs must seek legitimacy from the government.

The various process steps in implementing an industrial policy follow from its formation. Such a chain of events (e.g. decisions or procedures) is necessary to effectuate the industrial policy controls, for example, to issue various licenses. TNCs mainly participate in these networks because these constitute a basic condition for operating successfully in the host country. But there is also a possibility to affect the policy itself. Companies can participate in two main types of networks to influence the industrial controls. They could be interested in abolishing, changing or adding a control. In this way, the policy formation process will work backwards. By changing a control, for example the procedure for industrial licensing, the policy might also be changed, since it is implemented in another way. This could take place gradually. When small changes are accumulated in a certain direction, the result could be a total change of policy.

An action network can also be formed for the purpose of lobbying.[1] In action networks several companies share common interests, and therefore cooperate. Participation in such networks is also necessary for other reasons. The government could be influenced to interpret a rule to favour a group of companies, for instance local firms compared to competitors from abroad. Another reason for membership could be to get first-hand information on the policy formation process. This can also be achieved through direct contacts with the government. In either case, there would be some lessening of uncertainty.

As noted above, companies are interested in influencing the implementation of a policy in order to preempt competitors in acquiring a license or to hasten the processing of applications. For such purposes another network situation is valid. Its main difference compared to action networks is that companies act as competitors and not collaborators. Companies get a competitive advantage by getting an industrial license for a new product, improving their quality or efficiency by investing in new machines or through permission to increase their production capacity or to import products not allowed to the competitors. A competitor could in turn stop or delay rivals to benefit through its own good contacts with the authorities. The industrial policy domain thus consists of partly conflicting and partly cooperating 'political' actors. There are two main reasons why TNCs participate in these organization networks:

1. TNCs must gain legitimacy from government, in the form of licenses.
2. TNCs want to increase efficiency.

These two basic objectives presuppose each other. The more a TNC can improve its legitimacy position in various networks, the easier it is to reach efficiency goals, for example to increase its competitive advantage in the market by gaining the right to import high-quality inputs for the local production site. By gaining legitimacy with the government TNCs are in a better position to gain various types of licenses. As this happens they also could further improve legitimacy with the government. This shows to the society that the operations of a particular TNC take place in accordance with the national aspirations, rules and regulations. In the long run, efficient operations of a firm in a country may even alter national values and norms.

To reach efficiency and legitimacy objectives the TNC thus participate in the authorities' decision processes. It is not enough to merely apply for a license and await the processing and approval. The decision processes in a government are complex with enough scope for individual decision makers to use discretionary powers. Moreover, there are often shared interests between the parties, since the authorities are quite often dependent on TNCs for decision-making, for example in getting information. Furthermore, to increase its competitiveness TNCs try to influence decision makers to favour their own company. However, this objective is subordinated to the legitimacy goal and also to the speeding-up of the application process. (These latter goals are a precondition for being able to fulfil the competitive objective.)

Actions by TNCs towards government might have a direct effect on the implementation of policies by the authorities, which could have an indirect effect on the policy itself, for example altering it by showing that it cannot be implemented as thought. This is elaborated on in Jansson & Sharma (1993).

BUSINESS LEGITIMACY

The TNC network is primarily characterized as a rational structure of high technical development with a collective orientation towards efficiency. But since it is also embedded in highly institutionalized contexts like government and politics, the network is also oriented towards legitimacy (see Figure 2.2). A local unit within the TNC network reflects these two main interests in its organization by having a structure legitimated through being efficient in markets and another structure that reflects the political interest by legitimating inconsistencies in the environment, primarily by incorporating various government demands.

The issue of legitimacy of TNCs is bound up with the fact that organizations require resources from the environment to survive and to function, for example money, information and access to markets. Furthermore, their activities must be approved by society. Legitimation is "the process whereby an organization justifies to a peer or superordinate system its right to exist, that is, to continue to import, transform, and export energy, material, or information" (Maurer, 1978, p. 361). Legitimacy in this sense is externally supplied and externally controlled. Organizations can also try to achieve legitimacy by acting in a manner which is considered to be legitimate, or pursuing goals that are considered legitimate by the resource suppliers. Such a claim for legitimacy is not given and is not achieved automatically. It is acted for and can be influenced. A company must prove its right to operate in a certain country.

One way for TNCs to gain legitimacy is through efficient action. Efficiency has two connotations. In a technical sense, TNCs must be efficient in order to be competitive and survive in the markets. In a non-market and more ideological sense efficiency is a societal norm through which such a behaviour is legitimized by society. From an ideological perspective efficiency is regarded as a more fundamental legitimacy category because it justifies the technological, scientific or rational orientation of the modern welfare state. At this level legitimacy is regarded as expressing the TNC's adaptation to dominating values and attitudes in the society. However, we are not concerned here with this level. Legitimacy is viewed in a more specific context relevant with regard to the government and business sectors. In fact, in its more confined sense legitimacy is defined for three interest groups: the political and administrative sides of government and the foreign business sector. A similar approach is where legitimacy is defined from the perspective of different stake-holders, interest groups or coalition members of the company.

Society is large and complex, consisting of several groups and subgroups with varying norms, values and concepts of what constitutes legitimacy. In a parliamentary system, governments are expected to reflect the dominant values and norms that prevail in society.

Efficiency is defined as market efficiency, and denotes how efficient and competitive companies are in the market. It is a value-oriented concept, viewed differently by various interest groups in society. It is one basis among several, on which TNCs are accepted by government units. It is concerned with output, economic performance or the technical legitimacy. Technical legitimacy then connects efficiency and institutional legitimacy (see Figure 2.2). The latter type of legitimacy is broader than the former type and generally includes the modes of operation. Within the government sector efficiency in the market or technical legitimacy is thus one basis of legitimation among others, where cost-benefit analysis can be used as a basis for such judgements. In this work, efficiency is viewed from an outside angle, the government. This is technical legitimacy, when efficiency is viewed from the government perspective instead of being looked at from the company's standpoint. The vital question is now, how is this efficiency norm expressed in Government policies and rules, and how it affects the TNCs. For example, are the typical values and norms of a Western market economy found in Indian government. If not, how does a company justify its goal related to efficiency? Governments also attribute validity to TNCs on grounds other than economic, chiefly their general behaviour, for example if the laws, regulations and customs of the host society are followed (institutional legitimacy).

TNCs act politically to learn the rules of the game and how to gain legitimacy, for which they organize themselves. This organization is facilitated by a knowledge about how political and administrative organizations gain legitimacy. The industrial policy documents are public documents which an informed and experienced TNC will use to substantiate its case in the proposals submitted to the government.

Arguments dear to the government are highlighted to conform to the letters of the policy. Such conformity to publicly declared policies increases the chances of getting approvals. The arguments will be backed by calculations showing that stated policy is followed and that desirable results will materialize. TNCs also gain legitimacy from administrative units by learning the rules and procedures of the bureaucracy and sticking to them. Hence, legitimacy is achieved by adapting to both political and administrative interests.

STRATEGIC ISSUES OF THE GTN

Classical Weberian bureaucracy that is regulated by rules and regulations and in which each individual bureaucrat is a mere cog in a bigger wheel, will preclude the need for contacts. Since rules and regulations are well-defined and objective and the bureaucrat is guided by these rules and regulations, TNCs would face no problems in getting things implemented. TNCs would learn the rules and regulations and formulate proposals according to the criteria specified by the government. Once these are submitted to the government machinery it would not be necessary to establish contacts with the executive organizations or individuals within them. As stated earlier, this ideal picture is far removed from the real world situation in which TNCs operate.

The more the bureaucracy drifts away from this ideal type, the more opportunities there are for TNCs to influence the manner in which decisions are reached and implemented. There could be either too many overlapping rules and regulations or too few of the same. In either case there is a problem of knowing what the rules are and which rules are applicable in a particular situation. An information asymmetry may prevail between the bureaucracy and TNCs, which creates both opportunities as well as uncertainty.

Moreover, we see that in most government matters, more than one authority (department, unit and so on), either within the same ministry or from a number of different ministries with occasionally conflicting goals, is engaged. As a result the manner in which a particular issue is dealt with and is interpreted is contingent upon which ministries are engaged in the decision process. This also creates opportunities as well as uncertainty.

Which proposals are considered legitimate will be dependent on the above two factors regarding type of government matter and organization of the bureaucracy and will be reflected in the TNC–government interaction. The purpose of the contacts with the government is to show that the performance requirements (local content, export obligations and so on) improved by the government are fulfilled by the TNCs. It is also often in the TNC's interest to hasten the processing of permits and utilize the rules, to benefit its own company. This is related to institutional legitimacy, which also can be used specifically to increase the efficiency of the TNC (Figure 2.2).

To reach the main objectives related to legitimacy three main strategic issues are involved in TNCs' contacts with the Indian government. They are identified as below:

1. to get permits;
2. to hasten the processing of applications;
3. to utilize the rules to benefit the TNC in competition with other TNCs or local firms.

All these issues are connected to institutional legitimacy, while the last two are also related to technical legitimacy through their relation to efficiency. These main strategic issues are sub-divided into thirteen issues, which are ranked and shown in Table 3.1. They were identified through literature review and exploratory interviews with the TNCs in India and included in the questionnaires (see Appendix 2).

The thirteen strategic issues identified for investigation are further classified as those related to a particular application submitted to the government, those related to company's business dealings in general, and those which are 'purely' social in nature. The difference between the first and second categories strongly resemble the distinction between beneficial government decisions and facilitating intelligence, where the latter category concerns knowledge about the political environment, about relevant regulations, governmental decision structures and processes, and public opinion towards foreign products (Boddewyn, 1988, p. 350). As will be seen below both are relevant for our study.

The most striking fact from Table 3.1 is that so many issues are considered to be important for the relations with the government units. Only one strategic issue 'to get information about competitors' is unimportant. As mentioned earlier the Indian government has over a long period of time followed an interventionist policy and through various acts and regulations restricted the business operations of TNCs. They are required by Indian laws to seek permission from the

Table 3.1   *Reasons for contacts with the government: subsidiary's view*

Reasons	1	2	3	4	5	mean value
Application Specific Reasons						
To give information related to a particular application	0	0	1	6	11	4.56
To influence decision on a particular application	0	0	1	11	6	4.28
To speed up a particular application	0	0	0	8	8	4.50
To learn in advance if a particular application will be granted	2	0	3	5	6	3.81
To learn about decision on a particular application	0	0	1	10	5	4.25
General Company Related Reasons						
To learn new policy moves in advance	3	2	0	6	7	3.67
To seek clarification on present policies and procedures in general	0	2	0	9	7	4.17
To get information on competitors	8	4	1	2	1	2.00
To solve disputes	7	2	4	2	3	2.50
To inform the government about the company's adherence to the stipulated terms in licenses & collaboration agreement	0	2	2	9	4	3.88
To inform the government about company's difficulties	0	3	1	7	7	4.00
To give advice on technical matters	1	2	3	3	4	3.54
Social Reasons						
To make a social call	5	1	4	3	4	3.00
Others	0	0	0	0	0	0.00

Note: 1 = Very Unimportant, 2 = Rather Unimportant, 3 = Neither/Nor, 4 = Rather Important, and 5 = Very Important.

government prior to undertaking a new business operation or extending an existing one. Applications are submitted, which are then processed at the various levels and departments in the government and its numerous ministries. In this process TNCs must legitimize the proposals, since not everything works automatically and a number of hurdles develop. The process is slow. Therefore, it is important for TNCs to keep track of the applications and try to move them forward from one position to the other. Therefore, as soon as TNCs submit an application to the government, they need to develop contacts with the decision makers in the ministries to explain, what the company intends with the application and the license, and its impact on the country and industrial development. This means that TNCs invest in linkages with the government to convince the officials that the submitted proposal is feasible within the framework of the Indian laws, and beneficial to the country and its industry. It was expected that alternatives specified under application specific issues should be strong reasons for contacts with the government.

Application Specific Strategic Issues

Many nations have traditionally relied upon performance requirements to contain the activities of TNCs. In India, TNCs are required to meet a number of such requirements, which when seen from the TNCs point of view, are generally negative in nature. For example, TNCs are required to reach a minimal level of local content within a specified number of years. While submitting an application to the authorities TNCs must ensure that their proposal conforms to these official norms and rules specified under the performance requirements.

Five different strategic issues are specified under this category and the responses indicate that all are important. As firms submit applications to the ministries the officials seek clarification and additional information to assess and evaluate the merits of the application. Without a single exception, the strategic issue 'to speed up the processing of a particular application' is for example, specified as either very or a rather important for contacts with the government. Although there are time limits on how much time processing an application should take, there is no guarantee these will be followed. The processing may, and generally does, take longer than stipulated in the guidelines. Our investigation revealed that in 1982 merely 25% of the submitted applications were processed by the Indian bureaucracy within three months from the date of submission (Appendix 2). But by the year 1985 this figure had reached 55%. An important task is, therefore, to influence the speed with which an application is dealt with. None of the respondents specified this strategic issue to be unimportant.

A third important strategic issue is 'to influence decision on a particular application'. None of the respondents indicated that this is an unimportant reason for having contacts with the government. Contacts are also established to 'learn in advance about decision on a particular application'. The purpose is to minimize the time taken by the bureaucracy to intimate the applicant on the final decision. This supports our assertion that gaining legitimacy is a process, since establishing legitimacy does not start with the submission of an application, but much earlier. One may state that a certain degree of legitimacy for a project is already established by the time an application is submitted to the government.

Another strategic issue concerns the wish of the companies 'to assure in advance if a particular application will be granted'. TNCs do not want to submit an application to the government if the likelihood of its rejection is substantial. It is done only if there is a fairly good chance of acceptance. The rejection of an application may kill the venture for a long time and it is difficult to reverse the decision in future. Eleven respondents specified this to be very important or a rather important reason for the contacts. Only three respondents specified this to be either an unimportant strategic issue or neither important nor unimportant.

The purpose behind the interaction is to impress upon the government and most activities are directed at the executive bodies when particular applications are planned or processed. Information related to a specific application is given. Decisions on it are learnt and influenced in order to speed up the processing or to learn in advance if the application will be granted. To justify and legitimize its application the Government is informed about the company's adherence to the stipulated terms in licenses and collaboration agreements. The TNC also informs the authorities about its problems and difficulties. These two latter types of information exchange do not necessarily take place only in connection with specific applications. They are also part of the general exchange of information between the parties.

A failure on the part of a firm to execute terms of an agreement or application is less problematic if explained to the government. Indeed, such an information may be used as a strategy to enhance the legitimacy claims of the firm. It is generally difficult to hide this type of failure, since the competitors, the news media or others uncover such failures. It is better that the decision makers learn of these failures directly from the firms rather than through leaks and press reports. This supplies TNCs with opportunities to communicate with the authorities and seek an improved deal.

General Business Related Strategic Issues

These strategic issues are not directly related to a particular application and its processing, but are related to the general environment in the country. It is important to know of new moves in the industrial front as early as possible and to influence the same if possible. They are also important in order to detect the prevailing and the forthcoming business opportunities in the country. Indeed, TNCs can learn on some of the changes through the mass media, but that is not necessarily reliable. TNCs get such information by being members of different associations. However, face-to-face contacts with the decision makers in the government is certainly a more accurate and reliable source of information.

All the alternatives specified within the general business-related category, with the exception of two, are fairly strong but not a very strong strategic issue of the GTN. There are individual variations. Among these strategic issues one seems to be particularly important, namely, 'to seek clarification on present policies and procedures in general'. More or less all respondents (around 85%) specified this strategic issue to be rather or very strong for contacts with the government. To seek clarification is important as government laws do change. In the Indian case, radical changes in industrial policy are rather infrequent. However, the interpretation of the laws and their implementation do vary over time depending upon the political situation, among other things. It is therefore important to be informed along what rules or criteria actually apply and the alternative courses of action that are available.

Closely related to the above is the strategic issue 'to learn new policy moves in advance', which is also vital. This helps companies to plan and initiate measures to adhere to the government policies and changes. Similarly, government must be informed if the company has been able to adhere to the conditions imposed upon it in the past. This indicates a company's sincerity to the host country as well as its ability to keep its promises given in the past. This is closely related to another strategic issue, namely, 'to inform the government about company's difficulties'. These could relate to a particular application or to the general business climate (namely, tax structure or tariffs), or the inefficient functioning of infrastructure (transport or power). 'To give advice to the authorities on technical issues' is an unimportant strategic issue. Indian authorities rely upon their own institutions for advice on technical matters. However, such contacts do occur as in a number of areas the level of technical expertise of the Indian authorities is below that of the TNCs.

An even less important strategic issue of the GTN is 'to solve disputes'. In the general debate a point is made that companies pass through a cumbersome, lengthy, and complicated licensing procedure. The rules are vague. We had expected a significant level of conflict in government–TNC relationships. A majority of the respondents identified this issue as being either very or rather unimportant. This is contrary to the opinion that TNCs and governments are frequently in conflict with each other. Similarly, the strategic issue 'to seek information on competitors' is weak. Twelve out of sixteen respondents specified this strategic issue as being either very or rather unimportant. Only three respondents specified the issue as either rather or very important. We had expected that this strategic issue would be more important. As government seeks information from all the TNCs in India this could be a good source of information on the competitors. One explanation could be that leaking such an information is illegal in India. Moreover, this is not considered legitimate and in tune with the free market ideology propagated by the firms.

The above figures indicate an emphasis on a conflict aversion behaviour rather than a conflict resolution behaviour. Case is taken to see conflicts do not arise. In this sense TNCs can claim to be good citizens of the nation. The above may also have to do with the nature of the Indian bureaucracy. The government officials are highly status conscious and showing respect is important. A conflict may imply that TNCs do not accept the opinion of the official bureaucracy, which can be taken as a sign of disrespect.

Application-specific and general business-related strategic dimensions are related. In the short run, they may survive independently of each other, in the long run, however, they either support or contradict each other. Our assertion is that TNCs that are able to gain a high level of legitimacy in their contacts for general business related issues are in a superior position to gain licenses and applications approved for a particular business proposition. On the other hand, those firms that have a better legitimacy concerning specific licenses may build upon these, a position with the government, even for the future.

It is concluded from a study of these responses, that the GTN is not utilized to compete head-on with other companies. Influence positions are not primarily built up to favour business efficiency but to gain institutional legitimacy, and therefore efficiency primarily has an indirect bearing on the TNC–government relations. The study shows that business legitimacy is achieved in various ways. In order to get it from the political system it is necessary to learn new policy moves in advance, which is not a one-time process but a continuous process. This is an important aspect with a profound impact on the organizational arrangement to manage TNC–government relationships. Such clarifications are also sought from the administrative organizations. This pattern is confirmed by the answers to the question about 'how important are the following reasons for the Government of India to take the initiative to contact your company?' The answers to another question show that the importance of the company's contacts with the Government is mainly unchanged regarding these strategic issues since 1984. There is a small increase for certain strategic issues. Two reasons appear important. First, these show that implementing liberal policies take time. The prevailing network structure and contacts therein take time to dissolve or re-structure (see Jansson & Sharma, 1993). The fact that it is unimportant to solve disputes indicates that the GTN is characterized by cooperativeness.

A conclusion drawn from the answers to these questions, and directly confirmed by a direct question on the matter, is that the contacts in the network are initiated by the TNCs. When applying for industrial licenses, import licenses and licenses for import of technology contacts are established with different government units for the strategic reasons stated above. This is in accordance with the rules stipulated by the government. Thus the initiative for individual applications rests with the TNCs, while the initiative for setting the general guidelines for such applications rests with the government. The contacts are normally taken within the context of already established relationships within the GTN.

Socially Based Strategic Issues

Only one strategic issue was mentioned within the third category, namely, 'to make a social call'. Social calls could be a good mechanism to maintain a continuity in the relationships. Firms do not always have applications lying with the government for processing.

Inbetween the processing of applications, relationships with the government officials can be maintained through social calls. In the survey this is only a fairly strong reason for contacts with the government. Seven respondents specified this strategic issue to be either rather important or very important, whereas six identified the same as either unimportant or rather unimportant. Another four specified this issue as being neither of the two above categories. Two different interpretations are plausible. Firstly, officials avoid such contacts. As TNCs are rather suspect, it is possible that a close association with TNCs is 'officially' unacceptable and not recommended. Too close a social contact with TNCs could be considered as unsuitable for maintaining objectivity. Officials in the various ministries, therefore, avoid social contacts. Secondly, it is possible that TNCs believe that such contacts are not a source of legitimacy. A more important reason for the above pattern is, however, that such social contacts are purposive and act more as supportive contacts, which strengthen other contacts mentioned earlier. In this respect the existence of social contacts is surprising and shows that official decision making is removed from the process defined in the traditional decision making theory.

GAINING BUSINESS LEGITIMACY

As mentioned earlier the business operations of TNCs in India are regulated. There are laws on ownership structure, product composition, imports, and royalty payments, among others. TNCs operating in such an institutional environment cannot survive by being efficient in only the technical sense. A TNC may have an excellent record, produce products desired by the market, and have an outstanding technology but this is not helpful as long as the institutional environment is hostile.

TNCs investigated in this study have been successful, both in India as well as in the rest of the world. In the Indian market these firms are highly appreciated for their high quality products and services. Over the previous decades these TNCs have penetrated the Indian market and there is no dearth of clients in the market. A number of these firms can quite easily increase their production significantly in the country, if only the institutional environment is willing to allow them the opportunity to expand. Their equity shares in the Indian share market are highly valued and investors are willing to supply financial resources. These firms can easily finance their expansion and growth programmes.

But all the TNCs investigated here operate in a highly institutional-ized environment and their operation is influenced by the characteris-tics of such an environment (Selznick, 1948; Singh, Tucker, & House, 1986; Scott, 1987). Firstly, as mentioned earlier, there are elaborate rules and regulations on the type of business operations these TNCs can engage in. TNCs are more or less banned from operating in the consumer goods industries, mining industry, and small scale indus-tries, to name a few. In principle, the operations of the TNCs are confined to the hi-tech priority sector, where operations must be sanctioned by the government.

Secondly, as mentioned earlier, there are elaborate rules and regu-lations governing the ownership pattern of the Indian subsidiary. In general, TNCs are not permitted to hold more than 40% of the equity shares in an Indian subsidiary. A change in the equity ownership must be sanctioned by the government.

Thirdly, there are a number of other elaborate institutional rules and regulations concerning the use of local components and parts (for example, the subsidiary undertakes to procure more or less all the components and parts from local sources within 3-5 years according to the Phased Manufacturing Program), royalty payments, and trans-fer of technology. At the time of entry in the Indian market or when seeking an expansion of production, TNCs must seek sanction from the government on all these and many more issues. Officials in the government inspect the details and impose performance requirements.

There is an underlying belief (a myth) that these elaborate institu-tional rules and regulations protect the Indian society from the 'imperialistic design' of the TNCs. It is also stated that restriction on the operations of TNCs will enable the country to achieve a higher degree of self-sufficiency and autarky, should contribute towards a strong domestic industry, and to a more desirable form of economic and industrial progress.

TNCs operating in such an institutionalized environment adapt to these elaborate rules and regulations to gain legitimacy. A first step while seeking legitimacy is to acquire a good knowledge of the insti-tutionalized rules, regulations and practices. The last is important as the written rules and regulations frequently deviate from the manner in which they are applied. Indeed, a TNC may try to acquire this knowledge by going through the guidelines and legal documents. This is insufficient as the rules are cumbersome with a number of 'ifs' and 'thens'. Moreover, knowledge on how these rules and regulations are

interpreted and applied is crucial. In a way neither the interpretation
nor the application of these rules and regulations is 'objective', that is
independent of time and people involved.

Keeping these elaborate institutionalized values, rules and regulations in mind, TNCs first prepare and then submit proposals to the
government for processing. A good source of knowledge on how to
prepare an application, what aspects to include (or exclude), what to
emphasize, is the government itself. Contacts with the decision makers
and the avenues to seek their views and opinion are valued and a
source of advantage. These contacts help TNCs to comply with the
institutionalized rules and regulations. Hence, the importance of contacts for the 'general company related strategic issues'. Such contacts
also help TNCs to gain an understanding about such important issues
as which proposals to submit and when. The same also helps TNCs to
ascertain which technology to use in a project (the most advanced
technology or a second hand technology), the scale of production, and
where to locate a plant (a backward area with possibilities of subsidies
from the government or near an established industrial location).
Discussions in advance on issues such as 'if an application will be
granted' helps to legitimatize the project with the government.
Similarly, strategic issues such as 'to inform the government about a
company's adherence to the stipulated terms in previous licenses and
collaboration agreements' and 'to inform the government about company's difficulties' are directed towards influencing the manner in
which the institutionalized environment (the government) perceives
and treats a TNC.

After submitting the applications contacts start due to 'application
specific strategic issues'. A TNC must legitimatize to the bureaucracy
that its application for a license is in conformity with the rules and
regulations. Each piece of a proposal must be legitimated. Claims
made by the TNC on technology, import requirements, use of
domestic parts and components, and foreign collaborations must be
vindicated and questions must be answered. In this process, TNCs
first must show a willingness to listen to the government and then
comply with its wishes. A technically correct answer to a query by
the officials is insufficient. Also important is the willingness to introduce changes in the original proposal in keeping with the official
interpretation of the laws, rules, and regulations. This willingness on
the part of the TNC is a source of legitimacy, since it allows the TNC
to claim that it is a good citizen of the country, and illustrates willingness to participate in the industrial uplift of the country as inter-

preted by the government. The firm can show, for example, that the technology import is not repetitive and that the firm makes a positive contribution to the country through imports of improved technology, training of local people, employment creation, and uplift of industrially backward areas.

The central point is that through contacts TNC gain an understanding of the institutional environment and the methods and the means to comply with the same. A mistake is fatal, as the application will be rejected.

Through contacts TNCs are able to convince the government about their willingness and intentions to adhere to the government's rules and regulations. At each level in the bureaucracy, an appropriate mix of information is supplied to seek legitimacy. Contacts permit TNCs to ascertain what information to supply, which, in turn, is contingent upon requirements put out by a particular official. Consequently, it is not unexpected that contacts for the strategic issue 'to solve conflicts' are less important. A conflict situation is dangerous for TNCs as the institutional environment is too powerful and can refuse to supply legitimacy (Aldrich, 1979). Conflicts may change the perception of the government of a TNC and create hostility. This may create difficulties for a number of years to follow.

These contacts contribute little to the efficiency of the TNCs. Indeed, in the majority of the cases the entire process only delays the venture, leads to cost escalation, and restricts freedom of action. Through years of experience in the Indian market the TNCs in our study know that they can easily sell their output in the market. The technology is already developed and tested by the parent company. Contacts with the government are established merely to seek institutional legitimacy, although in the process, valuable investment could be lost and alternatives available to consumers restricted.

In the process of acquiring legitimacy the general company related contacts and the application specific contacts are tightly coupled. The former helps the latter (Weick, 1969; Orton & Weick, 1990). The better the contacts for the general company related issues, the better the chances are to adjust to the procedures, rules, regulations, and myths. In our opinion legitimacy achieved through social means is a necessary but not a sufficient condition for business success. To achieve success in the long term would demand that TNCs adhere to the norms and values of a host society irrespective of the rationality of these norms and values.

NATIONALITY: DOES IT MATTER?

The survey does not indicate significant differences in the response based on the nationality of the TNC. A cross-tabulation shows that the response pattern is similar for the TNCs. As seen in Table 3.2 there are differences regarding a few of the issues. For the Swedish TNCs, for example, the general business related contacts with the government officials is more important than for German TNCs. The single largest deviation is for the strategic issue 'to learn new policy moves in advance'. This is a more important strategic issue for the Swedish respondents than for the Germans. The same is true, but to a lesser extent, for the strategic issue 'to seek clarification on present policies and procedures in general'. On other issues mentioned in Table 3.2 the deviation is slight.

Table 3.2   Nationality & differences in general company related contacts*

Reason for	Swedish				Germans			
contacts	1-2	3	4-5	sum	1-2	3	4-5	sum
To learn on new policy moves in advance	1	0	10	11	4	0	3	7
To seek clarification on present policies & procedures	0	0	11	11	2	0	5	7
To solve disputes	4	3	4	11	5	1	1	7
To inform authorities about company's difficulties	1	0	10	11	2	1	4	7
Give advice on technical matters	0	2	5	7	3	1	2	7

*   On the issues not mentioned in this table the deviation in response is insignificant. Moreover, the alternatives supplied are the same as table 1.

Although the number of TNCs researched is limited, the German TNCs seem to maintain contacts with the government more for social reasons than their Swedish counterparts (Table 3.3). This is somewhat surprising and unexpected. None of the respondents in the German firms specified the alternatives either very or rather unimportant,

Table 3.3   Nationality & contacts for social reasons

Nationality	1	2	3	4	5
Swedish*	4	1	2	2	1
German*	1	0	2	1	3

*   The alternatives supplied are the same as in table 1.

whereas three Swedish respondents did so. On the other hand, three German respondents specified these strategic issues as very important whereas only one Swedish respondent did so. Due to the small number of TNCs studied, a definite conclusion is, nevertheless, difficult to draw.

A major result of the study is that no significant distinction between the Swedish and the German firms was uncovered. This indicates that the contacts with the host government are dictated by the characteristics of the institutionalized environment in India rather than by the nationality of the TNC and that this environment exerts a 'similar' influence on TNCs is the matter of submitting an application to gain legitimacy. This is rational as the laws and the demands exerted on TNCs in India are local-specific and based on local industrial structure and supply conditions. Similarly, the individual components of the performance requirements and their respective importance vary over time. In the Indian case importing has been problematic in those product areas, where local capacity exists, and imports are only accepted if the quality of the local product is very much inferior in comparison with the requirements. All these aspects require liaison with the government and need a very high degree of familiarity with the local economy and the local production structure. The need for decentralization within the TNC network is obvious.

The equivalence in dealing with government does not imply that there is a standardized way to do it and that all TNCs pursue the same strategy. Rather the similarity lies in the fact that through trial and error, TNCs learn which units, sections, and departments within a ministry that are more powerful and yield a stronger influence in the decision making process, which issues are emphasized, and at what stage and level in the decision making process. There seems to exist an Indian way to manage relationships with the government, to gain access to the officials, approach them, and pay respects to the same.

Since the TNCs included in the survey are well established in India with years of experience they have learnt the Indian way. It also implies that the decision regarding why, how, when, and whom to contact in the government is carried out by the Indian subsidiary and not imposed by the parent firm from outside India. The subsidiary is familiar with the institutionalized environment and legitimacy requirements in India and the manner in which to secure the same. This knowledge is based on experience (Penrose, 1966). The process is organic and based on imitation and evolves over time. This is not an outcome of a centralized decision at the head office of the TNC. Imitation plays an important part in the whole process. TNCs observe each others' ways of managing contacts with the government and pursue a 'similar' strategy.

COOPERATIVE AND COMPETITIVE ASPECTS OF THE NETWORK

The discussion in the previous sections may have created the impression that the interaction between the government and TNCs is always harmonious and peaceful. In reality this is hardly the case. Interaction between TNCs and government is characterized along two main dimensions: the extent of cooperation and competition. These aspects are not mutually exclusive but rather, are complementary. The degree of competitiveness as well as the degree of cooperativeness are characterized in Figure 3.1 to be either low or high. When both these aspects are low, the Government–TNC network is defined as a peripheral strategy on the part of the TNC. This strategy is not valid in India. This is a typical strategy when TNCs do not have to deal much with government and therefore can concentrate on the business or efficiency aspects.

Figure 3.1   Network strategies

	Degree of cooperativeness	
Degree of competitiveness	**Low**	**High**
High	DOMINATION	CONSENSUS
Low	PERIPHERAL	COOPERATION

The other three strategies are part of the Indian scene. The co-operation strategy is signified by high cooperation among the parties, while competition is low. In this situation government as well as TNCs are familiar with each other's needs and find that they are complementary. This strategy is practiced by TNCs that are in a very strong position in the host country, in that they are in high demand by governments due to the advanced technology they can offer or their good export potential or because they are considered to be highly efficient. However, we know from the present study and our general knowledge of the Indian situation that this strategy is uncommon in India or any country following an import-substitution policy. This strategy is prevalent in countries that have an export-promotion strategy, for example, Malaysia, Singapore and Thailand in Southeast Asia. These countries favour an industrial policy founded on Western market ideology, where foreign companies usually are mainly evaluated on market performance, making technical legitimacy more important than institutional legitimacy.

The opposite case, the domination strategy is the typical situation in which each party wants to dominate the other party and when the use of bargaining power is common. Either one or both may perceive the demands put by the counterpart as illegitimate, still lacking alternatives. Network relationships may continue. The use of bargaining power may, however, deteriorate the quality of the relationship. A change in the bargaining power in favour of the counterpart may create difficulties in the future. For this reason this could be an unstable situation. A major conclusion from this research is that the domination strategy is not typical in India and not suitable towards the Indian government. This is also shown by two well-known historical examples of this strategy, namely the IBM and Coca-Cola cases mentioned below. One might even say that this strategy has been more practised by American TNCs than by European or Japanese TNCs, and therefore this strategy may have a certain cultural bias. American companies are usually stronger advocates of the 'free-market' ideology, and are being considered to be more conflict-oriented, than Asian or European TNCs.

The strategy which involves both a high degree of cooperation and competition is complex. This consensus strategy seems to be typical of how European TNCs act in India. There is a high degree of dependence between the parties. This creates a basic understanding about each party's position and an awareness of the need for each other as well as the existence of a basic conflict between them. In such situations creativeness and ingenuity are called for to evolve solutions in order to accommodate the conflicting positions. It is important to avoid securing gains at the cost of the counterpart. Adjustments by the parties may be introduced either in the goals, or in the means to achieve the goals. One alternative could be for both parties to achieve their goals but not at the same time, by a de-coupling along the time-dimension. Alternatively, TNCs and government accommodate each other in different areas. TNCs may, for example, agree to export a portion of their production in return for freedom to import technology, raw material or equipment. It seems plausible that in such circumstances, subsidiaries of TNCs enjoy a particular advantage, since they are part of a world-wide network. This may provide the subsidiary with a better possibility to develop a 'mix' acceptable to the government in return for a 'suitable' treatment.

The possibilities of a satisfactory deal with the government do improve as governments are a coalitions of interests. A number of ministries and interest groups with conflicting views on what needs to be done participate in the decision making process. TNCs can form coalition with a few of the powerful interest groups in society and offer to 'satisfy' the view of a few ministries or groups in exchange for their support.

BUSINESS EFFICIENCY

The primary basis for collective orientation of the group network of the TNC is efficiency/effectiveness or business efficiency as it is defined here. This concept thus concerns both internal and external efficiency as seen from the perspective of the TNC, since it emphasizes the technical aspects of organization structure. What could be expected from different structures regarding the possibilities of achieving a certain degree of collective orientation? A pronounced orientation towards efficiency is typical of the Western business firm, notably the TNCs of this study. Cultural factors do determine how efficiency is viewed and how efficient an organization is, and how the organizational process is viewed. Organizational processes in firms in the West are seen as a systematic coordination of discrete parts, which can be synthesized and analysed. Organizational structures are designed to accommodate the individual and expect him to function in an individual capacity. Japanese firms, as representative of an oriental collectivist culture, are seen as an interconnected whole, a collective, where only the totality of the whole, not the individual parts, can be judged. In the latter, there is an element of higher moral involvement in the organization, as compared to Western firms.

This orientation towards allocative efficiency by TNCs in the West is most clearly revealed in transaction cost theory and expressed as a goal to minimize transaction costs. The efficiency logic that is related to administrative rationality is best captured by transaction cost theory, whereas the pattern of the TNC network could be explained from this theory. This is analysed further in Chapters 5 and 6. As discussed there, efficiency is mainly accomplished by promoting unity in action, where organization is primarily focused on consensus around common solutions to problems and decisions are consistent with the solutions and based on common efficiency goals and values that support these (ideologies). This breeds enthusiasm, competence and efficiency.

RELATION BETWEEN BUSINESS EFFICIENCY AND LEGITIMACY

As stated earlier, companies cannot survive solely by being efficient. The fact that efficiency is defined differently in various cultures is the main reason why technical legitimacy is important. This type of legitimacy provides a direct link between efficiency and legitimacy. There are other bases too according to which companies are accepted in different societies. This institutional legitimacy is more indirectly connected to efficiency. Indeed, neither efficiency or legitimacy are absolute categories and are present simultaneously for all the organizations. There is also a conflict between the two, the more of one may lead to less of the other. There is a continuum along which organizations can be ranked. There are organizations with strong emphasis on efficiency in market terms. They produce goods and services no less effectively than the competitors. These organizations emphasize the management of their internal and external relationships. Internally they must efficiently divide the work, establish an organizational structure to produce the goods and services, evolve a hierarchy to achieve coordination and resolve internal conflicts, develop information collecting and interpretation routines and procedures. Externally they must manage their relationships with the actors in the environment, that is, the players in the market place: the customers, the suppliers, the distributors, and so on. Organizations such as TNCs are primarily validated on commercial norms imposed by the environment, for example, profit and growth. Failing to meet these criteria will jeopardize their chances of survival. In addition, these organizations must also accede to institutional norms regarding pollution control, regional development, consumer needs and so on.

This relation between business efficiency and legitimacy is illustrated in Figure 3.2. In cells 2 and 3 are found stable cases. A TNC found in cell 3 is in a bad position, since the company is neither competitive nor legitimate. A plausible option is to withdraw from the host country voluntarily or be forced out by competition or government. The opposite position is found in cell 2, where the high legitimacy has been achieved by being efficient. In cells 1 and 4 unstable cases are shown. In cell 1 the position with the government is good at present, where the TNC through the high legitimacy is protected from competition by government. But since the legitimacy position does not rest on a solid efficiency ground, it could be undermined in the future by a change of government, which also may jeopardize the TNC's competitive strength in the market by taking away the protection. Cell 4 illustrates that efficiency is not enough. There must also be legitimacy. The high efficiency is here undermined by too low a legitimacy. This is a classical issue regarding the effects of TNCs on host LDCs. An efficient TNC may drive less efficient local firms out of business and monopolize domestic markets. It may also hinder domestic firms to emerge, thereby stifling local entrepreneurship. When host country governments fear such consequences, it is harder for TNCs to justify their operations in the country, to be seen as good citizens. The IBM and Coca-Cola cases in India, during the 1970s prove the point. Both firms were exceptionally successful in business efficiency terms, being profitable and having a satisfactory growth. Still, neither company fit well in the political situation prevailing at that time and Indians did not see any benefits in having such TNCs. Coca-Cola was perceived as an extravagance in a country where the

Figure 3.2   Relation between legitimacy and efficiency

	Efficiency	
Legitimacy	Low	High
High	Cell 1	Cell 2
Low	Cell 3	Cell 4

majority of the population lacked drinking water. The conflict resulted in the expulsion of the two companies from the country.

Overall, the TNCs studied are found in cell 2, where an acceptable trade-off between efficiency and legitimacy has been found by operating in India for many years, thereby gaining lot of experience. However, this has not always been the case. We know from our earlier research in India that some of the companies have come into unbalanced situations due to large shifts in government policies. Even if no larger unbalanced situations were found for the period under study (1984-1989), this does not mean a stable situation, however. A main result of this research is how the continuous balancing between efficiency and legitimacy perspectives take place with changes in markets, within TNCs and governments. Social norms and values change over time as do demand and competition in a market. As a consequence the technical legitimacy as well as institutional legitimacy are in state of flux and tension, and where the main strategic issue is to seek a balance between the two. Since efficiency aspects primarily are an internal issue for firms, the real problem lies with the legitimacy dimension, that is the trade-off between technical and institutional legitimacy.

Companies could attain a competitive advantage over their rivals through legitimacy, which can be utilized to further business aims. These advantages that are mostly specific to the subsidiary, are created and are not equally available to every firm (TNCs or local). Their distribution is unequal and their access could be viewed as an entry barrier. In the Indian market, as in a number of other markets, it is the ability of a TNC to gain such a subsidiary specific competitive advantage that to a large extent determines its success.

The ability and the feasibility of combining the firm specific advantage at the group level (Hymer, 1976; Dunning, 1988; Rugman, 1979, 1986; Jansson, 1994a) with the subsidiary level, thereby creating a subsidiary specific advantage, is the source of the real strength of TNCs, particularly compared to local competitors.

In shifting our perspective to the government side we notice that a problem faced by governments when trying to change industrial policies and their implementation, pertains to 'softening' the strong legitimacy positions enjoyed by many TNCs, particularly since they often have been achieved from grounds other than efficiency. This justification of business operations in ways (institutional legitimacy) other than through being efficient (technical legitimacy), can be advanced as the main reason for the low efficiency in the protected

Indian markets and the markets of many other developing countries. From the government's point of view, then, the legitimacy/efficiency situation might be unbalanced and found in cell 1, where TNCs, but chiefly certain Indian business houses, enjoy a high legitimacy resulting in inefficient markets and companies.

SUMMARY AND CONCLUSIONS

In this chapter the strategic issues involved in the government relationships of Swedish and German TNCs have been studied and the evidence presented. The strategic issues are divided into three different categories, namely, application specific, general business related and socially-oriented. Our conclusion is that TNCs operate in a highly institutionalized environment and that contacts between TNCs and the government are shaped by the desire of the former to achieve legitimacy in the institutionalized society.

In the overall research some changes in the strategic issues came to light after the government of India liberalized some of its policies towards the TNCs in the year 1984. The most significant changes concern the category application specific strategic issues. This indicates an increasing activity of TNCs in India.

Legitimacy is achieved through the GTN, a crucial impact being the evolution of more stable and permanent network structures in which both parties are interwoven. Contacts between the government and the investigated firms are frequent and evolve into stable network structures in which the parties act and learn to communicate. Government personnel and company officials develop familiarity with each other. The real issue is to find the right people, since without their cooperation not much can be achieved (Weinberger, 1988, p. 79). Friends inside the bureaucracy are a useful resource. They also help to identify adversaries, that is, those who might oppose a particular position or proposal (Yoffie, 1988). Such operational characteristics of the GTN will be presented and analysed in detail in the next chapter.

To reiterate, it is through frequent contacts with the government that TNCs keep the network intact. It is not merely important to maintain contacts when a licensing application is submitted for processing but to sustain the same over time. Contacts which result from general company related strategic issues and social circumstances are, consequently, important and serve to strengthen and solidify the network. Even if social contacts are less important and not a primary strategic issue, per se, important cementing effects are produced in the government relationships together with other strategic issues. These networks evolve their own code of conduct and communication channels, which on certain occasions may complement the legally sanctioned procedures, while on other occasions may contradict them. An impact of the rigid network structure is that the liberalization put into practice is limited (Jansson & Sharma, 1993).

Legitimacy is the main purpose behind the organization of the GTN. Parties of the GTN claim from and give legitimacy to each other and other parties outside the network. TNCs claim validity for their actions by establishing linkages with different government units. Communication channels with the executive bodies of the government serve many purposes: help to know of policy moves in advance, provide clarification on present policies and procedures, provide information about, and influence, decisions on specific license matters, to inform about the company's adherence to the stipulated terms in licenses and collaboration agreements. Social calls by themselves, are a rather important part of these relationships. The contacts in this emergent arm's-length network are mostly initiated by the TNCs. To gain business legitimacy it is thus up to the TNCs to act towards government. In the process efficiency goals are achieved as well, for example by speeding up the licensing process and to utilize the contacts in competition with other firms. It is important to achieve a balance between these two basic objectives. Allocating too much resources into gaining and maintaining legitimacy with government rather than into market activities could benefit the company in the short run as long as the present government is in power. This is demonstrated by a recent change of government in India, the most striking example being changes of favour of a specific business family. The opposite unbalanced situation is equally unfavourable, where the TNC is acting too much in markets and too little in government corridors.

NOTES

1. An action network is defined as a temporary alliance for a limited purpose. It is also called an action-set (Aldrich & Whetten, 1981, p. 387). Cartels, trusts and organized lobbying groups are examples of action networks formed by companies.
2. An institutionally based theory to the organization of transnational corporation is found in Jansson (1994a).

4. Operational Characteristics of the Government–TNC Network

In chapter 3 we discussed the main objectives and the strategic issues involved in TNCs' quest for business legitimacy. We consider here the role of the TNC–government network in utilizing the strategic means in attaining the objective of business legitimacy.

INFLUENCE

As discussed earlier, a claim for business legitimacy is accepted by government after assessing whether TNCs act according to the ideology, values and norms represented by the government. If these norms and values were exact and stable, TNCs would only need to adapt to them to gain legitimacy. But as we have seen this is not the case in respect of industrial policy and its implementation, where there is always the potential to influence the ideology, norms and values of the government. Influence is both dependent on the hierarchical position of a person or a group of people and on positions within the arm's-length government–TNC network. The direction of influence can therefore be both horizontal as in the latter case as well as vertical as in the former case. In order to exert influence, parties communicate with each other and engage in exchange. Influence is thus different from authority which is entirely hierarchically legitimate.

Our research shows that TNCs are successful in convincing the Indian authorities on what the firms consider as prudent and correct (Table 4.1). It is therefore interesting to know how this was achieved at the operational level, that is what the network looks like in such situations. The survey shows that in all the cases TNCs are able to convince the Indian decision makers on the suitability of their proposals. This is true irrespective of the nationality of the TNC. This response is further supported by the fact that, in the area of expansion of production capacity, for example, the TNCs which were studied have always been able to acquire licenses.

Through early contacts with the government at the preparatory stage, TNCs prepare a sound ground for seeking various types of licenses. Through their network of relationships TNCs are in a good position to ascertain in advance how to apply for a license, how the licensing application will be interpreted in the bureaucracy, and when to submit the same to the authorities for approval.

Thus, as illustrated in Table 4.1, TNCs are often or very often successful in getting government officials in India to accept their arguments. In addition, Table 4.2 shows that material resources in the form of services or favours such as presents, transport, entertainment and speed money are exchanged. Presents are given to the government officials and a kind of 'taxi service' is operated for them. They are also normally invited to restaurants for dinners and other amusements, and are paid extra 'fees' for their services. This highlights the need for contacts with the government.

Table 4.1   How often TNCs are able to convince the government on their argument

Nationality of TNCs	1	2	3	4	5
German	6	7	0	0	0
Swedish	4	3	0	0	0

Note: 1= very often; 2 = often; 3 = now and then; 3 = seldom; 5 = never.

Table 4.2   The importance of providing favours to government officials

	1	2	3	4	5	NR
Presents		1	5	5	5	1
Free transport (cars etc.)		1	2	9	4	1
Entertainment			6	6	4	1
Guest houses	1	1	1	7	4	3
Speed money		2	4	4	5	2

Note: 1 = very unimportant; 2 = rather unimportant; 3 = neither nor; 4 = rather important; 5 = very important; n = 17.

CONTACT PATTERNS

The contact pattern of the GTN tended to follow a specific procedure and take place between certain organizational levels. However, as observed earlier in the book, the study demonstrates that decisions and action according to this procedure and at these levels do not entirely take place as prescribed by the authorities or which is expressed through the formal network. There is also room for other decisions and action occurring in emergent networks in order to adapt to changing conditions. Therefore, the arm's-length Government–TNC network becomes a mix of prescribed and emergent networks.

The procedure followed by the GTN in seeking the four types of licenses, is divided into two stages, namely the preparation stage and the processing stage. The former is before an application is submitted to the government. The latter starts when the application is submitted to the government until it is approved. The study shows that the contact pattern is almost the same for the preparation as well as the processing stage. People seem to meet a little more often in the processing stage, but not much. On the other hand, each meeting seems to take a slighter longer time at the preparation stage. This is on account of the fact that at the preparation stage TNCs seek information on rules, regulations, and procedures. At the processing stage they try to push the application through the bureaucracy which we expected to be more time-consuming. Since no main differences in the contact pattern between these stages were found, general results are mostly presented for the whole process.

Government Level Contacts

In the government four levels of contact were identified, while TNCs are divided into three hierarchical levels (see Figure 4.1). The political level is found at the top and involves various ministers. Of the three administrative levels, the high level includes the major positions of secretary, additional secretary and joint secretary. The positions of director, deputy secretary, under secretary and section officer are found at the middle administrative level, while the low administrative level mainly includes clerks.

It is often stated that the political leadership interferes in industrial policy implementation and that the political leadership in India and other developing countries too often intermingles with firms. Favours are traded and the political leadership in these countries often reacts

Figure 4.1   Position tables for government and foreign subsidiary

GOVERNMENT

Level P	Political level	Cabinet Minister State Minister Deputy Minister
Level A1	Administrative levels High	Secretary Additional Secretary Joint Secretary
Level A2	Middle	Director Deputy Secretary Undersecretary Section officer
Level A3	Low	Clerks

FOREIGN SUBSIDIARY

Level C1	High	Chairman of the board Board members M.D.
Level C2	Middle	Business Area Manager Company Secretary Functional Manager Department Manager "Liason officer"
Level C3	Low	Clerks

in favour of TNCs. Consequently, one would have expected that TNCs' contacts with the political level and the high administrative level would be important. The response from the TNCs, however, lends no support to such an expectation (Table 4.3).

Not a single respondent specified the contacts with the political level as very important, whereas two thirds of the respondents specified that these contacts are neither important nor very unimportant. Even more surprising is the response received which stated that contacts with the lower level in the government are more important than those with the political level. The most important contacts are those with the middle level bureaucracy, which are followed by the high

Ta. 4.3   *Importance of contacts with the different government levels at the preparation stage (A) and the processing stage (B)*

LEVEL (see Figure 4.1)	1		2		3		4		5		NR	
	A	B	A	B	A	B	A	B	A	B	A	B
Political	5	2	1	2	2	3	4	1	0	0	7	9
High Administrative	1	0	2	0	5	1	8	13	1	2	0	1
Middle Administrative	0	0	1	0	0	0	6	8	10	9	0	0
Low Administrative	3	0	4	1	4	1	4	9	2	5	0	1

Note: 1 = very unimportant; 2 = rather unimportant; 3 = neither nor; 4 = rather important; 5 = very important.

level. Obviously, both the preparation and the processing of license applications are the responsibility of the bureaucracy. The political level is less engaged at these stages. The reasons are that political leadership is less familiar with such executive issues, particularly since the details and the rigours of the rules and regulations are voluminous and cumbersome with several clauses and exceptions, of which it takes time to gain an insight and a deep knowledge. The politically elected leadership is thus in no position to gain this type of deep knowledge compared to the bureaucrat, who has a permanent employment contract and who after years or decades of service in the same department commands a good insight regarding these issues.

Company Level Contacts and the Initiative Structure

According to Figure 4.1. there are three major levels at the foreign subsidiaries in India involved in government contacts. At the high level is found the chairman of the board, the board members and the managing director. The middle level comprises possible business area managers, functional managers, department managers, the company secretary and the 'liaison manager'. The main responsibility of the company secretary is the legal matters of the company, which often gets this person involved in government matters. The company secretary could then also become the 'liaison manager', that is the person responsible at the subsidiary for managing the contacts with government. But this responsibility could also be given to another manager, for example a functional manager. By a liaison officer is meant a person working directly in the government corridors with creating and maintaining government contacts. This could either be a person employed by the TNC or a hired representative (agent).

Table 4.4 shows the levels at which TNCs are important for the government contacts. The response shows that the high and the middle level managers are important for nurturing government contacts, but not the lower level. High level management is involved, mostly in the more strategic aspects, mainly in dealings with the political and high administrative levels. Seeking licenses is a strategic issue with the subsidiaries, the primary responsibility for which lies with the top echelon of the local subsidiary.

Table 4.4   Importance of different company levels for the government contacts at the preparation stage (A) and the processing stage (B)

LEVEL (see Figure 4.1)	1		2		3		4		5		NR	
	A	B	A	B	A	B	A	B	A	B	A	B
High Administrative	1	0	1	1	3	2	4	10	6	2	2	2
Middle Administrative	0	0	0	0	1	1	3	4	13	12	0	0
Low Administrative	5	5	1	1	6	6	1	1	0	0	4	4

Note: 1 = very unimportant; 2 = rather unimportant; 3 = neither nor; 4 = rather important; 5 = very important.

The table also reveals the importance of the middle level managers in TNC-government contacts. These managers prepare applications to 'conform' to the laws of the land and fit in the official interpretations. Together with the liaison officers they operate the GTN. The senior level management, then, functions partly as the door opener and legit-imizer in the corridors of power and assists the middle level man-agement to gain access to the bureaucrats. In the contacts with the high level bureaucracy it is important to involve the high level com-pany management. The Indian bureaucracy, not unlike bureaucracies in other countries is highly status conscious. Seniority and position matters a lot. The participation by the top level company executives has a symbolic value as well. It shows that from the point of view of the company, contacts with the government are a high priority area in par with the other strategic decisions made by the top level executives.

The high and middle level managers together convince the bureaucracy about the desirability of a proposal from the national point of view. The middle level managers know the details of a proposal. This explains the predominance of the middle level managers in the TNC–government contacts.

Hence, all administrative levels in the subsidiaries are involved in the contacts with the government. The role of the middle administrative level is by far the most important one in both stages, followed by high administrative level. The low administrative level is unimportant during the whole application process.

Our study also shows that the initiative for these contacts lies with the subsidiary and not with the government. Figures show an 'imbalance' in the initiative taken by the parties. At the license preparation stage this was expected as the TNCs have limited information on the details concerning laws and regulations. Exceptions were found in those cases in which TNCs posses the strategic advantage of high technology. The imbalance at the processing stage is more revealing and results from a number of factors. Licensing applications are dealt with on a case to case basis. As a result it is the responsibility of the license seeker to vindicate the claims made in the application, as we shall subsequently see.

Deliberations with the government illustrate a number of aspects. The outcome of the deliberation with the government is contingent upon the adeptness, the diplomatic skills and the relationship building of the TNCs. As we shall observe gradually, the importance of these contacts lie also in the fact that these allow TNCs to collect information on the various aspects of industrial policy and its implementation. In addition, this also allows TNCs on a particular course of action, and thereby, gain a better position in the Indian market.

This shows two more aspects. The first is the disability of the Indian bureaucracy to deal with the license applications in time. Without these contacts an application may remain with the bureaucracy for long time periods. Secondly, that contacts and relationships with the government are a source of strategic advantage to keep the firms competitive edge intact. TNCs gain access to soft information through these network relationships, and ahead of the competitors.

INTENSITY OF CONTACTS

The intensity of the contacts are determined by the frequency of contacts and their informality or openness.

Frequency and Breath of Contacts

Structural characteristics of the network regarding frequency of contacts and types of contacts are given in Tables 4.5-4.10, illustrating some common traits of the entire GTN of the study. Table 4.5 shows that the direct person to person contacts between the government of India and the company officials is frequent but more or less equal at the preparation and processing stages of the application procedure. The frequency of contacts is generally high, where eleven respondents at the preparation stage and twelve at the processing stage have more than five contacts with the bureaucracy. Evidently, face-to-face TNC–government contacts are frequent. As observed in Table 4.9 the number of people in contact with the government is moderate. In around half of the responding companies three or less people maintain government liaison. This implies that the face-to-face contacts between the company and the government authorities are concentrated and limited to a few people. Because of the intricacies and the sensitivity of these contacts only a limited number of people engage in such contacts. Since government contacts are a critical resource for the TNCs these contacts are a source of power for the people having them.

Personal Media

Personal contacts are the main medium of contact as observed in Table 4.5. Table 4.6 shows that more than half the number of respondents were in face-to-face contact with the government at least once a month. Often the contact frequency was more than twice a month. This demonstrated the importance of the social linkage of the GTN, which gives the network an informal character with a low degree of formalization. In addition, people other than the respondents were in face-to-face contact with the government at least twice a month. In four TNCs these contacts took place more than twice a month and in another four TNCs, between 13-24 times a year. Government officials are met no less than three times a month and in a few cases there are even daily meetings, which were mainly attended by the liaison officers, based in Delhi. From Table 4.7 it is observed that for all contact persons at the subsidiaries these meetings usually lasted for half an hour each for every contact person.

The above pattern implies that TNCs meet government officials frequently, but that each individual meeting is short. This further indicates the importance of 'face showing' in pushing matters ahead,

Table 4.5   Frequency of personal meetings with government officials for respondents at the preparation (A) and processing (B) stages

Frequency	Number of respondents	
	A	B
Quarterly or more rarely	4	3
Bimonthly	3	3
Monthly	2	1
Fortnightly	0	2
Weekly	1	1
Twice or thrice a week	1	1
Daily	1	1
No reply	5	5
	17	17

Table 4.6   Frequency of personal meetings with government officials for major contact persons at the subsidiaries

Frequency contact	Respondents	Other persons
Quarterly or more rarely	2	2
Bimonthly	3	1
Monthly	5	0
Fortnightly	1	5
Weekly	0	2
Twice or thrice a week	3	1
Daily	1	2
Twice a day	1	0
No reply	1	4
	17	17

Table 4.7   Average time in minutes per personal meeting (excl. of travelling time)

Number of minutes	Respondents	Other contact persons
10-15	2	2
20	2	2
30	9	6
35	1	1
40	1	0
45	1	0
No reply	1	6
	17	17

Table 4.8   Frequency of other contacts than personal meetings (e.g. telephone calls, letters, telex etc.) with government officials for major contact persons at the subsidiaries

Frequency	Respondents	Other contact persons
Quarterly	2	1
Bimonthly	1	0
Monthly	1	0
Fortnightly	1	2
Weekly	1	3
Twice or thrice a week	3	2
Daily	4	1
Twice a day	1	0
No reply	3	8
	17	17

such as by reminding the officials of the existence of files. In these meetings firms also receive official reaction to a proposal and come of with matching suggestions. It is rather doubtful that in such short meetings prolonged and very deep discussions on each individual issue

Table 4.9   Number of persons from the subsidiaries in contact
(personal meetings, correspondence, telephone etc.) with
the government of India

Number of persons	Number of subsidiaries
1	1
2	2
3	4
4	0
5	1
6	2
7	0
8	1
9	0
10	2
	13

take place. The above argument is validated by the figures presented earlier in Table 3.1, where it was shown that an important purpose behind contacts with the officials is to 'speed up the processing of a particular application', 'to influence decision on a particular application', or 'to learn in advance decisions on an application'.

This critical importance of personal contacts demonstrates the importance of the social linkage of the GTN, which gives the network an informal character with a low degree of formalization. The frequency of personal meetings with government officials is high for both the respondents and other contact persons at the subsidiaries.

The Complementarity of Personal and Non-Personal Media

Contacts also take place in ways other than through personal meetings, as seen in Table 4.8. The response shows that more than half the respondents were in contact with the government through a non-personal media no less than twice a month, while other people in the firms frequently used non-personal media for contacts with the government. In a majority of firms contacts through non-personal media are more than twice a month, where a few firms are in contact with the government on a daily basis.

Such impersonal contacts through telephone calls, letters and telex messages are frequent at both the stages, but especially at the processing stage, indicating an 'exchange of views', 'discussion' and 'negotiation' between the parties. Firms discuss issues with the bureaucracy and negotiations are undertaken. The important point is, however, that the structural characteristics of the GTN presented here imply that these negotiations are not power-based zero-sum games but more oriented towards consensus. The purpose of the negotiations is to find a common ground and reach a solution considered to be legitimate by either party. The use of power by TNCs would be doubtful as it will readily lead to government taking on a rigid, defensive position, in an assertion of national sovereignty and independence. The consensus approach is usually possible, since industrial policy agencies are engaged in negotiations with TNCs that have widely different outlooks, goals and perceptions. Obviously, this allows firms a wide opportunity to accede to some demands without foresaking their own goals. For the same reason, however, there is a significant possibility that the entire process of granting licenses will be delayed.[1]

In this negotiation process personal and non-personal contact media are complementary. Face-to-face interaction with the bureaucracy is superior to impersonal contacts when the intentions with an application is to be explained to the bureaucracy, and how these suit the national priorities. Face-to-face contacts are also superior in creating trust, to prove sincerity, as well as making the communication more accurate. This kind of communication is more than just a use of language, since it also conveys a message on the importance assigned to a meeting and to an authority. Face-to-face contacts also allow the use of posture and facial expressions, which are important. It has been estimated that as much as 70 per cent of the message transferred during a face-to-face contact is non-verbal (Hall, 1959). Information richness and reliability is improved (Daft & Lengel, 1984; Weick, 1987), and particularly in a relationship-oriented society like India (Pye, 1985; Kakar, 1971). Face-to-face contacts develop into durable, stable, and reliable networks. Once established the same channels and networks can be used to communicate with the bureaucracy at a later occasion.

Face-to-face contacts with the bureaucracy at the application and preparation stages are also a source of commitment. By legitimating a proposal at the preparation stage, and through learning in advance if a particular application will be granted TNCs are able to gain commitment from the bureaucracy. This is a source of legitimacy for a proposal at the processing stage as well (Staw & Ross, 1980). A smooth processing of the application is achieved.

Impersonal communication channels are more suitable to communicate hard information (like figures on production, imports, exports, equity ownerships, etc), whereas these complement face-to-face communications.

According to Table 4.9 the breadth of linkages varies considerably, since the number of persons from each subsidiary in contact with the Government of India through different means such as personal meetings, correspondence and telephone varies between 1 to 10. The variation is large with a slight concentration to 3 persons. As seen in Table 4.10 these interviewed contact persons have a long experience from dealing with the Government. As many as four persons have between 20-24 years of experience. One person even exceeds that with his 25-30 years of experience. Everyone has been involved with government for at least two years. In our opinion this stable pattern is not contingent upon a formal decision by the firms, and is more a consequence of a trial and error process, through which such patterns emerge. In addition, these are critical resources within a firm. Developing relationships with the government is time and resource consuming, and once developed the firms try to keep them intact.

Table 4.10 Number of years engaged in personal meetings with government officials for respondents at the subsidiaries

Number of years	Number of persons
2-5	4
6-9	3
10-14	2
15-19	3
20-24	4
25-30	1
	17

Informality of Contacts

The study also clearly demonstrates that social exchange is a critical ingredient of the networks. Table 4.11, which illustrates the importance of friendships in the GTN, shows that a majority of the interviewees at the TNCs have friends among the government officials they deal with. Eight of them even considered most of the officials to be their friends. Five of them, on the other hand, did not have any friends at all among this group of people. Friendship is closely related to trust and Table 4.12 shows that the respondents at the subsidiaries very much trust government officials to give them correct information and trust them to act in a way promised. This is vital since it was noted above that exchange of information and influence is important in the GTN.

Table 4.11   Number of friends among government officials

Number of officials	Number of persons
All	1
Most	8
Some	2
Few	1
None	5

Table 4.12   Extent of trust in government officials by respondents regarding the following aspects

	1 A B	2 A B	3 A B	4 A B	5 A B
To give correct information				2 1	5 3	10 13
To act in a way promised				2 1	5 3	10 13

Note: 1 = not at all; 2 = only a little; 3 = neither nor; 4= rather much; 5 = very much.
A = Trust in Government officials by subsidiaries
B = Trust by Government officials in subsidiaries

Friendship is found to be rather calculative and instrumental, since there is a professional trust among involved persons, who can be labelled business friends and not family friends (Table 4.13). Most of the friendship or all of it is characterized as professional personal friendship and a private personal friendship is uncommon. Social relations are also established for other reasons. Belongingness to the same social groups, mainly kinship, as well as membership of professional groups are important connections for the organizational linkages. Cultural groupings, primarily language groups and to some extent regional groups are also part of the connectivity of the organizations. On the other hand caste groups and religious groups are unimportant. All in all, this further demonstrates the importance of the social linkage. Diffused future obligations are created, which are an essential part of the long-term character of the relationship. In spite of that, the main conclusion from Table 4.13 is that coalitions dominate the GTN, since most of the friendship or all of it is characterized as a professional personal friendship and that a private personal friendship, typical of cliques, is rare.

Table 4.13   How much of the friendship is a result of the following types of contacts

	1	2	3	4	5	NR
A professional personal friendship	6	4	1	1	2	3
A private personal friendship		1	2	2	5	7

Note: 1 = all of it; 2 = most of it; 3 = some of it, 4 = a little of it; 5 = none of it.

Trust in the network

Information is an important element of exchange of the Government–TNC network, as is keeping promises. In both cases trust is important, which was defined in Chapter 2 as being reciprocal in nature and related to confidence (Fox, 1974). In the long run it is difficult to maintain a one-sided trust, since relationships then become unstable. For this reason trust is time-consuming, experience-based, and does not evolve over night. It is also future-oriented, and is not absolute. Trust is a legitimacy creating mechanism that reduces the need for checking and controlling what network actors do and promise. Deviation between promise and action is reduced.

The opposite is mistrust, where parties would move apart from each other, causing the relationship to thin out. Mistrusting actors will reduce interaction and their ties will be weak in nature and fewer in frequency.

Trust in information

At the preparation stage of the application process TNCs collect information from the bureaucracy on such issues as relevant rules and decision making criteria. At the processing stage TNCs supply information to the authorities to process the application and to advance the company's cause. This exchange is mutual as TNCs and government officials receive and supply information and promises to and from each other.

Table 4.12 shows that TNCs as well as the authorities find the information supplied by the counterpart is reliable. The general opinion of the respondents is that trust is high on both sides and that government officials trust the information that TNCs supply. The high level of trust was found to be independent of the nationality of TNCs. This response is understandable. The TNCs researched by us have been operating in India for decades, their local operations having been started long ago, when these firms served the Indian market through exports. Gradually, local production started, and since then these firms have been exchanging views and information with the authorities in order to get licenses. The parties have had a long time to gain familiarity with each other.

Informality and openness are critical ingredients of the network and create strong ties between government and TNCs, these linkages remaining undisturbed by the industrial policy liberalization measures introduced in 1984. In addition, this continuity of linkages is true irrespective of the nationality of TNCs. This means, as was argued above, that the relationship between government units and TNCs is a local phenomenon: decided, developed, and managed by actors located in India. These ties are sometimes strengthened and cemented by kinship, caste, and regional considerations. These factors act to create a feeling of commonality of interest and purpose among the actors engaged in industrial policy implementation. Consequently, temporary and minor changes introduced in industrial policy do not have any major impact on the government–TNC network. However, it is possible that changes in these network relationships are a long term, gradual phenomena which will be observed only after a few years. However, what the most recent developments in India demonstrate is that very drastic changes are required in the factors influencing legitimacy for industrial policy to have an impact on the GTN (Jansson & Sharma, 1994).

Our analysis does not lend support to the hypothesis that trust varies with the legal status of the subsidiary. Trust remains whether the Indian company is a wholly, majority or minority owned unit. There is a high degree of relationship-specificity among the actors involved, which has not changed since 1984.

From a purely ideological point of view the above analysis could be problematic, but from a pragmatic and policy implementation point of view it could be positive and pose no major problem. It could even be beneficial. Because of the trust that prevails between the actors in the TNC–government network, the functioning of industrial policy is smoother in many ways. Company executives, for instance, return to the same sources of information which improves the probability that TNCs will be able to convince the Indian authorities about the suitability of their proposals. Policy implementation becomes less cumbersome and less time consuming.

A major conclusion from the analyses above is that the GTN relationship is stable, consisting of several linkages between the parties that have been in place for many years. There is also a mutual interest in having these contacts, particularly for the TNCs, since there are no alternatives to these linkages. The bonds are strengthened and sustained by the social linkage, of which trust is a critical part.

CHANGE IN GTN DIMENSIONS

Hence, the above implies that, in the absence of drastic changes in factors underlying legitimacy, the changes in the network are gradual rather than radical. As executives from TNCs interact with the government officials bonds between the two get strengthened, among other ways through the social contacts. A change in the policy may only gradually, if at all, affect the nature of these contacts. A positive impact could be that the network structure functions as a buffer against the short-term, politically motivated and opportunistic behaviour of the industrial policy formulating bodies. As has been observed in several developing countries that a change in government (or even of a minister) may result in changes in the industrial policy. Strong ties between the national policy implementing bodies, on the one hand, and investors, on the other, could buffer policy implementation from vagaries of the policy formulaters. One function of these contacts is to minimize variations, which is shown in Table 4.14. The moves to liberalize industrial policy have all resulted in increases in the dimensions illustrated in the table, for example the number of personal meetings at the preparation stage and at the processing stage.

The importance of high government administrative levels seem to have increased more at the processing stage than at the preparation stage, while the importance of high company administrative levels seems to be increased equally in both the stages. As procedures to seek licenses remain very much unchanged, applications have to pass through the same long bureaucratic apparatus.

Table 4.14   Extent of changes in the following aspects since 1984

	1	2	3	4	5	NR
The importance of high government administrative levels at the preparation stage	1	2	12	1		1
The importance of high company administrative levels at this stage	1	4	11	1		
The number of personal meetings at the preparation stage		5	12			
The average time of personal meetings at this stage		2	15			
The importance of high government administrative levels at the processing stage		5	10	1		1
The importance of high company administrative levels at this stage		4	13			
The number of personal meetings at the processing stage		3	14			
The average time of personal meetings at this stage		1	4			12

Note: 1 = increased very much; 2 = increased rather much; 3 = unchanged; 4 = decreased rather much; 5 = decreased very much.

To us, this suggests that the moves to liberalize industrial policy implementation up to 1991 have had an opposite effect on the bureaucracy. These moves have resulted in increased uncertainty among the middle level decision makers. It is probable that although policy changes were introduced, few detailed guidelines on how to implement the policy were issued. This resulted in a vacuum at the middle level of decision making in combination with the increased resistance from the opponents to liberalization moves. The uncertain middle level managers moved all the papers, documents, and applications to the higher level in the government, which resulted in an increased need for contacts with the higher level bureaucracy. Decision-making became more centralized at the top of the bureaucracy. The same also explains the increased time taken to decide on the licensing application.

Data analysis does not show any differences on these issues based on the nationality of TNCs or their size of operations in India. Somewhat contrary to our expectations there was no systematic difference in the response pattern based on the legal status in the Indian case of FERA and non-FERA TNCs. Similarly, whether the subsidiary was registered under the MRTP law or not did hardly matter. Again this indicates the point made earlier that these relationships are firm specific and unrelated to the legal provisions of the country. The TNC–government network structure operates through its own norms.

CONTACT PATTERN AND LEGITIMACY

The political level represents the ideological streams in society. Ministers and deputy ministers incorporate the divergent opinions, beliefs, values, and norms that prevail in the country to ensure that the policy is balanced and supported by a wide spectrum of society. TNCs influence the decision making at this stage primarily as a collective (through industry associations). The strategy is to gain institutional legitimacy by showing that TNCs accept the aims and the goals held by society.

There is legitimization of the policy at the political level, as well as of its implementation, through speeches and debates in the Parliament, its Committees and subcommittees, as well as in the public. These help the government to interpret the industrial policy in terms of the accepted social norms and values. This political legitimacy is analyzed in greater detail in Chapter 5.

Administrative and Procedural Legitimacy

Applications submitted by TNCs are inspected by the bureaucracy to ensure that the proposal conforms to the laws and priorities of the land, irrespective of their technical and commercial viability. The official scrutiny adds little to the technical or commercial viability of proposals. Foreign investors assess the commercial viability of projects and determine appropriate technical production processes. Contacts with the bureaucracy are, however, a source of administrative and procedural legitimacy that help TNCs to comprehend the involved legal and procedural aspects (see Figure 2.2). At the preparation stage TNCs collect information on industrial laws, regulations, and procedures. In a majority of the developing nations, as in India, the procedures for evaluating license applications are lengthy and complicated, and several stages are involved. At the preparation stage it is important to ascertain the following: that the product that the TNC wants to manufacture is not reserved for the domestic small scale industries,[2] that the manufacturing technology does not already exist in India (to avoid repetitive import of technology which is against the law); that the proposal will not lead to increased imports; that the TNCs will try hard to improve the use of local components or equipment in the manufacturing process to reduce imports; and that the necessary imports will be kept to a minimum. The practice among the developing countries varies. The Korean industrial policy, for example, specifies a negative list restricting the entry by TNCs. In the 1980s government declared around 200 products off-limits for the large indigenous conglomerates and TNCs. The Indonesian industrial policy contains similar clauses. The Indian industrial policy forbids TNCs to operate in industries reserved for small scale industries.

With the help of all available and necessary information a company, then, prepares applications to meet the official requirements and interpretation of the laws and regulations. If the bureaucracy disapproves of a foreign collaboration agreement which restricts, for example, exports from the subsidiary, an application submitted to the government is unlikely to include any clauses of this nature. But the same can be achieved by informal agreements between the parent company and the Indian subsidiary (UNCTAD, 1971; Frankena, 1972, pp. 572-592). Similarly, knowing which individuals or groups are influential in government is helpful. As processing starts, TNCs come in contact with the lower level bureaucrats, who collect papers and documents. Here contacts are important to push the matter, so that the papers are dispatched to the concerned ministries for comments and views, or else the application documents remain unattended and delays arise. In addition, several applications are rejected outright as these are not prepared in accordance with the official 'instructions'. The lower level bureaucracy is not engaged in evaluating proposals. Applications are scrutinized primarily at the middle level, and to a limited extent at the higher level. The details of an application must be legitimated with the bureaucrats. The purpose is to convince the bureaucracy that the proposal conforms to the laws and priorities of the country. Through the network TNCs influence the evaluation of an application.

The TNCs may introduce minor changes in the application to satisfy the bureaucracy, but these do not alter the nature of the proposal. On major issues (the technology to be used, the size of the project, the quality of the final output, etc.) changes, if any, are minimal. These issues are determined more by the internal logic of the firms and the market conditions in the country than by the bureaucratic rules, regulations, and procedures. However, there are negotiations. TNCs may agree to locate an industrial plant in the election constituency of an influencial politician in exchange for the speedy approval from the government and the bureaucracy. Stopford & Strange (1992, pp. 151-152) state that accepting figures and information presented to the bureaucracy by TNCs is rather common despite the fact that the accuracy of these figures is highly doubtful. An example given is that in most of the projects financed by the International Finance Commission (IFC) the stated rate of return was higher than the real rate of return.

At the processing stage securing legitimacy is often a 'bottom up' process starting from the lowest level in the government. TNCs first legitimize a proposal at the lower and the middle level in the government. This also indicates that the additional scrutiny at the high government level is rather limited. At the preparation stage, on the other hand, this is not the case. The process is experience-based as TNCs seek information from those sources which they conceive as reliable and with which they are experienced. These are randomly distributed in the bureaucracy.

Passing through such a lengthy process is itself a source of legitimacy for a proposal. This shows that the proposal has passed through the correct channels and procedures. A tall bureaucratic structure implies that the decisions are subject to more and repetitive analysis (Carzo and Yanouzas, 1969, p. 190). Thereby, the government as well as TNCs claim that the accepted proposals are legitimate.

ROLE OF THE SUBSIDIARY

The study shows that the strategic management of government relationships is decentralized and carried out by the subsidiary. The arrangement is host country specific and there is no centralized policy on the subject. As a subsidiary operates in a country, it comes in contact with the bureaucracy and learns by trial and error how the official bureaucracy works, what its preferences are, who wields the major influence in decision making, and what the cultural nuances are. Channels are, then, developed to secure legitimacy.

This indicates three aspects of TNC–government relationships. First, rules, regulations and procedures are complex and it is most rational that the same persons maintain contacts with the government from TNCs' side. A change therein could be expensive as learning about the counterpart is both time and resource consuming. Similarly, developing trust is time and resource-consuming. Second, TNCs are greatly interested in these contacts with the government, since they are a source of advantage for the firm in competition for the resources controlled and owned by the government, for example, access to the local market, financial support and incentives supplied by the government in the shape of tax holidays or export incentives.

Lastly, the continuation of relationships also indicates the importance of trust, friendship, and other social interactions between the government and TNCs. This may have repercussions on the power structure within the subsidiaries. People having contacts with the government officials probably gain importance unconnected with their formal position and designation in the subsidiary. Such employees are a critical resource of a company.

Another impact is the distribution of power between the Indian subsidiary and the head office of the TNC. Since the government contacts are controlled by the subsidiary, the decision making power on a number of important operational issues might be influenced. One consequence would be that the integration of the Indian subsidiary in the international operations of the TNCs is made difficult. Government contacts may develop into a power base for the subsidiary as they monopolise these contacts. In addition, the head office, in general, lacks sufficient knowledge and information about the local network, its actors, and its relative power distribution. Due to the complex nature of the network, public disclosures are avoided and the participants keep this knowledge and information to themselves. It is not that a subsidiary avoids passing on this type of information to the head office. The problem is rather that only a part of this information is coded in formal rules and regulations, and the major portion is informal and difficult to articulate. Therefore, even the decision makers in the subsidiary may not be fully aware of such aspects. As will be analyzed in detail in Chapter 6 the group's influence varies with different types of licenses.

SUMMARY AND CONCLUSIONS

In this chapter the operational qualities of the network between the Government of India and TNCs are investigated. It is argued that the types of linkages found and their structure reflect the desire of TNCs to secure institutional legitimacy in the host society. These two parties are in frequent contact with each other through a communication network, of which a professionally oriented social exchange, called professional trust, is an important part. The established GTN is mainly characterized as an emergent arm's-length network. The middle level managers and the middle level bureaucrats dominate such contacts and there are few contacts at the political level. Through these contacts TNCs gain legitimacy and, in turn, are rewarded by a protected market. The TNCs who can better accommodate the wishes of the host government secure a stronger position in the market and face less competition. Thus, technical legitimacy is often subordinated to institutional legitimacy.

The GTN permits a rapid access to the government officials, and improves the quality and the reliability of information exchange. A negative consequence could be, however, that such networks are strong, invisible and evolve a life of their own separated from the laws, rules, and regulations of the country. For this reason the changes (for example, liberalization) introduced by the government could be less effective and difficult to implement. There could be a rather wide discrepancy between public statements of the formal policy and the actual implementation of the policy. These networks can be effectively used to block new policy measures initiated by the government. These matters related to the Government side of the GTN will be analyzed at depth in the following chapter.

The frequent TNC–government interaction evolves into stable network structures, which are dominated by rather frequent face-to-face communication, but in which impersonal contacts also play an important part. Social, mainly work-based, relationships develop. Bureaucrats and managers from TNCs gain familiarity and develop trust. Within the network communication and exchange of views are made easy and reliable. Such networks are a resource and a TNC turns to the same government officers for information and assistance.

The GTN is managed by the middle management at the local subsidiary, and where the involvement of high-level management is important for strategic reasons. Although the number of people at the TNCs engaged in the contacts varies a lot, generally three persons are very experienced in handling the contacts. People from other parts of the group do not take part. The strategy in this field can thus be characterized as country-centred (Porter, 1986). This part of the GTN, the TNC network, is analyzed in detail in Chapter 6.

The structure of linkages of the GTN is characterized as rather broad, frequent, durable and dense. In addition, trust prevails. This results in an organizational structure that is signified as an arm's length network, mostly of the emergent type, but determined by the prescriptions laid down in the main mandate, that is the guidelines. Therefore, the GTN is stable and rather highly coupled, and found in an uncertain environment.

There is no likelihood that a whole GTN will emerge from the bottom up. Rather, the characteristic of emergent networks are vital to consider in order to get a complete picture of the GTN. Arm's-length relations are thus viewed as a combination of prescribed and emergent networks. In a mandated situation, voluntary exchanges may still take place and where many relationships start out as voluntary and later become standardized. Arm's-length networks are a mix of these pure forms.

NOTES

1.   See for example Stopford & Strange (1992, ch. 4).
2.   In 1990 around 830 different items were solely reserved for small-scale firms. They are defined as firms with a capital investment in plant and machinery of no more than 3 million rupees.

5. The Political and Administrative Organization of the Government Network

In this chapter we study how the government network operates, both at the political (or policy) level and at the administrative (or executive) level. We consider the main objectives or rationale behind these two main types of organizations on the government side. The legitimacy aspect of the network is developed further and compared in greater detail to the efficiency aspect of the network.

In the TNC–government network three pure types of organizations or actors are identified, that is, TNCs or business organizations, participative organizations consisting of political actors, and bureaucratic organizations consisting of government authorities. Although the focus of this book is on business organizations, the other two cannot be ignored. Participative and bureaucratic organizations provide opportunities to TNCs but also restrict their freedom of action. The participative organizations, for example, formulate the rules and regulations that guide the actions of TNCs. Participative organizations are analysed first in this chapter, followed by administrative organizations. These are ideal types and may not be present in practice. Moreover, it is possible that within a single organization all these ideal organizations are present but in varying degrees. We introduce a distinction between political and administrative organizations as the two work according to different principles and nurture different aims and goals. Our analysis emphasizes that in the field of industrial policy implementation, official bureaucracy is at once an independent and a powerful actor, and should not be ignored.

Two main interests are found to determine how the government network is organized. The political interest, which reflects the political, ideological streams in society, acquires legitimacy by reflecting the inconsistencies in the environment. The administrative interest gets external support by acting chiefly according to the prescriptions from the political side, that is, by implementing policies. These two interests coexist within the government network. The political interest is a very important subject of study because of its large impact on processes within the administration, and directs its indirect influence on the TNCs. The government network consists of different mixes of political and administrative organizations. Even in a typical political organization such as a political party, there are also administrative tasks. In a typical administrative organization such as a government body or set up, on the other hand, there are important political influences. Other organizations, such as a government ministry, are more mixed.

The focus of the chapter is on industrial policy implementation, since TNCs' relationship with the government is chiefly evident at that stage. However, implementation cannot be properly understood without putting it into the context of policy formulation, which is therefore, discussed first in the chapter. Policy execution is analysed from the perspective of political legitimacy. The political process itself is not analysed.

POLITICAL ORGANIZATION

The industrial policy in any country is formulated and implemented by the government and the discussion on the subject is based on the metaphor that governments are rational decision makers like any other organization and acting in the best interest of the society. The underlying assumption is that organizations are rational, with well-defined goals that guide the actions undertaken by them. In this perspective decisions are made to be implemented and any gap between the decisions and their outcome is an unsatisfactory state of affairs and must be eliminated. A failure to carry out a decision is attributed to the irrational behaviour of the participants and faulty structuring of the organization. If every participant executes his part of the task efficiently, an optimal solution will be obtained.

A discussion on industrial policy in general, presumes (a) that policies are formulated so that they may be implemented; (b) that the government is in a position to implement the decisions and achieve its goals; and (c) that the government is willing to do so.[1]

Traditional models of policy formulation processes are based on rational decision making. A common way is to divide the policy process into five stages: problem identification, problem development, programme implementation, programme evaluation and programme termination.[2] The traditional central planning system in

India is based on this thinking. The policy was formulated and goals were established according to a rational decision-making process, where cause-and-effect relationships between country-wide goals and industry sector goals were established through input-output analysis of sectors and cost/benefit analysis of projects. Defective results were mostly attributed to faulty implementation, rather than mistakes in formulation.

In the above perspective, the national leadership does the job of industrial policy formulation, with the goal of national well being as the overwhelming, if not the sole, purpose of this exercise. As in the traditional organization theory, it is presumed that the national leadership does not entertain any aims other than the development and maintenance of competitiveness of the national industries. The policies thus formulated are then implemented in the most effective manner to optimize returns to the nation. In this metaphor, the central bureaucracy too is presumed to be acting in the best interests of the nation while implementing the national industrial policy. In a typical rational perspective any discrepancy between the formulated policy and its implementation is explained as a deviation which should not have been. In this view the gap between the industrial policy and its implementation is eliminated by way of enacting administrative rules and procedures which are more rational and which assign well defined tasks to each position in the central bureaucracy. According to this perspective governments are pro-active players in shaping and changing the industrial situation in the country, and decision making is merely a means to achieve an outcome (to act). Otherwise decision making lacks an independent value.

It is presumed that by rationalizing rules and streamlining the administrative procedures and the administrative structure, it should be possible to eliminate the gap between the industrial policy as formulated by the national leadership and its implementation by the national bureaucracy. The root of the entire problem is identified as the nonrational administration and bureaucracy. By streamlining the administration (that is, the various ministries) the goals of the national industrial policy can be achieved.

Political Legitimacy

This implementation doctrine pays no attention to the fact that industrial policy is both formulated and implemented by governments that are also political and representative democratic bodies. This vital political aspect of government cannot be overlooked. Governments are significantly different from bureaucracies as well as commercial organizations (Brunsson, 1986, 1987). Political organizations achieve legitimacy through reflecting inconsistencies in their environment. They remain viable and powerful as long as they reflect conflicts, opinions and interests prevailing in the society. Political legitimacy is defined according to Brunsson (1987, p. 143) as follows:

> A legitimation policy involves activities on the part of the political system directed towards creating legitimacy for itself. The main strategy of the political organiza- tion for creating its own legitimacy is to reflect in its structure, its processes and its production the norms and values and interests that obtain in the environment. This represents a direct way of creating legitimacy. But legitimacy can also be created indirectly, through the agency of the industrial system. This indirect aspect of legitimacy is connected with the question of the responsibility resting with the political system.

One may even state that the existence of a broad array of different and conflicting goals is a precondition for the long term survival of the parliamentary form of government. In other words, the success of a democratically elected government depends upon its ability to enter- tain the conflicting opinions and goals that prevail in the society. The greater the number of conflicting goals a government is capable of accommodating, the more 'successful and viable' it is likely to be. This is, however, feasible only as long as governments entertain a weak ideology in comparison to bureaucratic and commercial organ- izations which promote one single but strong ideology promoting action.

This definition of political legitimacy means that we build on interest group models, where policy formation and implementation are to a large degree influenced by powerful interest groups in the society. Lobbying is important. Policies can be characterized as 'minority politics' rather than 'majority politics'. Various interest groups are very visible on the Indian political scene.

In our study, we populate the government policy model with in- terest groups in order to understand what is going on. But we extend traditional interest group models beyond goals and strategies to also include their norms and values. Political behaviour then becomes more complete. We also take up more general societal norms and values, particularly when cultural influences are analysed. Our study analyses two main interest groups in the Indian society, foreign com- panies and the bureaucracy.

The characteristics of political organizations are summarized in

Table 5.1, which illustrates the large differences between political organizations and the main type of hierarchical organizations studied earlier, that is the TNC. This table compares political legitimacy with business efficiency.

Table 5.1   Main organization characteristics according to two main orientations

BUSINESS EFFICIENCY	POLITICAL LEGITIMACY
Consistency	Inconsistency (hypocrisy)
Unity	Conflict
Solutions	Problems
Integration	Dissolution
Implementation is an integrative force	Implementation is a dissolving force
Change induced	Change obstructive
Talk and decisions used for mobilizing and coordinating internal actions	Talk and decisions used for external purposes
Irrational decision processes	Rational decision processes
Enthusiasm (self-confidence)	Depression (uncertainty, criticism)
Common goals and values	Divergent goals and values
Myths of efficiency and competence	Myths of inefficiency and incompetence
Action	Ideological outputs
Hierarchy	Loose coupling

Source: Brunsson (1986)

Participative Organizations

The political side of the government is characterized as participative organizations. This is especially true for a democratically elected government such as in India.

Divergent goals and values
The goals of such organizations are unclear and so are the preferences about the outcome. The causation is unambiguous but not the means

and the procedure to achieve the same (Thompson & Tuden, 1959). In the process, goals lose value and meaning whereas adherence to the social rules and procedures acquire importance. The norm in these organizations is not to pursue any fixed rules, regulations, or procedures but to reflect inconsistent norms and values.

Rather than reflecting a single dominant goal at one time, political organizations reflect a number of goals or none at all. A clear ranking of the goals is not found. The aim of the organization is survival and in the struggle to survive organizations co-opt a number of divergent and conflicting goals and aims which are a source of legitimacy (Selznick, 1948). Indeed, the organization may lack a clear cut goal. These organizations have few internal rules and the purpose is to freely exchange views and opinions. Too much dependence on rules could be detrimental to their purpose. The principle that guides the working of these organizations is that 'we agree to disagree'. In extreme cases these organizations could be characterized as 'crowds'. These organizations seek rationality in participation and significant amounts of resources are devoted to 'demonstrative' activities. This is political legitimacy, and the outcome is speeches, papers, meetings, directives, and documents and so on. Therefore *myths of inefficiency and incompetence* are easily established.

One example of a participative organization is the Parliament. Birgersson and Westerståhl (1979) describe the Swedish Parliament as a forum in which the various actors present their respective alternatives and preferences. Such an organization has a symbolic value; there is no instrumental value. Olsen (1983) described the Norwegian Parliament as an arena which represents the divergent thinkings, values and norms in the country. Its capacity to influence the substance of the political activities of the nation or to act as a pro-active political force was limited.

The same interest groups are, then, represented in the various committees, sub-committees, and the other political bodies of the Parliament. During the deliberations on national industrial policy, representatives of different societal segments struggle to get their special interest included in the policy, although with no guarantee of its inclusion in the final policy document. However, these efforts, even if futile, have a symbolic value (Larsson, 1986). It is important not to take initiative, but to wait and see future unfolding (Jacobsson, 1989, p 16; Brunsson & Jönsson, 1978).

Inconsistent and conflicting interests

In India, industrial policy formulation acts as an instrument for the legitimation of the policies pursued by the government. Existence of such a policy allows political organizations to alter it, when the need arises. Changes may be either covert or open. This is a situation prevailing in all elected governments and India is no exception. The Indian government is exposed to a number of inconsistent and conflicting demands and forces from society. There are a large number of *problems* that call for attention. Agriculture competes with other sectors of the economy for more resources. Various state governments seek regional balance and vie for industrial projects. Labour unions want job protection to keep their members satisfied. Consumers want better quality products and services. The Indian government is expected to balance regional demands, modernize industry, preserve existing jobs, create competition in the market place and still not allow firms to close down their operations. The rise of the Indian middle class has resulted in a demand for more and better quality products. There is rising demand for more money and resources for the poorest sections of the society. Furthermore, as we will see below, bureaucracy has demands of its own, for which it tries to create legitimacy.

These demands are partly reflected in the sectoral composition of the society, the distribution of GNP, and so on. In the beginning of the 1960s the farming sector contributed around 50% of the national GNP, while the industrial sector contributed a much smaller percentage of the GNP. Over the last two decades the figures have gradually changed and by 1989-90 the contribution of the agriculture sector was down to approximately 33%, whereas the industrial sector contributed slightly less than 30%. The farming sector is strong and influential in shaping the industrial policy. Farmers demand more resources for agriculture and want the development and establishment of industries which serves their interest (fertilizer industry, agro based industries and so on). Another strong influence is the village sector, as around 70% of the Indian population lives in villages. No government can alienate either of the two groups, and therefore, these two main influential segments are accommodated in the industrial policy formulation and implementation in a number of ways. Firstly, there are clauses in the industrial policy which protect the interests of these segments. The development of fertilizer and agro based industries is encouraged. Around 40% of the national budget is spent on the agriculture sector and allied industries. The same is achieved through highly visible acts such as establishment of separate ministries or departments. There is a separate department for fertilizer industry and the agro-based industries. To further improve the legitimacy of the government in the rural areas there is a separate department for small scale industries, cottage industries and so on. A number of incentives and subsidies are supplied.

The different regions in the country demand development as well. Poorer regions want a larger resource allocation since industrial development is seen as an instrument for improving their economic lot. State governments vie for industrial projects and want to advance their own interests. Through representation in the national Parliament and the National Development Council, states influence the industrial policy formulation and implementation. The interests of each state and region impinge upon the industrial policy decision in a number of ways. Customarily, representatives from each region and state are included in the cabinet, where they can safeguard their respective interests. The Indian industrial policy, therefore, advocates regional balance and minimization of disparities among states.

Organized labour is another powerful influence group, which wants more employment and wishes to preserve the interests of their members. Deindustrialization through closing down and relocation of industries, is resisted. This interest is then served by policies that prohibit or restrict lay-offs and re-locations. Although the middle class is not organized, it is large, around 200 million, and therefore an essential segment of the society. The middle class demands improved consumer goods and services, which in turn implies modern and efficient industries. With the growth of the Indian cities, the influence of the Indian middle class on industrial policy has become stronger. Encouragement to consumer goods industries (especially electronic goods) is thus a way to accommodate this group.

The established domestic industry developed since Independence (through the policy of import substitution) wants continued protection against imported goods. A new generation of industrialists, on the other hand, wants import restrictions to be lifted, inter alia, to improve the international competitiveness of Indian firms. The industrial policy is expected to seek a balance between these two conflicting interests, which is achieved through a progressive liberalization of import laws and through incentives to export.

The government on its part tries to accommodate as many of these divergent demands as possible. This allows the government to seek support from the powerful segments in the Indian society. The government appears to serve the interests of the farmer, the labourer, the middle class, and the domestic industry alike.

Dissolved policy formation and implementation

Trade-offs between conflicting demands are difficult to balance. A better regional balance may slow down the rate of industrial growth. Increased imports create competition, but also result in a trade deficit and may jeopardize the survival of a number of both large and small domestic firms. Moreover, since not all demands are economic in nature, there is frequently a problem in quantifying and comparing them. In such a situation the use of objective criteria in decision making is difficult. Industrial policies formulated are expected to address all these issues. In addition, no powerful group in the society would appreciate being excluded from the policy.[3] Hence, formulating industrial policy with one single objective in view is impossible. From an implementation point of view, the system then becomes irrational, as vague policies can be implemented in many different ways.

As has been seen, industrial policy is important for government, not merely as a rational process aimed at improving the growth rate of the industry, but also to achieve legitimacy in the various groups represented in society. The industrial policy document is expected to indicate or signal to society that government is interested in doing a number of things to improve the industrial situation of the country. In doing so, government would avoid alienating any group. Implementing a single well defined goal is not conducive to this aim. Instead, industrial policy is expected to be vague in nature to allow for a number of different interpretations. This makes it possible for various groups to interpret policy in their own way. Government can, for instance, signal one goal at one time and another goal at another time depending upon situation and audience.

Talk and decisions

Output from the political system is mainly ideological, and it gains legitimacy in a number of ways. One way is through action, that is, by actually taking steps to alter a situation in keeping with an aim. Such action results in a tangible outcome, for example government may change an industrial policy and create an improved industrial climate by an increase in the number of industrial licenses issued and rising industrial production. Legitimacy is thereby created through the agency of the industrial system.

Two other means to achieve legitimacy is through talk and decisions. For these the outcome is intangible, since no action is involved. Such 'products' are flexible and can be made more inconsistent in order to reflect different interests in society. Through both these means government is able to change perceptions held by different groups in the environment about the government and its ability to do things. Government also gives an account of action without really acting, for example, by burying a burning issue under deliberations. In other cases industrial policy decisions may be taken without the likelihood of their being carried out. These decisions are, however, made public, e.g. to show that government is capable of and willing to change policy. In reality little changes may occur.

In India, many industrial policy changes seem to be introduced merely for symbolic reasons. Most talk and discussions about the inefficiency created by the elaborate control framework are, for instance, interpreted in such a way. Both government and industry gain legitimacy through such output. At the same time they have a mutual interest in preserving the actual situation. The procedures are rather cumbersome, but parties concerned have learnt how to obtain licenses. Therefore, decisions on streamlining licensing procedures may not be followed by implementation. Such *hypocritical outcome* does not imply that government tries to cheat. It signifies that in the industrial policy arena a number of forces are at work, which exert opposite and contradictory influences. These must be considered in policy analysis. The use of traditional rationality criteria only gives a partial explanation.

Hence, political organizations reflect inconsistencies in the environment by using three kinds of output in different ways. Through talk organizations highlight the value they assign to the norms and the values of the environment. Talk is not expensive and provides flexibility to the organization to wait and watch. Talk is also suitable as an intermediate solution until the future course of action becomes clearer. Decisions about the future are postponed until a suitable and a more appropriate solution is available.

Similarly, when a decision is taken and presented to society, it creates the feeling that something is being done. In the minds of people a decision is more or less synonymous with its implementation (action), although the decision maker may have shown no such intent. This signals the willingness of the organization to adhere to the norms and values of the environment (Jacobson, 1989). A decision is more definite than talk, but like talk, it could be vague and varied. For instance, in order to keep the options open, a definite timetable is not given for implementing the decision. Or, decision makers are not provided with the criteria to be able to select between various alternatives. There are also advantages involved. First, the decision makers have freedom of action, and are still able to achieve legitimacy. Second, due to the inherent ambiguity, decisions are interpreted differently by the conflicting interest groups.

One specific aspect of talk is denial. Policy makers may consistently deny complaints that the interests, values, and norms of a specific segment is being neglected either at the policy formulation stage or at the implementation stage. This is done either vocally or in writing.

Organizations may simultaneously make use of all these three mechanisms to achieve legitimacy.

> They can talk in consistence with one group of norms, decide according to another and produce according to a third. Organizations dealing with inconsistencies have reason to be hypocritical. When other methods of reflecting inconsistencies are difficult to use, they should even be expected to be hypocritical. (Brunsson, 1986, p. 171)

Loose coupling

The three ways of achieving legitimacy are loosely coupled or decoupled (Weick, 1969). The loose coupling could be precised along a number of different dimensions, namely, in time, by subject matter, by type of environment, and by type of organization unit (Brunsson, 1989; Jacobson, 1989). Organizations blend the three mechanisms differently. They can talk at one time, decide at another, and act on a third occasion. Organizations may also use all the three simultaneously, but talk to one segment of the environment, make decisions for another, and act for a third. This can be done by various parts of the organization, that is, by giving responsibility for a specific vehicle of legitimacy to a certain organizational unit. Thus, both means and units are decoupled. Within certain societal segments the organization may seek institutional legitimacy, while for other segments it seeks technical legitimacy (Meyer & Rowan, 1977; Jacobson, 1989, Ch. 6). Loose coupling can also be based on subject matter, that is talk on one subject, decide on another and act on a third. Segmentation is also possible by project group. Consequently, loose coupling is a mechanism to manage environmental demands and not a mechanism primarily developed to resolve intra-firm conflicts.

The advantage of loose coupling is that organizations can function in a more adaptive manner. It also allows segments of the environment to gain representation in the policy, at different times and locations, and to different extents. The main disadvantage is the difficulty in knowing how decisions are made, by whom, and when. The holistic approach is lost. Only some of the problems are solved at one time, and various parts of the organization may move in different directions.

In the industrial policy arena all these mechanisms are applied. As noticed before, policy formulation and implementation are more or less decoupled. The former is more a political process and achieved on the principles valid for participative organizations. The latter is done by the government ministries which are administrative organizations. We shall study this in a following section.

Cultural Elements

Inconsistent or hypocritical behaviour to gain legitimacy is explained by the fact that governments as democratic organizations have to consider many interests, values and norms. These factors are in their turn influenced by the national culture. An extension of the analysis including cultural factors produces further insights into how the political organizations work and how the TNCs' network strategies and operations are influenced.

Dual political cultures
A dual political culture prevails in India: an elite culture and a mass culture. Power at the national level responds to ideologies of planned economic growth and liberal democratic ideals. These are myths that reduce uncertainty and create stability. By living up to these myths legitimacy is created for the political system. At the local level, politics is more pragmatic and based on exchange relationships. This dichotomy between formal legalistic power and personal human relational power continues to exist (Pye, 1985, p. 317).

The politics of personal relations is based on the Indian politicians strong moralistic outlook which produces a moralistic political rhetoric. From this perspective plans can be viewed as a way to impress others with one's own superiority and virtuosity, as well as an Indian leader could be seen as legitimizing his search for power by saying that his inner life has made him particularly sensitive to morality questions.

In fact, the combination of British rule and Gandhian response turned Indian political culture inside out by making it appear to be moralistic, when in fact it still contained many of the amoral, but subjectively gratifying, qualities of traditional Hindu political culture. (Ibid., p. 143)

This separation between thought and action in Hindu society and the reasons for the split is a vital knowledge for understanding the large gap between policy formation and implementation. Where physical things are an illusion, the failure of a policy does not matter much.

The contrast between the dual systems of power as formal structures of state power and informal patterns of power relations is generally and explicitly acknowledged in Indian societal life.

Patron–client ties
Dependency relations, arranged in a patron–client network are vital in India. This is most visible in the Indian party system, which is a mixture of ideological or policy oriented politics, and patronage politics. Caste and kinship ties and factional affiliations based on the quest for status, prestige or material rewards are important. Few businessmen, for instance, believe they can operate without personal ties with the government officials. Also the administrative organization, possibly except at the highest union government levels in New Delhi, can be characterized as a complex network of patron–client ties. Since Independence this patronage has also been increasingly controlled from the centre. This system is kept together by a nurturent and supportive patron, who gives favours and receives praise and homage from the clients. The system is built on the fact that the patron gives protection and support, often in the form of money, to clients, while they show loyalty and give votes. The exchange of these types of resources maintain the interaction and strengthen the bonds of obligation. The network is rather loosely coupled with no binding ties and a low emotional bonding.[4]

THE ADMINISTRATIVE ORGANIZATION OF THE GOVERNMENT NETWORK

We investigate and analyse here how the administrative structure works vis-à-vis TNCs. As stressed above, this will give us a vital insight into why the Indian bureaucracy is unable to implement industrial policy and how this has influenced the behaviour of TNCs towards government. The failure on the part of the bureaucracy manifests itself in a number of ways, namely, delay in processing and granting industrial licenses, the implementation of inappropriate projects, administrative irregularities, corruption and so on. Our basic point is that the goal of improving and streamlining the implementation of industrial policy through changes in administrative rules, regulations, and procedures is unlikely to be achieved. The problems are more fundamental.

We start with a discussion of the traditional view on policy implementation, and point out why this view is inappropriate for the purpose of our study.

Executive bodies are 'rule following' organizations, which do not necessarily seek and encourage participation by the different segments of the environment. But indirectly administrative organizations integrate and reflect the values and norms of the environment by pursuing and following rules, regulations, and administrative procedures set up as guiding principles by political organizations. Therefore, it is not essential that the different segments of the environment are represented in the organization or that a free exchange of views is encouraged.

On the other hand, these organizations are also different from business organizations and lack well-defined goals. In a sense, the main goal of these organizations is to follow rules, regulations, and procedures. The measurement of their output is not done in the same manner as in business organizations, namely, through profit, growth rate or market share. The output of these organizations is hard to quantify. There is much controversy regarding what these organizations do and how effective they are. The officials are expected to be objective without their own preferences or goals influencing work tasks. As discussed below, the rationality of administrative organizations is mainly expressed through rules.

An example is the ministerial level bureaucracy in India. The ministries are manned by bureaucrats with permanent employment, who are expected to follow the rules and regulations enacted by the National Parliament. The structure is hierarchical. Before any decision is taken, files have to move. The composition of the bureaucracy is not supposed to be based on group interests and bureaucrats are not the representatives of the different segments of the Indian society. They are an independent force, employed to interpret and enforce rules and regulations. These organizations, consequently, seek procedural rationality and action has little independent value, whereas rules, regulations, and procedures are valued.

Relationships between the public and private sectors are seen to be typically governed by laws and regulations. The cabinet or the parliament is a third, external agent that imposes specified sets of interactions, resource flows and boundary interpenetration on a group of organizations that otherwise may have remained unconnected. By making policy decisions this central agent structures the implementation network and then more or less 'withdraws'. It also manipulates incentives for organizations to form networks on their own. This is a top down or mandated process of network formation.

Hence, relationships among government agencies normally operate on the basis of mandated domain and sequential interdependence. The domain is often subdivided so that the transorganizational network becomes a situation of sequential interdependence, in which there is a value added system of officials, each performing his portion of a larger task and passing the job onto the next one. These vertical and horizontal patterns of implementation events are usually highly structured by charters, laws, administrative policies and procedures. They are usually bureaucratically organized with rational planning, specified goals, prescribed means, and clear authority and sanctioning patterns. Decisions are implemented by a network of agencies and authorities. Authority is centralized in the different units in such a bureaucratic network. Although centralized within themselves with clear vertical division of authority and responsibility, these bureaucratic units may lack unity, with more or less uncoordinated offices trying to exercise control. Horizontal coordination between them is difficult to achieve.

Administrative Rationality

Administrative organizations work according to the hierarchic metaphor, particularly in their vertical organization. They are looked upon as a rationally structured hierarchy with an efficient division of labour, well-defined authority lines, objectives, rules and regulations. Rules are rational and objective and independent of the preferences of individual decision makers. Organizational structure achieves preference over the individuals, wherein rationality lies in the structure of the organization and not in people. Structure is defined as 'the pattern or regularized aspect of relationships existing among participants in an organization' (Scott, 1981, p. 13). Control is personal (commands) or impersonal (rules). Organization as a hierarchy of office with a fixed division of labour is emphasized. Officials up in the hierarchy issue orders to the subordinates at lower levels and thereby curtail their decision making autonomy. Surveillance and control of the subordinates are high (Scott, 1981, p. 150). Decisions are made to be implemented and any gap between decisions and outcome is an unsatisfactory state of affairs and must be eliminated. Indeed, these are machine like organizations in which cause and effect relationships are well established. The organizations avoid conflicts that are a symbol of deficiency of the organizational structure and may result in undesirable outcome (sub-optimization). Therefore, conflicts must be reduced to a minimum and this is achieved through objective structures, rules and regulations (ibid., Ch. 3). Failure to carry out a decision is attributed to the irrational behaviour of the participants and faulty structuring of the organization. If every participant executes his part of the task efficiently, an optimal solution will be obtained.

Administrative organizations become rational (efficient) by pursuing the bureaucratic rules, regulations and procedures. The situation becomes problematic if these organizations' goals, rules, regulations, and procedures are unclear, and they fail to provide guidance in decision making. Either there are too few rules to follow, or there are too many of them (with a number of 'ifs' and 'buts'). The latter is more common. In either case, this provides either too little or too much latitude in decision making. Rationality is reduced or may be lost.

Competence and honesty of government officials

For an administrative organization to be rational, officials have to be competent and honest. Competence implies that the holder of a position must possess sufficient knowledge and expertise to exercise the task assigned to him. The office holder may acquire knowledge and competence either through formal education or through on-the-job training. Honesty implies the sincerity of the officials to their assigned task, which implies an emphasis on official responsibility rather than on personal gains from the office. Competence and honesty are the corner stones of any bureaucracy and its successful working. An important reason for the failure of a bureaucracy to implement industrial policy could be that the incumbent of an office is incompetent or dishonest.

As shown in Table 5.2, the survey figures show that the degree of competence varies between the different administrative levels specified in Figure 4.1. By and large it is high at middle and high administrative levels with a preponderance at the latter level. At the high level, TNCs consider most or all officials to be competent. At the low administrative level, however, this is not so. Fewer officials at the

Table 5.2   Competence and honesty of government officials

1. Degree of competence of government officials at different levels.

LEVEL (see Figure 5.3)	**1**	**2**	**3**	**4**	**5**	**NR**
Political			3	2		12
High Administrative	1		2	8	5	1
Middle Administrative		1	7	7	2	
Low Administrative		3	9	3	1	1

2. Degree of competence of government officials at different ministries.

Ministry of Industry & Company Law Affairs	1	11	2	3
Ministry of Finance	2	9		4
Ministry of Commerce and Trade	2	10	2	3
Other important Ministries (please specify!)	1	2	1	13

Note: 1 = none is competent; 2 = few are competent; 3 = some are competent; 4 = most are competent; 5 = all are competent.

3. Degree of honesty of government officials at different levels.

LEVEL (see Figure 5.3)	**1**	**2**	**3**	**4**	**5**	**NR**
Political			3		5	9
High Administrative	1	8	3	2	1	2
Middle Administrative		5	6	4	1	1
Low Administrative		1	6	7	2	1

Note: 1 = all are honest; 2 = most are honest; 3 = some are honest; 4 = few are honest; 5 = none is honest; n = 17.

low levels are competent. It is hard to draw any firm conclusions from the few answers regarding contacts at the political level. The high no-response figure is interpreted in the way that contacts at the political level are rare. Moreover, the political representatives who occupy the office of ministers and deputy ministers keep on changing. The few answers indicate that the level of competence is not considered to be particularly high at the political level. Another main conclusion is that most officials are competent at the main economic ministries.

The honesty level follows a similar pattern as the competence level. Most officials are considered to be honest at the high administrative level, while a more mixed picture is shown for the middle administrative level. Overall not very many are honest. But more officials are honest at the middle level than at the low administrative level, where only some or a few are honest. There are two cases where none is considered to be honest. At the political level, five of eight respondents believe that none is honest. How strong this tendency is is not known, since there are very few answers regarding the political level.

The present research, therefore, indicates that one reason for the problems in adequate implementation of industrial policy is the dishonest behaviour at some of the administrative levels. The competence of the officials is, on the other hand, not problematic with the exception of those at the low level. In other words, many incumbents of positions in the official hierarchy seems to behave as if they own the position and extract rent to make personal gains.

The above may also explain to some degree why the average duration of a meeting (as shown in Table 4.7) is merely 30 minutes. Exchanging favours in the shape of gifts, money and so on does not require much time. At the same time the main purpose of this exchange, from the standpoint of the TNCs, is to reduce processing time.

Degree of rationality of transorganizational relations

A conclusion from the previous section is that the degree of administrative rationality can be questioned, since relations with government are not a rational clean process. The government is not objective and incorruptible and company officials do not entirely pursue public or company interests. Government officials do not just grant permissions, they also have something to sell. And TNCs have something to offer. Thus, the possible bias of individual parties trying to create favours with opposite parties in order to increase their influence cannot be overlooked. Legitimacy is constructed on non-rational grounds. Different units of the TNC (the buyer network) offer extra favours to the government (the seller network) to get the service demanded. The temptation to bend the rules in a particular instance could be strong, particularly since there is a shortage of this monopolized service. Favours can be created in ways other than monetary gifts, for example, through the employment of relatives and contributions to charity.

As was observed in Chapter 4, (Table 4.2), the relations with the government are neither a perfectly rational nor a perfectly clean process. Favours of various kinds are provided to government officials.

Presents, free transport, entertainment, use of guest houses, and speed money are all important. In the preceding discussion on bureaucracy, the objectivity of the rules, regulations and procedures was emphasized. Objectivity in decision making also implies that the officials are 'equally' available to all the 'service seekers'. Any one who wants to seek a service has the right and opportunity to do so. The subjective or the emotional feeling of an official should not impinge upon whom the official serves. Previous research has shown the inadequacy of the bureaucratic models in this respect, where the inadequacy of industrial policy implementation emerges in our research.

Another result observed in Table 5.3 is that different connections are vital for getting access to government officials. Particularly kinship, language group and membership of professional groups stand out as important. Caste group (jati) and religious group are unimportant, while regional group is only important in certain cases. Another obvious observation is that relationships are built on friendship, particularly of the professional type, created through contacts in connection with the preparation and processing of applications for licenses and import of technology. A private personal friendship caused by contacts outside work, for example meetings in family, kinship, and common religion exists, but is less common. Even if the figure is high for this aspect, it is moderated by answers on other questions about friendship.

Table 5.3   Connections to government officials

	1	2	3	4	5	NR
Kinship	4		2	2	8	1
Language group	3	1	3	7	1	2
Caste group (jati)	6	2	5	1	1	2
Regional group	4	2	4	4	1	2
Religious group	5	2	4	1	2	3
Membership of any professional group (association etc)	3		3	9	2	
A professional personal friendship	2	1	1	3	9	1
A private personal friendship	2		1	3	8	3

Note: 1= very unimportant; 2 = rather unimportant; 3 = neither nor; 4 = rather important; 5 = very important; n = 17

The responses to these two questions do not necessarily show that government administrative processes are irrational and work in a haphazard manner, but rather that they are imperfect as compared to the rational model of administrative efficiency discussed above. How these imperfections are used and why the favours are given determine how effective the processes are. A general result of the study is that the linkages are still instrumentally determined. Connections and favours are instrumental. Dishonesty also leaves room for favours. These things are seen as operative conditions utilized in a calculative way to achieve business legitimacy and to reach a certain level of business efficiency. In addition, the strong differences in levels of competence makes it necessary to approach the officials differently. Incompetence, for instance, gives an impetus for giving assistance in order to speed up the administrative process. In that way, TNCs help officials in their work, thereby contributing to the administrative rationality of the Indian bureaucracy. This can be viewed as an interesting spin-off effect from the operations of the TNCs in India.

Administrative Legitimacy

Administrative legitimacy is achieved by furthering the interests of the administrative subunits with other organizations – mainly the political organizations, but also TNCs. As seen above it is not obvious that administrative organizations are rational, that is to say, that they follow the rules, charters and so on, as they should. They may have to prove themselves and convince different interest groups, particularly politicians, that they are rational. In addition, administrative organizations have their own interests that they want to promote. According to Brunsson (1986) interaction between administrative agencies and political organizations is of two kinds.

> When the initiative is with the political subunit – which then makes decisions prescribing the actions of the administration – the interaction can be called a process of implementation. When the administration has the initiative and tries to convince the politicians to make decisions describing the actions that the administration has completed, or wants to complete, the process can be called legitimation. For both implementation and legitimation, the political decision is the bridge between the two suborganizations; in implementation the decision is supposed to be the starting-point and in legitimation it is supposed to be the result. (Ibid., p. 178)

We describe this type of legitimation as administrative legitimation. As seen in Chapter 2, we see legitimation as a more general concept that is valid for any legitimation process. Therefore, implementation is also closely connected to legitimation or what we analogously define as political legitimation, when political units further their interests.

Administrative Legitimacy or Rationality?

The dissimilarity of political and administrative organizations could also result in separation of the systems. Vague policies, typical of political organizations trying to gain legitimacy by incorporating conflicting demands in their organization, could create confusion and misinterpretation at the administrative levels, when the policy is implemented. Policy objectives do not provide clear direction and selection criteria for decision makers at these levels. Three main things might happen. First, it could open up the administration to political influences, and at the same time increase the possibilities for the executive bodies to be part of the political process. In these cases, political legitimacy is achieved through the executive bodies so that these organizations are controlled more by the political legitimacy rationale than by administrative rationality. Second, the bureaucracy might feel insecure about how to implement decisions, since it is unclear how to interpret the rules. Depending upon how the rules are interpreted, they may annoy one or the other powerful group and be a target of attack and criticism. In this case the combination of insecurity and the wide discretion may create passivity, since the result of following the rules is uncertain. In an uncertain situation, an administrative organization legitimates itself by literally following the rules. Third, the situation of high discretion and uncertainty may be taken advantage of by officials to further their own private interests ('rent-seeking'). In all three cases policy implementation is made more difficult.

A great deal of discretion is left to decision makers at the executive levels, who may subjectively interpret policies in their own way. Thereby, one fundamental prerequisite of rational organization is lost, namely objectivity in implementing decisions. As a consequence, industrial policy formulation and execution become loosely coupled. The deviation between the two may be either denied or not made public. Indeed, occasionally the whole issue may be treated as either a mistake or a misinterpretation of the policy followed by government.

In India, as shown in Table 5.4, government officials at different administrative levels do not generally deviate from the guidelines. From the responses to another question it is concluded, except for a few cases, that the possibilities to deviate from the guidelines have not changed since 1984. These answers indicate that the administrative organizations very much follow rules and that there is a certain objectivity in implementing decisions for the studied issues. The administrative process is not much influenced by political considerations and administrative legitimacy is achieved from zealously working by the rules, that is by seemingly being rational. Another indication in this direction, as observed in Chapter 3, is a concentration of linkages in the GTN to the administrative levels at the expense of the political level. However, this does not necessarily mean that the discretion of individual officials is low, since these answers do not tell anything about how the guidelines are formulated. The more general they are, the more diverse are the actions covered by them, with loss control over decisions. Furthermore, this chiefly concerns the prescribed arm's-length network. There is also an emergent network that is more informal in character and where the social linkage plays a major role. Connections and favours are important in this network. The loose coupling between policy formation and implementation is thus mainly explained by how this emergent arm's-length network is established and maintained.

Table 5.4   *Deviations from guidelines by government officials at different levels from the stated guidelines regarding industrial, import, and technology license matters*

LEVEL (see Figure 5.3)	**1**	**2**	**3**	**4**	**5**	**NR**
Political	2	1	3	1	1	9
High Administrative	7	3	2	1	2	2
Middle Administrative	9	2	3	1	2	
Low Administrative	9	4		2	1	1

Note: 1 = not at all; 2 = only a little; 3 = rather much; 4 = much; 5 = very much; n = 17.

Hence, vague industrial policy documents provide little assistance and guidelines. Results of the survey show that implementation is guided more by bureaucratic practices and traditions. It is dependent on who implements the policy. Industrial policy implementation then very much becomes a bureaucratic phenomenon. The policy is implemented by the bureaucracy manned by people who have worked in the same department for years. A number of ministries (the Ministry of Industry, the Ministry of Textiles, the Ministry of Chemicals and Fertilizers, the Ministry of Heavy Industries) are involved in implementation and these are loosely coupled to each other and the environment.

This high degree of rationality is also the common theme found in the answers to questions put to government officers about their contacts with TNCs. Five officers at the middle administrative level were interviewed with a special questionnaire developed for the government side.[5] The general picture given by these answers is that the government–TNC network also exists when viewed from the government side. But it does not seem to have the same significance from the standpoint of the administrators. Between 1984 and 1989 number of contacts with the companies decreased sharply. The network is much broader and less intensive, where the officers have contacts with numerous company representatives. Generally, these contacts are important, since the officers interviewed meet company representatives daily, in one case they had arranged two 'consultancy' hours per day. The government–TNC Network is used for making better or more rational decisions. Only two reasons why companies use it were rather important according to the officials, namely to 'seek clarification on present policies and procedures in general' and 'to give information related to a particular application'. All the other reasons were rather superfluous or very unimportant. Similarly, there are two instances where it was found that it is rather important for the administrative unit, where the interviewed person works, to take the initiative to contact the companies, namely 'to inform about decisions on a particular application' and 'to seek information about the company's adherence to the stipulated terms in licenses and collaboration agreements'. There were no change in these reasons between 1984 and 1989.

Social aspects of the network are unimportant. The officers do not consider themselves to be friends with the company representatives, there are neither professional nor personal friendships involved, and connections are very unimportant. But, on the other hand, officers trust company representatives rather much to give correct information. TNCs rarely offer favours to the officers. One officer admitted that he received presents only during festivals and another officer responded that '30 % of the people get influenced by all these things'.

Moreover, as observed above, rational decision making is handicapped by the unequal competence among officers. This is aggravated by an imbalance of expertise between administrative organizations and TNCs. In the policy implementation processes a number of gaps develop. Firstly, as previously discussed, it is the responsibility of the companies seeking a license to formulate an appropriate proposal. They possess expertise, are familiar with the technology and the production processes as well as the clients. This knowledge is mainly held by the subsidiary, but also by the parent company or some other sister company in the group. They enjoy business-related, first hand information, and they are also commercial risk takers. In the ministries dealing with the license application a corresponding level of information and knowledge is missing. Moreover a majority of the people engaged in the decision making are non technicians and have never been engaged in business.

The performance of the administrative organizations, like ministries is instead based on surrogate measures, for example time taken to process an application, number of questions asked (which illustrates the thoroughness with which the rules are applied), the number of papers and documents sought and dealt with and the number of applications sanctioned or rejected. There is, then, a natural tendency in the bureaucracy to seek more and more information, papers, and to ask questions. In this manner the ministries show to the environment that they are effective, and exercise control over what the business firms do, and protect the interest of the environment.

Moreover, what the ministries may see as a necessary piece of information and knowledge for making decisions according to the rules, the companies may see as useless, irrelevant, and unnecessary. But the bureaucracy may justify queries and inquiries as they share responsibility in case the venture fails. Since they have processed the application, its failure can initiate criticism. An official clearance for a project proposal confers legitimacy on the project and in case of failure the bureaucracy may have to share the criticism. Decisions are illegitimate in the eyes of the politicians.

A proposal under consideration or scrutiny, however, implies no such commitment from the bureaucracy. In a resource scarce society there is an excuse to prolong the process to grant licenses merely to keep the state's commitment to a proposal low. Applications under consideration merit little or no official commitment.

Rent-seeking behaviour

Bureaucratic decision making is frequently guided by aims and goals not mentioned in the formal rules, regulations, and decision making procedures. Kinship, caste, family ties, and personal gain seeking impinge upon decision making. Hypocrisy is common. The visible (to the public) talk, decisions, and actions are de-coupled from the invisible or illegimate ones. The former conforms to the rules, regulations, and procedures, the latter need not do so. Hypocrisy is rewarded as well rewarding. Behind the scene inspectors enjoy sufficient means to further their own ends. In reality a number of questions are asked by the inspectors merely to gain favours and personal gains. The invisible behaviour allows the bureaucracy to 'feather its nest', namely to use the organization for personal benefits (Perrow, 1986, Ch. 1). The people who occupy a position in the bureaucracy behave as if they own the position and successfully try to achieve personal ambitions. Survey results prove the point. Familiarity with and the ability to understand and adjust to the invisible aspects in the industrial policy implementation is important.

The legitimacy of the bureaucracy is now not contingent upon its ability to implement the industrial policy in conformity with the intentions, but its ability to hide and minimize the exposure of the invisible aspects of behaviour. Important is the ability to explain the anomalies in the industrial policy implementation with reference to the existing (missing) rules, regulations, and procedures.

Promoters vs. Inspectors

The actual administrative legitimacy prevailing in India is compared to another possible and common interpretation of political intention. If the industrial policy is expected to lead the industrial development the bureaucracy should be awarded a pro-active roll. This would mean that goals are specified and operationalized, alternatives are derived and weighed against each other. Lastly, corrective action is taken. The pro-active player should know what he wants (Jacobson, 1989). The state should not only remedy the prevailing industrial problems but should also foresee the problems and eradicate the same in advance. In fact the policy implementation agencies are expected to be the pro-active catalysts in industrial development and transformation, and are expected to act as the promoters and the pro-active partners in policy implementation. To be a pro-active promotor, the bureaucracy should formulate the proposal, analyse the market, master the technology, be informed about the market competition and, lastly, but not the least, be willing to take risks.

In reality, however, the situation as demonstrated above is different and the bureaucracy merely acts as inspector. The study demonstrates that the TNCs initiate the licensing process. They formulate an appropriate industrial proposal, since they are familiar with the market, technology, and competition. The bureaucracy is rather reactive, which corresponds with its traditional role of operating according to the administrative rationality, which implies a controlling authority.

Indian ministries and the people employed therein mostly lack competence or suitable attitudes for exercising such a promoting authority. Lower level clerks have no business and industrial experience, and this often holds true for all levels in a ministry. Very few of the higher level decision makers have ever worked in business. Most of them were recruited into the bureaucracy directly as college or university graduates. These people have spent their entire life within the government organizations and gradually advanced to the higher position in the hierarchy. Their position in the bureaucracy is contingent upon the number of years of experience in the ministry, which bears little relevance to the future direction of industrial development of the country. In addition, a number of decision makers are educated in subjects other than technology or business. They are handicapped in making suitable judgements on complex commercial and technical issues.

Inspectors enjoy a controlling authority, implying that the bureaucracy enjoys all the power and authority to seek information on every aspect of an industrial proposal, and where additional information on the parent company can be asked for. How the information should be used and whether the claims made by the firms are to be rejected or accepted, are issues which are decided by the bureaucracy. This authority is primarily negative. This power to deny permission or acceptance is often exercised by referring to the existing rules, regulations, and procedures, irrespective of the merits of the denial.

There is, consequently, an inbuilt bias in the authority structure in the Indian system of industrial policy implementation, which favours the bureaucracy rather than the business enterprises. The result of this conformity to a controlling authority is that authority is executed through the rules. In the process, however, the bureaucracy skilfully tries to prove that this kind of authority is legitimate by being in conformity with the interests of society. This is a kind of illusion created with reference to the rules, regulations, and procedures, since they are supposed to have been based on rational goals enunciated by the government. As a consequence, the implementation of the policy diverges from its intentions. At the same time it is difficult to pin-point the responsibility for the failure to implement a policy.

This imbalance between an actual controlling authority and a desirable promoting authority, is strengthened by the illusion that legitimate authority is achieved by following rules. The inspector can, by referring to the rules, deny any proposal put forward by the firms or may keep it pending while seeking invariably additional information related to a venture. Moreover, vague rules and regulations at higher administrative levels make the application of negative authority easier. What is done is not as important as what can be legitimized with reference to the existing rules, regulations, and procedures. If the number of rules and regulations are large and detailed this leads to a perverse democracy (Crozier, 1964), that is, a system in which no one enjoys the authority to make decisions. It is hard for anyone to keep track of the rules. The situation deteriorates even further, if the many laws are conflicting. A proposal that is acceptable from one point of view (industrial growth rate) is unacceptable from another point of view, (regional development or balance of payment). The avenues for rejecting or delaying proposals, but which will nevertheless confer legitimacy, are infinite.

Administrative Legitimacy as Ritual and Ceremony

As found within the Indian administration, a controlling authority favours a ritualistic, ceremonial behaviour, which is a source of legitimacy for the bureaucracy as it reflects presumed rational behaviour. It also provides a sense of control. The more questions are asked the larger is the feeling of control. To the society this gives the impression that the bureaucracy is doing the task assigned to it and that through its officials, the state is in control of industrial development. In the absence of such an exercise the industrial policy is characterized as laissez faire, directionless, and much too favourable to the TNCs and other private sector firms. Indeed, it is considered pro-capitalist and possibly dangerous and fatal, since control is lost over the destiny of the nation. In this process little attention is given to the relevance of the questions asked for implementing the intentions of the industrial policy. Questioning has a ceremonial value and is synonymous with control (for the sake of the society) by the Inspector. Rules, regulations, and procedures create an extra value or illusion of pro-activeness, control and desirability. In this process of gaining legitimacy the visible behaviour is important, that is 'what things look like'. It deviates from the real or the invisible part of the behaviour, that is, 'how things are' (Selznick, 1965). The two are either de-coupled or loosely coupled. Evidently, to understand how industrial policy is implemented, the invisible behaviour is more significant than the ceremonial and ritualistic visible behaviour.

This discrepancy between visible and invisible behaviour may also imply that authorities work not as inspectors or promoters but as rent-seekers, which behaviour was described above.

Cultural Elements

Traditional authority patterns or authority ideologies influence ad-ministrative organization in India.

Authority ideologies
Authority is defined by Kakar (1971) as

> a relationship between two individuals, one the superior and the other the sub-ordinate, the relationship lying not in the individuals but in the positions they occupy in the formal hierarchy of the work organization. (Ibid., p. 298).[6]

Kakar distinguishes four basic ideal authority patterns (see Table 5.5). The parental ideology has two dimensions. The authoritarian or assertive aspect, where emotional affiliation is low and task control by the superior of the subordinate high, emphasizes the superior's right of decision. The nurturant aspect, where emotional affiliation is high,

Table 5.5   Authority ideologies and types of superiors

Ideology	Image of superior	Behaviour of superior toward subordinate	
		Emotional affiliation	Task control
Parental	Nurturant	High	High
	Assertive	Low	High
Professional	Impersonal	Low	Low
Fraternal	Helping	High	Low

Source: Kakar 1971, p. 299.

emphasizes the concern of the superior for the subordinates. In an assertive relationship the status is not only legitimized on formal hierarchical grounds but also contains a cultural or ideological element. In a nurturant relationship a superior takes responsibility for aspects of the life of employees outside actual work, for example, the families of the subordinates. According to the nurturant ideology a superiors's area of competence is vaster compared to a modern bureaucracy. In the nurturant relationship, the parent–child relationship is extended to the superior–subordinate relationship in organizations. The nurturing mother is the dominant person in the Indian family and the mother–son relationship the basic dyad and ideal for human relations. The father is a distant figure, usually stern and aloof, who is not much involved in the child's upbringing. According to Pye (1985, pp. 148-149) the surrender to family and caste authority together with the very distant relationship with the father may be the root of Indian passivity towards authority.

The parental ideology is a relic from a traditional pre-industrial society. It is personal and the legalization is based on everyday routine and an unchanging past. People obey out of respect for the ruler's traditional status and decisions are limited by customs and traditions. As noted above, however, the authority in Western organizations is legitimized by impersonal laws and rules, which are based on agreed principles of rationality. Authority is limited to areas of competence defined by these laws. This type of authority is usually called formal or hierarchical authority. The right to a competence field is determined by the capacity of a person within this field and is not as in traditional societies, considered to be the property of a person's family or caste. In a Western organization with a professional ideology superiors legitimize their power and control of subordinates by their formal authority. The essence of civil-service integrity and fairness involves acting in a stately, considered manner according to invariant, impersonal rules. The emotional affiliation and task control are both low in such a rule determined organization. When the emotional affiliation is high, the ideology is characterized as fraternal. From the parental authority patterns, conforming to the Hindu society, follows a social interaction which is characterized by obedience and conformity and not by a personal power of initiative. Security for the subordinate is obtained by relying on the superior.

> The available evidence on superior–subordinate relations indicates that the parental type in general and the assertive superior in particular, dominate authority relations in Indian organizations. (Kakar, 1971, p. 299)

One factor responsible for the inefficiency in carrying out programmes is the Hindu belief that matters of spirit are more important
than material things. Following the strict rules of one's Dharma,
(social or moral law) is considered important. This authority pattern
also further substantiates why following rules often becomes ceremonial in the way discussed above. Hindu cultural factors result in a
propensity to stick to the rules of rank and status, thereby proving
worth by faithfully obeying the administrative regulations. Administration becomes more of a ritual, where effective government means
carrying out each action in the correct way. Matters of form and
trivia thus become more important than substance. The administrative
service is thus influenced by the traditional system, where everybody
has an ascribed position in a rigid system. These rules of conduct,
obligations, and customs are determined by a person's caste category
and subcaste grouping. This also results in a tendency not to reward
subordinates, since they only do what is expected of them. Superiors
should instead, according to the traditional way of Indian ruling, rep-
rimand, punish and give away as much work as possible. An outcome
of the system is an elaborate specialization of Indian social order.

This traditional assertive parental authority pattern was also characteristic of the colonial British way of treating Indian subordinates.
This was a highly authoritarian relationship of emotional aloofness
and high control of Indian civil servants by British superiors. It was
later imitated by Indian superiors and is still in existence (Kakar,
1971, pp. 300-301).

SUMMARY AND CONCLUSIONS

Policy formulation is done at the political level in which the different
segments in the society participate, either through parliamentary representation or through some other political act. The various segments in the environment try to gain representation in the industrial
policy through political parties, trade associations, lobbying groups,
and so forth. Efforts are made to bring in labour representation,
industry owners, regional interests and so on. The wider the representation of these interests in discussions and deliberations, the greater
the scope for conflicting and divergent interests to participate. Prior
to its finalization, the industrial policy draft is circulated to elicit the
views of the divergent interest groups. The idea is not necessarily to
include all these interests in the industrial policy but make sure that as

few as possible are left out. The opinion of the state governments are taken into consideration as well.

Political organization is thus far from the ideal traditional bureaucracy, where employment is based on a technical and rational criteria, namely possession of knowledge and skills to perform a task. Such organizations also function in a radically different manner and follow radically different principles, as compared to the commercial organizations. An additional feature of this normative literature is the compatibility between decision making authority and the responsibility for the outcome. Those who enjoy the authority to make decisions are also held responsible for the outcome.

This, however, does not imply that national governments are either less rational or are not interested in industrial development. Rather, there are inherent features in governmental organizations which make the task of industrial policy formulation and implementation difficult and less feasible in the manner prescribed by the traditional writers on organization.

Hence, industrial policy formulation and to some extent implementation, are political acts guided by the principle of survival for the political actors. An important goal in industrial policy formulation is to assure survival of the policy formulating bodies and this is achieved through gaining legitimacy and support of the powerful actors in the environment.

Industrial policy formulation is an act undertaken by governments with the aim to gain legitimacy and to show that the government is doing something about the problems in the society. This is a response to the demands to which a government is exposed. Governments proclaim that they exercise control over the affairs of the state. Whether the government can really do so is entirely a different issue. Through a formal industrial policy formulation and a formal procedure to implement the same, government signals to the environment that it is both capable of and is actually responding to the demands of the society. The society presumes that the measures outlined by the government will be implemented. Otherwise, there is no reason why the government should go through the tiresome process of formulating an industrial policy.

Political organizations are primarily exposed to the institutional environment and must respond to the same. By their very nature these organizations are political, with inbuilt conflicts. A clear, measurable output is missing. These organizations succeed because of their ability to identify with the institutional rules and regulations rather than by their ability to produce goods and services required by the environment. They survive because of their ability to integrate into their structure and processes, the norms and values entertained by the environment. Such organizations are exposed to two crucial problems. Firstly, the institutional rules and myths are inconsistent and conflict with one other. The different segments of the environment entertain different myths, institutional rules, norms, and values. Secondly, achieving institutional acceptance may conflict with the organizational ability to rationally produce the licenses and services required by the technical environment, mostly companies, which is a crucial problem for the administrative organizations.

We conclude from the above discussion of the role of the Indian bureaucracy, that it is more or less an independent power and pursue's its own rules, regulations and procedures. The purpose of the bureaucratic actions is to gain access to legitimacy and this is achieved through following rules.

Political legitimacy often stands in direct conflict with the implementation doctrine. Vague political goals can be executed in many ways and give little guidance. Sometimes they are not even meant to be implemented. One must not forget that the political system has a broader repertoire to claim legitimacy, for example through talk and decisions.

Policy formulation and execution become loosely coupled. Objectivity in implementing decisions, which is one fundamental prerequisite or rational organization, is lost. The rationality of the administrative network does not correspond to the rationality model of administrative efficiency. The competence and honesty of the officials are generally too low, and connections are vital for getting access to government officials. Kinship, language group and membership of any professional group are particularly important.

One conclusion of this result is that the rational model of administrative efficiency needs to be complemented. This is mainly done by developing the cultural factor of the network theory, in this chapter how culture affects authority patterns in Indian government organizations.

In spite of loose coupling mandated arm's-length network, on the whole, works as prescribed. Guidelines are followed and few linkages are established at the political level. But there is an emergent network that functions in another way. The social linkage is very important as shown by the significance of connections and favours. The Indian bureaucracy thus pursues a number of goals and aims of its own, of which not all are overt and visible. These behind the scene activities are important to know how policies are implemented. This is made easy as the authority structures deviate, making it unclear if officials operate as inspectors, promoters, or rent seekers. This allows the bureaucracy a wide latitude in decision making and pursuing its aims. In this process decisions are delayed, if there are ever made.

NOTES

1. Traditional cost-benefit analysis of TNC investments is also based on this metaphor as can be understood from the following quotation from Caves (1982). It also demonstrates the limitations of viewing governments as rational entities.

    The traditional view of rational industrial policies and its implementation in rational organizations has its counterparts in traditional welfare economics, where it is assumed that the government wishes to maximize real income for its citizens and merely needs help with the technical details of its policies. Our behavioural approach to public policy assumes, instead, that governmental decisions result from self-interest agents interacting in a political setting. This positive treatment of policy decisions does not lead to a single all-purpose model like that of neoclassical welfare economics, but the specific applications to date share a coherence of general approach. Policy towards MNEs has not generally attracted a behavioural treatment and so this research project is only based on tentative suggestions.

    In the government-policy model the focus is shifted from utility-maximizing electoral behaviour to the utility of a coalition of government officials whose tenure in office is not explained within the model. It is assumed that the government pursues numerous policy objectives but that it lacks policy instruments that are reliably sufficient to attain them. Perhaps powerful interest groups prohibit or restrict policies that unavoidably (if perhaps incidentally) harm their welfare. Perhaps norms of convention or constitution keep the government from imposing or fully enforcing policies that theoretically could suffice for the intended objective. The government periodically desires to change the economic allocations that result from market transactions (e.g. by liberalization certain industrial controls). But the insufficiency of instruments leaves the government constantly uncertain about whether or not it can make its allocative preferences stick. Private economic agents then become odious to the government in proportion to their ability to dodge its allocative designs. If MNEs enjoy better alternatives than nationals (they can spread the transaction cost of dealing with the government over more business, or they can credibly threaten to cut back their local activities sharply), they draw unfavourable glances from the government and invite overall restriction or special regulation of their activities.

    If the median-voter believes (or the bureaucrat, or the politician) that allocative preferences announced by the government are intrinsically superior to those cast up by the market, any proposal to restrict or regulate MNEs will receive approval, because the median voter's restraining concern with effects on real income from private-sector transactions is defined away.

2. The equivalence of this approach on the company level is where company strategy is looked upon as a plan (Mintzberg, 1988), e.g. Chandler (1962) or Ansoff (1965).

3. Compare the 'soft state' (Myrdal, 1968). In this state there are too many

conflicting group interests that government tries to align which has a severe effect on policy implementation.

4.   The role of patron-client relations in the political arena is developed further in Landé (1974) and Eisenstadt & Roniger (1980).

5.   As is discussed in the appendix on methodology a standardized questionnaire was developed in the research project to study how the government–TNC network functions from the government perspective. The intention was to put similar questions to government officers at different levels and in different ministries and authorities that were put to the company representatives. However, despite the fact that these interviews were carried out by people from a well-known Indian research institute with good government contacts, the access was severely restricted. Only 5 officers volunteered to answer the questionnaire in personal interviews, all of them working at the middle administrative level (A1 and A2 in Figure 4.1). Even if this is a very small and biased sample there are some general tendencies found in the material, which is presented shortly in this chapter.

6.   Authority is a power concept, which deals with inequality in organizations. The definition used in this work emphasizes the power of the superior and whether the bases of power are traditional or not. The concept power distance, used by Hofstede (1980, chapter 3), is different, since it is a measure of interpersonal power or influence between two persons as perceived by the subordinate.

6. Control of the GTN by the Group Network

In earlier chapters we have analyzed how the subsidiary relates to government through the government–TNC network. It was found that this network is heavily influenced by the subsidiary's linkages to other units within the TNC, that is to say, by its position in the group network. This aspect is being analyzed in this chapter, with the focus on the TNC as a whole and its relation to the GTN. We will primarily study how well the Indian subsidiary is integrated within the group, mainly in matters involving strategy towards government, but also where other business functions are concerned. The degree of integration or coupling with the group would depend on how much coordination there is with regard to decision-making over the main issues between the subsidiary and other units within the group. From the perspective of the GTN, this integration may be of the following kinds :

- A direct participation by other group units in the GTN or through a parallel network.
- A direct control of the GTN, for example by including such issues in the normal reporting routines, or requiring license applications to be approved by the group before being submitted.
- An indirect control of the GTN by directly controlling the decisions or strategic areas for which applications are sought and the GTN is organized, that is, production, imports of products and technology transfer.
- An even more indirect control where the GTN is part of a general control of the subsidiary as a whole.

The local autonomy of the GTN and indirectly of the Indian subsidiary is analyzed along these four dimensions. A distinction is made with regard to levels of control: direct participation; control of specific government matters; control of specific business functions related to government matters such as manufacturing, and technology transfer; and general controls of the subsidiary. The control of the government strategy by the group and thereby the autonomy of the Indian subsidiary varies along these dimensions, forming four distinct grades of control. When the GTN is controlled by the group, so also their related business functions, which means that the subsidiary as a whole is heavily controlled and the autonomy is the lowest at this first grade of control. Autonomy is likewise the highest where there are no specific controls and only general controls over the subsidiary exist. Thus, the integration of the subsidiary–government network with the subsidiary–group network is of variable degree. A direct participation makes for higher integration, while an indirect participation results in a lower integration. It can also be assumed that the more integrated the subsidiary is into the group network and the reason behind integration being efficiency, the more difficult it is to decouple the 'legitimacy' part of the subsidiary.

TRANSNATIONAL CORPORATION AS A HIERARCHICAL NETWORK

These grades of control are rather crude indicators of the degree of co-ordination and thereby of the autonomy. This is specified with the help of the general network model in Chapter 2. First it is necessary to transform the specific organization studied in this chapter – the TNC – into a network. According to the main grouping of types of transorganizational networks indicated in Chapter 2, the TNC is classified as a hierarchical network. Central to the network structure of this type of organization is the trade-off between integration and differentiation or between tight and loose coupling on one hand, and strong and weak ties on the other. It is a well-known fact from organizational network studies that tightly coupled or dense networks with strong linkages are vulnerable to external disturbances. Changes travel fast through such networks, which could create an information overload and too many conflicts. Loosely coupled networks with weak linkages have the opposite characteristics. Since independent individual units do not have much contact, information and resource exchanges are low. Disturbances are confined to parts of the network, which reduce the number of conflicts. The problem is to find the right trade-off between these extremes for various tasks as for the network as a whole. One way is to create linking-pin organizations as 'bridges' in the network, for instance, through teams, task forces, committees, integrators and integrative units such as regional head-quarters.

Following Ghoshal & Bartlett (1990) we combine internal and external networks in our study. The entire network would consist of organization sets. The main internal network studied is the TNC, while the main external network is the GTN. Internal as well as external networks consist of organization sets, where each set or cluster is coordinated through linkages within itself as well as between or across themselves. We also use the term density, which is defined as the percentage of actual to potential ties among members within organization sets and between them (Ghoshal & Bartlett, 1990). Consequently, the term 'within density' is used to describe the density of linkages within one organization set and 'across density' for the density of relationships within the whole network. It also follows that loose or tight coupling concerns both these types of densities.

Figure 6.1 Factors influencing the autonomy of individual subsidiaries

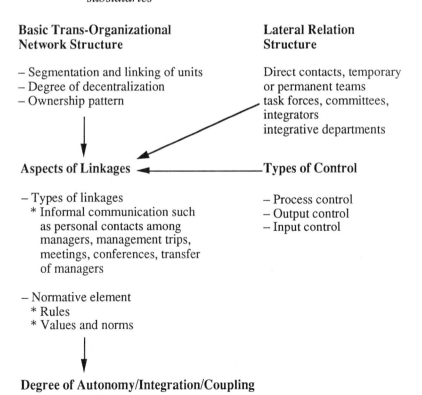

Basic Trans-Organizational Network Structure

– Segmentation and linking of units
– Degree of decentralization
– Ownership pattern

Aspects of Linkages

– Types of linkages
  * Informal communication such as personal contacts among managers, management trips, meetings, conferences, transfer of managers

– Normative element
  * Rules
  * Values and norms

Lateral Relation Structure

Direct contacts, temporary or permanent teams task forces, committees, integrators integrative departments

Types of Control

– Process control
– Output control
– Input control

Degree of Autonomy/Integration/Coupling

The network model in Chapter 2 is re-arranged to fit this transorganizational pattern of a hierarchical network analyzed in this chapter (see Figure 6.1). The focus is on the across-density, that is, on how the focal organization of the local organization set (the subsidiary) is coupled to or coordinated with the group network. Consequently, two main aspects of linkages are important to study: types of exchange and normative elements such as rules and values. The degree of coupling, which could be operationalized as the across-density of linkages, is influenced by (a) the basic transorganizational network structure, (b) the lateral relation structure and (c) types of control. An essential part of the linkage pattern is prescribed through the basic transorganizational network through such means as segmentation and linking of units, degree of decentralization and ownership pattern. Linkages are also influenced by the existence of lateral contacts such as teams, task forces, committees, or integrators and the way these are established.

A most vital integration dimension for a unit within a hierarchical network structure is the manner in which different units within a TNC network are controlled. The more a subsidiary is controlled by the group, the lesser its autonomy, and the more its strategies are constrained. Three main types of controls are found for the linkages: process (behaviour) control, output (performance) control, and input (conditional) control. Before we analyze the degree of coupling of the local subsidiaries (Figure 6.1), it is important to develop and characterize this hierarchical network in greater detail than was done in Chapter 2.

THE HIERARCHICAL GROUP NETWORK RELATED TO OTHER RESEARCH

The transnational corporation is viewed as a transorganizational network. This approach to organizational research about the TNC is new and not much developed. A detailed study is made of how one specific external network (the government–TNC network) is connected to the internal group network. Such relating of an internal and an external organization is one of the great strengths of a network approach as emphasized by Ghoshal & Bartlett (1990). This advantage is improved further in this study by combining a network approach with an institutional organization theory.

Following such an approach, the TNC is thus classified as a hierarchical network. This is an asymmetric network, where the vital part of the linkages within and across organization sets is prescribed from the top, through three main factors as in Figure 6.1: that is, the basic transorganizational framework, types of control and lateral relation structures. This prescribed basic network structure is assumed to be constant and given for the groups during the period under study.

Our study confirms that not all subsidiaries in a group are controlled in the same way. Smaller subsidiaries on the group's periphery such as those in India are controlled differently from larger subsidiaries in Europe and North America. This corresponds with results from recent research on the organization of TNCs, which show that control is differentiated between units. Therefore strategic roles or strategic contexts vary for subsidiaries (Bartlett, 1986; Bartlett & Ghoshal, 1989; Ghoshal & Bartlett, 1990; Hedlund, 1986; Porter, 1986; Martinez & Jarillo, 1991; Gupta & Govindarajan, 1991; Forsgren & Holm, 1992). Another similarity observed between this literature and the results from the present study, is that behaviour is not entirely controlled by hierarchical power (fiat), but is also variable within the network. Emergent network structures, as well as types of controls and relation structures together adapt to changing conditions in a complex world. These prescribed and emergent parts of the hierarchical network interact in a complicated way. Informal communication, for instance, may improve control through the budget system by supplying additional vital, not prescribed, information. But if this information is wrong or biased, control through the budget system becomes more difficult.

However, the main difference between this and the other studies of TNCs at the individual subsidiary level is that the latter tends to overvalue the importance of such informal organization for subsidiary behaviour at the expense of formal organization structures (e.g. Martinez & Jarillo, 1981; Gupta & Govindarajan, 1991). As mentioned in Chapter 2, the main argument is that several studies have demonstrated organizational variables or internal management processes to change more often than formal structure. But it is also a reaction to earlier major studies that over-emphasized structure, since they are based on Chandler's strategy-structure perspective (e.g. Stopford & Wells, 1972; Franko, 1976). However, this is an over-reaction as judged from the evidence of the study reported in this book, which demonstrates that the prescribed organization structure is still a most important control of subsidiary action. Our conclusion is that finer graded formal macrostructures should be developed for a better understanding of how different types of subsidiaries are controlled, and that a network approach facilitates such a task considerably. In other words, it is important to consider both formal and informal organizations.

One major difference between the present network study of TNCs and most others is that hierarchical power through the formal structure is more pronounced compared to linkage-based power through the informal structure. This implies that linkage-based power counteracts hierarchical power rather than the opposite. A major reason behind this emphasis on linkage-based power in the other studies is, in our view, that they rely too heavily on traditional inter-organizational theories, which mainly concern non-hierarchical organizations. One major consequence is that the large difference between intra- and inter-organizational networks is under-valued and is not developed adequately. Since this research on non-hierarchical organizations also largely focuses on dyads, a network approach becomes too simplistic. For the same reason, there is also a bias toward the power of individual units (exchange power) rather than the positions within networks (structural power). This tendency is also reinforced by the fact that large subsidiaries in strategic locations have been the focus of earlier studies. The present study, on the other hand, mainly takes up smaller subsidiaries in more marginal markets. In addition, in earlier studies hierarchical power is poorly defined, and then imply that this type of power is executed through the formal hierarchy.

Of the three generic types of control defined in this chapter hierarchical power is gained or executed through ownership control and hierarchical control (see below). However, market control does not seem to be part of the picture. Therefore, the construct 'prescribed hierarchical network' used in this book is more precisely defined than the 'formal hierarchy', since it covers all three generic controls as well as the basic transorganizational network structure. It is also a broader construct than 'formal hierarchy', since the term 'prescribed' is added, a concept that is based on the construct 'deliberate action', which is the opposite to 'emergent action' (Mintzberg & Waters, 1985).

It can now be concluded that two main aspects are vital in order to determine the degree of coupling of the Indian subsidiary: the strategic network position (control position) within the group and the degree of actual control. These are detailed below for the partial TNC–

government network and for the entire internal group network using the model in Figure 6.1. The degree of autonomy of the Indian subsidiaries is expressed in two main propositions:

Proposition 1: The degree of coupling varies with the specific organization of the linkages.

Proposition 2: The organization of the linkages and, indirectly, the degree of coupling varies with the basic organization structure of the TNC, which is a prescribed network structure. It also varies with types of control pursued within the group network and with the lateral relation structure.

GENERIC CONTROLS OF THE NETWORK FRAMEWORK

The TNC network is mainly viewed as a control structure which, as shown in Table 6.1, consists of the basic transorganizational network structure, lateral relation structure and types of controls. These factors are divided into three types of generic controls: ownership control, market control, and hierarchical control.

Vital to the organization of the network framework is its legal basis. Ownership of different units within the group is one medium of control. It can be used to decentralize the organization structure by giving divisions or subsidiaries a more independent standing or autonomy. Ownership control through share-holding and personal representatives on the board is strategic and general. Research has established that TNCs usually prefer to control their operations by majority ownership. However, this was restricted in India during the period of investigation on account of the Foreign Exchange Regulation Act (FERA). But these rules did not hinder TNCs from taking full control of the Indian subsidiaries through controls other than ownership. This is one reason why the term subsidiary is used for the Indian company, even if its formal ownership status is that of a minority interest company or a joint venture. A TNC is able, through its multinational organization, to control its activities in various markets. This organization in its turn very much influences the way in which business is run in a specific geographical area like India.

Market control, the second type of general control, is based on the principle that a unit within the group is incorporated. Legally the firm is an independent unit and is left to operate on its own in the markets. Its relationship to the group is market-oriented and control is effected through the price mechanism rather than through hierarchy. Market control seems to be the practice for small subsidiaries in distantly situated countries than for large market companies in main markets (Jansson, 1994a).

The third main type of control used by TNCs is hierarchical control or administrative control. This is the main aspect of the prescribed network framework of a TNC. Commonly TNCs today have a divisionalized organization structure with a high degree of internal control with regard to the various units. The incentive structure is equally well established (Jansson, 1994a).

BASIC GLOBAL TRANSORGANIZATIONAL NETWORK STRUCTURES

The most obvious example of a prescribed hierarchical network is the basic transorganizational network structure, which comes close to the formal organization structure as was discussed above. Depending on the degree of coupling between different units within the network as expressed through the linkage pattern, a distinction is made between four different prescribed transorganizational network structures. While the discussion that follows emphasises the three structures most relevant for this study, a fourth is also considered, as it is relevant for TNCs not studied here. A more detailed presentation is also in line with the general purpose of the study to develop the network approach to transnational organizations.

The four basic transorganizational network structures are all decentralized. At one extreme the network is characterized by a low degree of prescribed coupling or a low across density, where organization sets are loosely coupled both vertically and horizontally. The coupling is high within the organization sets because of a high within density. This is the loose hierarchical framework. At the other extreme is the dense hierarchical framework where both the degree of coupling within the organization sets and between them are tight. A third form, in-between these opposites, is the clustered hierarchical framework. This basic transorganizational network is tightly coupled across organization sets vertically but loosely coupled horizontally. The dense vertical clusters are usually based on type of product. The fourth basic network structure is a mix of these three more 'pure' forms. Since it is the most varied form with changing degrees of coupling within organization sets and across them, it is called the differentiated hierarchical network.

Main Interest Groups

Divisionalized network structures are predominant in TNCs today. This is true for a majority of the TNCs studied here. The units within such structures are further globally organized with incorporated units, where the basis of the organization is either product or geography or both. Following the interest group approach developed in earlier chapters three main groups of interests are distinguished with reference to how linkages are organized and controlled within such a decentralized structure. This does not imply that legitimacy is important within the TNC network, since these interests are all economic in nature and based on an efficiency perspective, albeit from varying standpoints. These are basic interests within the group that represent different efficiency rationalities, which are all related to the instrumental purpose. Two are concerned with the spatial aspect of international activities (that distinguishes TNCs from uninational corporations): the global and local interests. Some units within the TNC represent the global aspect of an activity, for example a product or project. The primary task of other units is to operate locally, for example a market company. The third interest type applies to the company as a whole and is found in all companies. It is termed the company-wide interest. While the global and local interests are parochial the company-wide interest looks at the common interest of the firm. The main task of Executive General Management (EGM) at the group headquarters is to represent the company-wide interest, a mandate it gets from the board or ultimately from the shareholders and other stakeholders, as for example, the home government. This task is accomplished by having a transorganizational network structure, types of control, and a lateral relation structure that ultimately favour that interest. A primary task is then to control the parochial interests so they do not get out of hand and conflict too much with each other and the company-wide interest.

1. Loose Hierarchical Network

Some of the smaller TNCs studied are characterized as loose hierarchical networks. This network is usually based on the geographical dimension, where the local market interest overrides the global product interest, and is a more traditional organizational form of the

TNC. The local organization set is highly coupled, but the linkages between organization sets are loose. It has also been called a multi-national organization or a mother–daughter organization, because of the centrality of the group headquarters (the mother), which has direct linkages with the subsidiaries (daughters). In this traditional organization type, the market companies are very independent and subordinated to the Executive Group Management. Such a network structure based on an area organization promotes local responsiveness, and ill-favours the leverage of the global integration needs. In addition, the strong affiliation of the subsidiary to its local customers, suppliers or regulators makes it harder to control by EGM. This loose hierarchical network is a rather 'primitive' form of world-wide organization and has primarily been in operation in the earlier stages of internationalization. The interwar period, for example, favoured a multi-domestic pattern of competition developed on a country to country basis, where little coordination and multinational control was required (Dunning, 1988; Martinez & Jarillo, 1989). TNCs were not very diverse and were not divisionalized, as for example along product lines, but were functionally organized. Subsidiaries were loosely coupled and more controlled through informal means by 'the mother', as for instance through informal communication by the EGM and even by the chairman of the board and other board members.

2. Clustered Hierarchical Network

Our study of TNCs reveals that global integration on product basis is their most common feature. The basic prescribed hierarchical structure is clustered around the product companies/divisions. Such a cluster is tightly coupled within itself (the vertical dimension) but loosely coupled to other clusters (the horizontal dimension). The local market dimension is subordinated to the global product dimension. An efficient coordination of global product interests and local interests increases the competitiveness of the corporation, particularly if competition is global. This type of organization is called a clustered hierarchical network, one example being the global product organization. The authority of the product companies over the local subsidiaries extends to local decision making and implementation. But this rationality of favouring global interests in decision making or conflict resolution through the basic network structure is achieved at the expense of low product adaptation to local conditions and customized marketing, particularly if the overall density according to all main factors is high within the local organization set. Product companies are not supposed to accept decisions by their subsidiaries that do not conform with the global objectives. Such a situation could lead to sub-optimization as seen from the TNC as a whole (the country-wide interest).

In a clustered hierarchical network based on the product dimension and organized as global product companies the market company reports directly to the management of the product company, which reports to the EGM. With this organization the control of the market companies becomes more formalized and they are more closely connected to the product companies, which often means that their independence is reduced compared to the loose hierarchical network structure.

The clustered hierarchical network is a later form of international organization structure. The change to more global competition from multi-domestic competition affects the long-term competitive positions of TNCs and as a consequence of that, their goals. The global integration of local market activities becomes more essential for international competitiveness. In the earlier stages of internationalization, newly founded subsidiaries are not integrated into the group structure on the basis of functions or domestic product types, and are left more or less to themselves, as exemplified in the loose hierarchical network. With rising international commitment and growing interest is increasing the control of international operations.

3. Tightly Coupled Hierarchical Network
A third form of basic transorganizational network structure is found among a few TNCs, namely where organization sets are tightly coupled both internally and externally.[3] The across density, which is a global characteristic, is high, as is the within density, which is a country characteristic. This is a matrix of two separate hierarchical networks, one based on the product dimension and the other on the geographic dimension, which intersects at certain points. There is a balance between two parallel hierarchies, one based on the global product responsibility and one on the local market responsibility. Such a prescribed basic transorganizational network could be suitable to TNCs that operate in industries, where international competition is both global and local. This requires an integrative tightly coupled hierarchical network, where local responsiveness is balanced with global integration. In this network the geographic dimension is as important as the product dimension, which means that it is a more

symmetric network compared to the prescribed hierarchical networks analyzed above. The clustered network is asymmetric favouring the product dimension, while the loose network is highly biased towards the geographic dimension. These asymmetries are supposed to balance each other in the tightly coupled network. The main task for the company-wide interest in this network structure is to control this balance. Conflicts easily arise, since the two main interests are considered equal. These are meant to be solved by negotiation and the use of informal and subtle control mechanisms. However, conflicts also generate information within the organization, which can be used mainly for control purposes. In the process, conflicting local market and global product interests are expected to be reconciled.

Compared to the other two hierarchical network structures, global competitiveness originates even more from coordination of inter-related activities world-wide. With an established market position in most local markets of interest to the TNC and a rising global competition, growth comes more from an increased international involvement of the whole TNC than from initial entries in new geographic markets. It is vital to utilize synergistic advantages and to rationalize production and marketing, for instance. The competitive advantage from integration is more sophisticated than in the clustered network. Co-ordination is based on both the global interest and the local interest and not only on the global interest. More complex internal controls are developed. For the tightly coupled network it is more difficult to separate local competitive advantages from global competitive advantages, since they tend to intermingle. In developing a new propriety asset, for instance, it is also essential to assess its potential for creating advantages for global integration, e.g. where to produce it in the world and how to integrate that production with the selling of the products in the various local markets together with how to integrate these new activities with previous operations of the TNC.

4. The Differentiated Network

The tightly coupled network comes close to the 'globalized' transnational organization, which is both global and local (Bartlett & Ghoshal, 1989). But this organizational macrostructure is too highly prescribed, to be simply called a transnational organization. This network structure is closer to a differentiated network, which is a very complicated organization and is more than a highly prescribed two-dimensional organization (Ghoshal & Bartlett, 1990).

The network structures discussed above, seldom exist as pure

forms. They are combined in different ways. Even in heavily prescribed integrated network structures such as the tightly coupled hierarchical network there are loosely coupled units. This is often the case
for subsidiaries in India, where strict Government regulations make it
impossible to integrate the units within the group to the same extent as
for units in general. The main purpose of the import substitution
policy and other restrictions is to protect markets in India. Many
TNC would most certainly reduce production or buy less inputs in the
country if trade barriers were lowered.

In the structured network several dimensions are simultaneously
considered. It could for instance be a mixture of the more homogene-
ous types of networks described above. There may be large differences regarding the degree of coupling between units within organization sets as well as across them. Activities could be linked in
various ways both within the same function and between different
functions. Marketing of some industrial products, for instance, might
be more linkage-based than others. Furthermore, research and
development can only be plugged into local resource networks in
specific countries. In the differentiated network, the degree of
coupling between different organization sets varies both vertically and
horizontally. Some local organization sets are internationally coupled
through an exchange of products, since production is specialized.
Alternatively, organization sets are linked because they have common
customers or suppliers, for instance, other TNCs. Such a differentiated network has a more complex prescribed linkage structure with
varying controls. These complex structures also raise the question as
to how much prescription of the network structure is possible or
necessary. Ghoshal & Bartlett (1990) found considerable changes in
internal management processes of some TNCs during a 20 year
period despite no change in macrostructure. Internal roles, relations,
and tasks as well as controls changed. In a differentiated network it is
more vital to prescribe these aspects than the structure itself.
Emergent networks play a large role in the differentiated network.
Informal communication, for instance, is a vital part of this type of
multi-dimensional network.

TYPES OF CONTROL

The types of control, which are specified in Table 6.1, are mainly
based on hierarchical control and market control. The former type is
mainly executed through rules, while prices are used in the latter

Table 6.1   Internal network controls

GENERIC CONTROLS

- Ownership control
- Market control
- Hierarchical control

BASIC TRANSORGANIZATIONAL NETWORK STRUCTURE
(PRESCRIBED)

- Segmentation and linking (grouping) of organizational units, shaping the formal structure, e.g. by function, product, area, matrix.
- Centralization or decentralization of decision making through the hierarchy of formal authority
- Ownership pattern

LATERAL OR CROSS-DEPARTMENTAL/DIVISIONAL/COMPANY
RELATION STRUCTURE

E.g. direct managerial contact, temporary or permanent teams, task forces, committees, integrators, and integrative departments.

TYPES OF CONTROL

Process control

Direct (Behaviour control): Orders, advice, dialogue.

Indirect (rules): Information stored in texts (formalization and standardization): written policies, rules, job descriptions, and standard procedures, through instruments such as manuals, charts etc. They are used in the planning and budget system.

Output (performance) control

Financial performance, technical reports, sales and marketing data, mainly organized through a planning and budget system.

Prices: Transfer prices stored in numbers

Input control

Socialization, building on organizational culture of known and shared strategic objectives and values by training, transfer of managers, career path management, measurement and reward systems, informal communication (see above).

Sources: This table is mainly based on Collin (1990), Larsson (1989), Martinez & Jarillo (1989, 1991), Gupta & Govindarajan (1991).

case. Ownership control, on the other hand, is not taken up here, since it is entirely exercised through the basic transorganizational network framework. As emphasized above, this basic network structure is viewed as a control infrastructure according to the control perspective used in this chapter. Prescribed structural controls take place through this structure, which also specifies the hierarchy of formal authority and the ownership pattern. Within this transorganizational framework three main types of control are used. Output control mainly takes place through a planning and budget system that gives objectives and performance standards for individual action. Marketing, production and financial performance, for instance, are controlled through a reporting system and an internal price system. This performance control is normally based on an internal transfer price system in an organization consisting of fully incorporated units or, sometimes, profit centres.

Process control is often based on direct, personal surveillance (behaviour control). Examples of personal instruments in this case are orders, advice and dialogue. But process controls can also be manifested in rules through formalization and standardization of information, for example, written policies, job descriptions, manuals and charts.

The know-how of the individuals classified as input control, is also important. This is in its turn closely related to another input control, namely, socialization of individuals within the organization. This could, for instance, be achieved through the means of career path management, transfer of managers, measurement and reward systems, and informal communication.

Socialization is one way of globally integrating autonomous units through the use of normative elements, that is indoctrinating managers so that they acquire group values and ways of thinking in order to identify with the whole group and not only with the local subsidiary. The values and norms of managers become closely aligned to those of the group as a whole. This can be achieved through transfer of information, influence and people among various group units according to a management development and transfer programme. The budget system is also an important mode for socialization. The know-how, values and norms of the individuals are thus influenced by exchange through the linkages, for instance through informal communication such as personal contacts among managers, attendance at conferences and transfers of managers. Decision making is also indirectly affected.

This communication can only be broadly prescribed, within which emergent control networks are allowed to develop. Lateral or cross-divisional relations, for example direct managerial contacts and temporary teams, can be encouraged. But formation of such relations must be dependent upon actual needs. Similarly, more prescribed means such as courses, conferences and so on, can be arranged to impart understanding about the organization and how it should work. But these means should also give employees opportunity to meet to develop relationships. Therefore, how such venues are organized varies with subject and participants.

Traditional direct hierarchical controls of subordinates or indirect controls through rules, procedures and manuals are usually less important in the highly decentralized multi-level, multi hierarchical and multi-national TNC. The planning and budget system, which intends to control the results of organizational behaviour has greater weight. Another vital indirect control of behaviour finally takes place through the methods by which people are selected and socialized into corporate values and beliefs. In a divisionalized TNC, indirect input and output controls are supposed to be more critical for efficiency than the traditional hierarchical process controls which are more characteristic of a functional organization. As noted above, controls in the modern TNC take different rationalities of the organization into consideration, as for example local responsiveness and global integration. Direct intervention is thus selective in such an organization, where control is mostly of this indirect variety.

THE DEGREE OF COUPLING OF THE INDIAN SUBSIDIARY TO THE GROUP NETWORK

The response to questions about the degree of autonomy of the Indian subsidiary in general and for government matters in particular is taken up in this section. The direct and indirect controls of the government–TNC network is first analyzed followed by the general control of subsidiaries.

Direct Process Control Through Participation in the GTN

Group units outside India do not participate in the GTN. Our study revealed no such network operating between the group and the Indian government. It is evident from the answer pattern to a number of questions, that the direct contacts between the group and the Indian government are too few for linkages or network to exist between these parties. With the exception of one TNC, groups do not participate directly in preparing applications or applying for licenses. Group representatives rarely visit India to establish contacts with the government on license matters. Between 1984 and 1988/89 there were no visits in two cases, one visit each in two cases, two visits each in two cases, and three visits in one case (Table 6.2). For these cases the respondents stated that the direct contacts between the government and other units within the group increased a little. The majority of the respondents found these questions irrelevant, which indicates that there are, generally, no, or very few, visits from the group. It can thus be concluded that the network between TNCs and government is local, with the subsidiary as the acting party. This means that groups and subsidiaries are loosely coupled with regard to government matters, which are the responsibility of the Indian company and for which there is no direct control by other group units. The linkage between the group and the Indian subsidiary in decisions related to the main license types is therefore mainly indirect.

Table 6.2   Frequency of visits by group representatives to India to have contacts with the government of India since 1984

Times per year	No. of Group representatives
0	2
1	2
2	2
3	1

The subsidiary can be labelled an autonomous subsidiary (Martinez & Jarillo, 1991). The degree of integration with the group is low and the degree of localization high. Compared to Gupta & Govindarajan's (1991) classification of strategic contexts for knowledge flows, this position comes close to their 'local innovator' category because inflow of information for license matters is low. Equally, the outflow to the group is also low.

Indirect Control of the GTN

There is always some kind of linkage between the group and subsidiary in business matters which also require licenses. Production
investments, imports (particularly of capital goods) and technology
transfers are of strategic importance for the subsidiary, since they
constitute main resource flows within the group and substantially
affect the profitability of the Indian company. It is vital for the group
to control such flows directly and the coupling is therefore usually
tight. But as seen below the strength of the linkage varies with different resource flows and thereby for different license matters. In this
way the group mainly controls license matters indirectly.

As seen in Table 6.3 there are different control patterns for the
main types of license applications depending upon how much production investments are controlled. Process controls such as separate
approvals by the group and the obligation to inform the group before
applications are submitted, imply a higher control than an output
control of only supplying information after the event. Generally,

*Table 6.3   How the Indian company is linked to the group for
different license issues*

	1	2	3	4	5	NR
Applying for Industrial Licenses						
– for expanding existing production	2	3	1	4	4	6
– to manufacture new product	1	2	4	3	4	6
Applying for Import Licenses of						
– raw materials	8	0	1	0	5	6
– components	6	1	2	0	5	6
– capital goods	4	0	1	0	8	6
Applying for Licenses for Import of Technology						
– designs and drawings	2	4	2	1	5	6
– foreign collaboration agreements	2	3	3	0	5	7

Notes: 1 = not linked at all; 2 = information is only needed afterwards;
3 = information is needed in advance; 4 = approval is granted without an
independent examination by the group; 5 = approval is granted after an independent
examination by the group.

though, the indirect control of industrial licenses is rather varied. Information may be needed after application or in advance. But in the majority of cases an approval of some sort is required, with or without an independent examination of the investment proposal by the group. The group indirectly influences applications for manufacturing new products to the same extent as expansions of existing production facilities.

With regard to production, most of the Indian subsidiaries can be classified as implementors of group strategies. The inflow of information is high at the same time as the outflow of information is low. Our study reveals that many groups thus take an active interest in the subsidiaries' production matters. This is indicated by the fact that approvals from the group regarding important production matters are required as well as output controls such as manufacturing reports are an important part of the information system. As seen in Table 6.3. feedback from reports is considered an important control. No connection is found between how applications for industrial licenses are linked to the group and the importance of the budget and planning system, which indicates that this economic control system works as a more general type of output control, and not being specifically related to production.

For the three types of import licenses, the responses are more clear cut and confined to the extreme alternatives. The Indian company and the group are either not linked at all or, approval is granted after an independent examination. The import of raw materials is the least controlled, while for the imports of components the response is almost equally divided among the two extremes. The import of capital goods, on the other hand, is the most controlled one of the import license matters. Obviously groups are either heavily involved in controlling this resource flow or not involved at all. The former situation concerns imports from the group itself, while the latter situation mostly concerns locally bought goods. The Indian import substitution policy forces the companies to localize the purchasing of input products to India, which is normally managed by the local subsidiary (Jansson, 1982). When it comes to purchasing, Indian subsidiaries can either be classified as 'implementors' or 'local operators'. The same strategic roles are found for import of technology, although with more subsidiaries as 'local operators' than 'implementors'.

In the import of technology group involvement is less strong than that in industrial licenses and import of capital goods, but somewhat stronger than that is the import of raw materials and components. The control is either tight, in that approvals are granted after independent examinations by the group or loose, on account of absence of exchange of information. The evidence of loose linkage between subsidiary and group for import of technology is unexpected. Our study shows that such licenses are mostly applied for without prior approval of the group, and where it is mostly enough to inform the group afterwards. The general experience in this field is that TNCs carefully control technology transfer matters, since they concern the heart of the company. But we find that in India, this control is counterbalanced by the strong government control of these matters, which means that applying for licenses to import technology, particularly foreign collaboration agreements, is still very cumbersome. Another reason for this unexpected result could be (which has not been empirically studied) that the studied TNCs do not export the very latest technology to India, and hence they are less keen on controlling its transfer.

General Control of the Subsidiary as a Whole

Our conclusion, therefore, is that direct involvement by the group in license applications is almost nil. There is more control over business aspects of license matters such as ascertaining the profitability of production investments and export of components and capital goods to the subsidiaries. However, in the main, control over the subsidiaries seems to be of a more non-specific kind and oriented towards various business functions in general. General boundaries are set for the companies within which they can act. These boundaries are less concerned with government matters (legitimacy) than with business matters (efficiency). We will now analyze how this more general control system is organized.

We have partially discussed the main general controls represented in Table 6.4. As a rule, the budget and planning system is important. This is also true for the reporting system. Visits by group representatives in India and from the subsidiary to the group are not directly used for controlling business matters related to government. But they are vital general controls for other functions. The same thing can be said about ownership control through group representatives on the board. They are all vital means of influence by the Group on the Indian company. There are also a few other means of communication that are important in certain companies.

Table 6.4 *Importance of different means of influence by the group on the Indian company*

	1	2	3	4	5	NR
Through group representatives on the board	0	1	3	3	7	6
Through the budget system	2	0	3	1	9	5
Through the planning system	1	5	1	2	5	6
Through feed-back from reports	0	2	1	8	4	5
Through visits by group executives	0	0	5	4	6	5
Through visits by Indian company executives at the group	1	3	6	5	0	5

Note: 1 = very unimportant; 2 = rather unimportant; 3 = some importance; 4 = rather important; 5 = very important.

Output controls

Impersonal and prescribed output controls through budgets, plans, and reports are essential in today's TNCs, as is shown in Tables 6.5 and 6.6. Table 6.5 illustrates objectives and budgets, and Table 6.6, the reporting system. With the exception of three cases, local conditions strongly affect the group's setting of objectives and standards for the operations of the Indian subsidiary. This seems to be one reason behind the consent in the assessment of priorities between the Indian company and the group.

In most cases subsidiaries are firmly anchored within the group's budget system with most respondents believing that it is very important to strictly follow the group's budget procedure. It would seem that only minor deviations from budgeted performance are normally tolerated. Respondents were less willing to answer the question about tolerated deviations, which is interpreted as a sign of this issue being sensitive and related to the cultural factor 'harmony' as discussed in previous chapters. As regards the reporting system, although this system is an important control, it is less extensive than the planning and budget system. The importance of manufacturing and product quality reports are acknowledged, while it is only important to report on government matters for some subsidiaries. Financial reports are also important, while the importance of marketing and sales reports varies. Normally one major report is supplied to the parent company

Table 6.5   Degree of consideration of circumstances and conditions in India when setting group objectives and standards for the operation of the Indian company

1 = not at all	0
2 = only a little	3
3 = neither nor	0
4 = much	4
5 = very much	8
Missing	5

Frequency of differences in assessment of priorities between the Indian company and the group.

1 = very often	0
2 = often	1
3 = now and then	1
4 = seldom	9
5 = never	4
Missing	5

Importance of strictly following the group's budget procedure.

1 = very unimportant	1
2 = rather unimportant	0
3 = some importance	1
4 = important	1
5 = very important	12
Missing	5

Extent of toleration of deviations from budgeted performance by the group.

1 = not at all	0
2 = only a little	7
3 = neither nor	3
4 = rather much	1
5 = very much	1
Missing	8

Table 6.6   Extent of feedback on reports sent from the group

1 = on every report	1
2 = on almost every report	7
3 = on half of the reports	1
4 = on only a few reports	6
5 = on no report	0
Missing	5

Table 6.7   Degree of group's influence on decisions in the Indian company compared to its influence on other group units

1 = much less	1
2 = less	6
3 = no difference	5
4 = more	1
5 = much more	1
Missing	6

(group headquarters) every month, which contains most of these reporting dimensions. It is seen that only one subsidiary reports to other units within the group, in this case, to four product divisions. Generally, the reporting requirement in the subsidiaries is thus comparatively low, making these report a rather unimportant control instrument. The responses presented in Table 6.6 indicate that in approximately half the cases formal controls are only procedural, since there is feedback from the group on only a few performance reports. The majority of these groups are large TNCs. For the other half, mainly smaller TNCs, feedback is given on almost every report. These groups more actively use such controls, which is facilitated if the TNC is small.

Judging from the results presented above the Indian subsidiaries are a part of the groups' prescribed control system and follow the rules established by this system. But as was indicated earlier in about half the cases following rules seems to be enough, since reports are not followed up. It can further be established that most subsidiaries are less controlled than subsidiaries in general or equally controlled. According to Table 6.7 the degree of the group's influence on the subsidiaries' decisions are less in 6 cases and equal in 4 cases compared to its influence on other group units. Two subsidiaries are very independent and are mainly controlled through the board of the local firm. A general conclusion from this response is that the degree of control of the subsidiaries in India is different from other units within the group, which means that not all subsidiaries are controlled in the same way within the groups.[4]

Input controls

Mutual visits which reinforce relations and which open up for informal communication between subsidiary and group units, combine some main types of control. These visits for prescribed purposes are a basis for the creation of emergent networks. Even if transnational visits could be used to control people directly, they remain an expensive proposition and therefore mainly work more as a means of communication and socialisation. As shown earlier in Table 6.4 and in greater detail in Table 6.8 executives from the Indian company go abroad to visit group units more often than executives from the group visit India. The variation in the frequency of visits is large in both directions. Although there are two exceptions of 10 and 20 visits, executives normally visit India a few times each year (12 instances of 4 visits or less). Local managers go abroad either infrequently (once or twice a year) or frequently and even very frequently (6 instances of 10, 15 or 20 visits). Though the travelling is important it is expensive. Communication within the group therefore mainly takes place through other channels (Table 6.9). On the whole there is a rather dense contact pattern. The number of boundary spanning persons varies a lot, from 2 to 50 persons. In 5 cases 7-10 persons are involved with the group and in 4 cases there are 15-50 persons. Normally 10% of the respondents' working time is spent communicating – attending meetings, in making telephone calls, sending telexes, letters and so forth to other group units outside India. Very little of this communication seems to take place outside official channels. It is equally much initiated by both sides. These controls are less formal in nature. The contact pattern varies with the size of the group and the type of business. These visits indicate that trustful relationships are present within the studied TNCs, which is a prerequisite for informal control to work. This control also seems to take place

Table 6.8   Frequency of visits

A Frequency of visits by executives from the Group to the Indian Company.

B. Frequency of visits by executive from the Indian Company to the Group.

A		**B**	
Freq.	**No.**	**Freq.**	**No**
1	3	1	2
2	6	2	4
3	1	3	1
4	2	6	1
6	1	8	1
10	1	10	1
20	1	15	3
		20	2
Missing	5	Missing	5

through middle management going abroad than top management coming to India.

The nationality of top executives

The nationality of top executives, which is related to human resource management, is another vital input control. It is also an indicator of the managerial perspective. A polycentric perspective implies a low integration of the subsidiary into the group. A country national is here considered to be the best suitable to manage local operations, among other things, because of better knowledge of local conditions and better rapport with employees. In such a TNC subsidiaries are managed by locals from the respective host countries and the head-quarters by locals from the home country. The polycentric perspective reduces conflicts within group units, but increases them between units, for example between local and global interests. A foreign national as managing director on the other hand, signifies that integration of the subsidiary into the group is more vital than when a local country national occupies this position. This expatriate could

Table 6.9 *Number of persons from the subsidiary in direct contacts with other units within the group*

Freq.	No.	Freq.	No.
2	2	8	1
3	1	10	2
4	1	15	1
5	2	30	1
7	2	50	2

Per cent of working time per year spent in communicating (meetings, telephone calls, telexes, letters etc) with other group units outside India?

Per cent	No.
1	2
3	1
5	2
10	9

Per cent of communication taken place outside official channels.

Per cent	No.
1	2
5	1
10	1

Per cent of communication (in per cent) taken place at the subsidiary's initiative.

Per cent	No.
25	1
50	9
75	2

represent two different managerial perspectives. According to the geocentric perspective the managing director of a local company is primarily viewed as a representative of the company-wide interest. Then the nationality of the expatriate does not matter, since this is the best person for the job, seen from the company-wide interest. The main task is then to make the right trade-off or reconciliation between the global and local interests on the spot. Inter-unit conflicts are reduced at the expense of intra-unit conflicts. These conflicts could grow even more if the outlook of the managing director is ethnocentric. Then there is a belief that a home-country business culture is superior to the host country culture. In such a group foreign nationals dominate. The managing director might not represent the company-wide interest but a local home-country interest. Japanese TNCs, for instance, are often run in a Japanese way and populated by Japanese managers throughout the group. This is typical of the centralized global organization form discussed by Bartlett and Ghoshal (1989).[5]

According to Table 6.10 parent company executives are only found in certain key positions. Approximately half the number of companies have managing directors from the group. Expatriates are very rare in other positions, such as marketing or production. The dominance of local executives point out the importance of local conditions for the operation of the Indian subsidiaries.

Table 6.10   Positions of expatriate managers

	Yes	No
Managing Director	6	9
Marketing (Sales) Manager	1	14
Production Manager	1	10
Finance (Accounting) Manager	2	13
Controller	1	14

Ownership Control

Although board membership is important for control purposes, the limited response to the question about board membership makes it difficult to arrive at a conclusion.

Other variables used to assess the degree of autonomy of the Indian subsidiary, such as the degree of indigenous shareholding and the formal status of the Indian company within the group, were discussed in Chapter 1. According to these dimensions Indian subsidiaries are independent.

SUMMARY AND CONCLUSIONS

In a divisionalized network structure with incorporated units a critical question is how to make the right trade-off between the three main types of controls: ownership control, market control and hierarchical control. Subsidiaries in far-off and culturally distant markets such as India seem to have a low degree of coupling. The environment is so specific that it does not matter what basic global transorganizational network structure the group has or how large its business in India is. However, the degree of coupling is a relative measure, and does not mean that the unit is autonomous, only that it is comparatively less integrated than many other units within the network. For instance, it is vital to ensure that the operations do not lead to sub-optimization in the way that they conflict with the interests of the group. Functions at lower hierarchical group levels are separated to operate on their own, for example relations with government authorities usually belong to this category. Although the position is that control varies from a direct control of the GTN to the group not having even an indirect control of the strategy towards government, the integration of government matters into the TNC network is generally considered to be low. However, the general management of the subsidiary is not separated from the TNC as a whole and thus is integrated into the group through the different types of controls illustrated in this chapter. The main problem is here to differentiate between the three main controls within the group, since a standardized global type of control could reduce the profitability of a local unit. However, this does not seem to be the case for the groups studied, where controls are differentiated among subsidiaries, and where the lesser control of the Indian subsidiaries is a case in point. In addition, controls are used differently, as was also seen above. Yet, other controls are unsuitable due to specific institutional factors in a country, for instance, government policy and law, as is obvious from this study. Market control has been shown to be less suited for India with its highly regulated markets and the keen government control of transfer prices.

NOTES

1. These concepts are defined by Ghoshal & Bartlett (1990, p. 616).
2. An antithesis to the loose hierarchical network is a centralized network that neither promotes global nor local effectiveness. If this network is non-divisionalized the global interest and the world-wide interest coincides, which is the case in the global organization type found with many Japanese TNCs. In such an organization, costs are large for decisions regarding foreign markets, since they are taken far from the markets, which results in inefficient decisions, particularly where there is a need for local responsiveness. An overload of information could occur at the top; a well known phenomenon.
3. Another prescribed hierarchical network that is rather tightly coupled between organization sets is the global organization type (Bartlett & Ghoshal, 1989) or centralized hub (Bartlett, 1986). This is a highly centralized and ethnocentric organization, where the subsidiaries are heavily controlled by the headquarters. Many Japanese TNCs have such a configuration. But this structure is not valid for any of the TNCs studied in this project.
4. These conclusions correspond to results from a study of subsidiaries of European TNCs in Southeast Asia, and where in a few instances, the same TNCs were included (Jansson, 1994a).
5. To be complete it is also possible to hypothesise a more unlikely perspective – the xenocentric one – when the EGM might even represent a foreign interest. This is the case if an American multinational, for example, is run by Japanese executives, and if there is a belief in the superiority of Japanese management methods.

7. Implications for Network Strategies

Strategic implications for TNCs of the earlier chapters are taken up in this chapter and a strategy model in the form of a summarized experience is presented that can be used by TNCs in their operations towards governments. Illustrations are taken up from earlier chapters but also some new data are included. In that way the chapter is a retrospective one but at the same time general conclusions are drawn.

The transorganizational network theory presented in Chapter 2 and used throughout the book is now being transformed into a normative strategic model, in this chapter which is illustrated in Figure 7.1. This transformation is done by using strategic concepts from industrial marketing theory (Jansson, 1994b) and changing them into constructs based on the inter-organizational network theory. The strategic model so derived is built on the three aspects of linkages: purposes, types and structure. While instrumental purposes are looked upon as company objectives, types of linkages and structure of linkages are mainly translated into three major strategic concepts: linkage strategy, competitive strategy, and first-mover advantages. The structure of linkages is complemented by the strategic construct 'linking process', in order to explain how network linkages could be developed and maintained. The resource aspect of the network theory is developed further into a grouping of strategic resource profiles. Indirectly, the strategic model is also built on the transorganizational patterns.

THE ANALOGY TO PURCHASING OF INDUSTRIAL GOODS

The strategic implications from the GTN are analyzed as being similar to industrial marketing or more precisely as a purchasing matter. An analogy is drawn from a purchasing situation, where products or services produced by monopoly sellers are acquired. These exchanges are seen to take place in order to acquire an input needed to produce and sell an output. These linkages are not viewed as a marketing

173

Figure 7.1 The strategic model

activity, since a service/product is not offered by the firm and can therefore not be related to the output side. However, like any critical input, the impact on output is high (see below). A permit obtained from government is not a pure service, since it is not consumed and produced at the same time, as are bank services or repair and maintenance operations. Rather something is acquired that is better described as consisting of a mixture of hardware and software. The permit, for instance, manifests itself on paper that resembles hardware more than it does a software, and lasts for some time.

The analogy is not made with purchasing in general. There are fewer similarities with traditional organizational buying models than with models that view purchasing as the other side of 'relationship-marketing' or 'business-to-business marketing' (Jansson, 1994b). However, the resemblance is greater with the network approach to industrial marketing and purchasing, which, like the present study, is based on interorganizational theory. In both cases the centrepiece of the approach is the direct relationships or linkages between organizations, in the first case on buyer/seller networks, which are established and maintained in order to acquire products or services, and in the second case on the government–TNC networks, through which licenses, or more specifically legitimacy, are achieved.

Lobbying is defined in our study as a common activity of firms trying to influence government policies, which is mostly aimed at politicians. But individual TNCs act mostly on their own and towards the administrative or executive parts of the government in order to get permits for their operations.

The emphasis on network relations is pronounced, since the 'market situation' in the government case is similar to 'monopsony', where 'the seller' has a local monopoly since 'products/services' cannot be imported. The 'market structure' is thus concentrated on the 'supplier side'. At the same time it is mostly 'oligopolistic' on the 'buyer side', where 'buyers' compete with one another for the monopoly service/product. This leads to a rather lop-sided structure altogether, an unbalanced situation in favour of the 'seller', which results in the 'buyer' being the active party of the relationship in order to compensate for the inferiority. As was demonstrated earlier in the book one expression of this higher activity is that the 'buyer' initiates contacts. The TNC is thus very active in relations with government, where it is important to create influence (get legitimacy). Moreover, most of the 'service/products' are forced upon the company because it cannot operate without them, in which case there is a strong analogy to such inputs, for which there are no substitutes.

The resemblance to the industrial network approach is also strenghened by the fact that the 'service/product' demanded is complicated, as compared to simple products, which is one main factor behind the establishment of buyer–seller networks. In our case a simple 'standard product' is not 'bought' 'off-the-shelf', rather a complicated 'tailor-made product' is acquired. As was shown in previous chapters, the decision making process of 'the seller' is very complex, while the decision making process of the 'buyer' is rather complicated. The 'buyer' issues an 'order' (an application) for the 'product', which is 'produced and delivered' to the buyer. This 'product' is complicated to produce, requiring many contacts to get 'delivered'. One characteristic of this rather informal process is that individuals of the government network are more prone to extract monopoly 'rents' contrary to formal rules. Government and company officials are not completely impartial and incorruptible, where only public or company interests are pursued. Government officials grant not only permissions, but also have something to sell just as TNCs have something to offer. Individual parties try to dispense favours in order to increase their influence. Different units of the buyer network offer extra favours to the seller to get the service demanded. The temptation to bend the rules in favour of such companies is strong, particularly since there is a shortage of this monopolized service.

As the present study shows, favours can be created in ways other than through bribery to interest government officials in the welfare of the TNC, for example, by

> providing them with beneficial MNE decisions, valuable information for government decision-making, future jobs, employment for relatives and friends, etc. (Boddewyn, 1988, p. 355)

This is evident from the many strategic issues discussed earlier in the book. From the different issues involved in the GTN, it is concluded that relations with government are mainly a rational, clean process. As is evident from the present study the GTN does not work in a haphazard way, in which case it would be impossible to even approach objectives which themselves become superfluous.

Even if there are reasons to question how professional government officials actually are, there is no doubt that contacts within the GTN take place between 'professionals' (business people and officials), which, then, is another important similarity in buyer/seller networks.

Still, another similarity between the approaches concern stable and long-term network relationships. This is a well-known characteristic of buyer/seller networks as well as of government–TNC networks as observed in the present study.

The 'oligopolistic market structure' on the 'demand side' makes a company interested in influencing the 'seller' in order to get a license before the competitors or to hasten the processing of the permit. From this perspective, companies are competitors and not collaborators. Companies could get a competitive advantage by, for example, getting an industrial license for a new product, improving its quality or efficiency by investing in new machines or by being permitted to increase its capacity or import products not allowed for the competitors. Here the impact on output is evident, as for any critical input. A competitor could, on the other hand, stop or delay such actions and thereby keep its advantage through a good influence position with the authorities. There is competition for such positions, since the seller also offers protection. Moreover, an upper-hand could also result from a faster processing of a license compared to the competitors. As we have seen, these possibilities depend upon the discretionary range of a control and the success in taking up the limited resources of government. In addition this competitive posture of the TNCs studied is not as strong as expected.

Hence, there are important similarities between dealing with authorities through the GTN and doing business with sellers through the buyer–seller network. However, there are also basic differences involved, chiefly, in the overall objective behind activities: in the former case the objective is to be profitable or efficient; in the latter case, to be legitimate. This basic difference, which has been a leading theme of the book and elaborated in previous chapters, will also be considered in this chapter. As is observed in Chapter 3, for instance, there are essential trade-offs between these two major rationales behind TNCs' operations in foreign markets.

Due to the many similarities between buyer–seller and government–TNC relationships analysed above, the analogy to purchasing will now be pursued in greater detail. Because of the major difference mentioned above, however, the term purchasing is replaced by the more general term procurement. Similarly, the government network will be referred to as a supplier network and not as a seller network.

THE PROCUREMENT MARKET SITUATION

The main characteristics of the procurement market situation were discussed above: the skewed market structure with a local monopoly on the supplier side and oligopolistic competition on the procurement side; network relationships are direct, long-term, and complex; there are professional actors; complex inputs; and complicated decision processes on both sides with many units and persons involved. It was also observed that as a consequence, largely, of the market structure, companies are involved in competitive and cooperative organization networks. Actors on the public side are those organizations that administer and effectuate industrial policies, for example various units within the ministries (such as the SIA, DGTD and Chief Controllers). Because of the competitive situation, organization networks are grouped in the same way as industrial networks. It is possible to define one procurement network consisting of the TNC and parties affiliated to it, which demand the grant of licenses. This network is connected to the supplier network consisting of different processing units within the central bureaucracy and state bureaucracy which supply licenses (a monopoly). This partial network works in competition with the competitor network.

MAIN OBJECTIVES

To reiterate, there are two main instrumental purposes for which TNCs participate in the GTN, which are viewed as the two main objectives of the TNC:

1. to gain business legitimacy from government: this is the main reason why contacts are established with Government. By getting licenses legitimacy is achieved.
2. to increase efficiency: this is the objective behind measures to hasten the processing of licenses and to utilize the rules in competition with other TNCs.

As was observed in Chapter 6, efficiency is interpreted differently by various units within the TNC network, for instance, the local subsidiary more easily accepts the lower rationality of government than the group, where problems are viewed from a global perspective. Conflicting interests regarding technology transfer, imports and ownership may arise within the TNC as a consequence of differing views on the trade-off between efficiency and legitimacy. But as observed earlier, these goals may also support each other, for instance, the more a TNC is able to improve the legitimacy position in various organizational networks, the easier it is to reach efficiency goals such as a specific competitive advantage.

THE PROCUREMENT STRATEGY

To fulfil these two objectives, the TNC needs to participate in the authorities' decision making processes through the GTN. As already established, the granting of licences does not happen by itself, since decision processes of the supplier network are very complex with a high discretion for individual decision makers. Moreover, authorities are often dependent on information from TNCs to solve the complex issues involved. Also the low capacity and rationality of the government can be improved with help from TNCs. As discussed in Chapter 3, there are several strategic issues involved. Attempts to increase competitiveness through influencing decision makers to favour the own company, for instance, are subordinated to strategic issues related to the legitimacy goal.

The procurement strategy concerns how the TNC acts towards the government network, which is both determined by the ability of the company (assets, experience, and advantages of jointly managing government relationships within the group) and circumstances prevailing in the host country. Such abilities of TNCs are elaborated into a number of procurement profiles, which typify the abilities of a firm to handle different forms of government relationships.

The procurement strategy consists of two main substrategies – the linkage strategy and the competitive strategy – where the former strategy is directly related to contacts between procurers and suppliers, and is therefore based directly on two main aspects of linkages in the transorganizational network theory of Chapter 2: types and structure of linkages.

The Linkage Strategy

The linkage strategy is the first part of the procurement strategy, and is directly related to how TNCs act within the GTN. It is mainly a matter of combining the two main types of linkages in the network model: exchange of resources, mainly information, and social exchange for the main phases of the linking process (see below) and for getting the right mixture between the legitimacy and efficiency goals.

This is a kind of tie-up strategy of the supplier network to the procurement network. As was observed in previous chapters, procurers and suppliers often work together for long periods, during the preparation and processing phases. The stable, intense, and rather informal GTN was classified in Chapter 4: contacts were seen to be frequent and mostly personal, social, durable, professionally-based and trustful. In Chapter 3 the application-specific and general business related strategic issues involved in these contacts were analysed. These were observed to be either information-based or socially based. It was further established that when developing and implementing a 'project' in the form of a new product to be manufactured and sold on the local market, inputs such as permits are needed. When procuring these, the parties become enclosed in their relationship, making it difficult to substitute each other for a third party. The supplier, for instance, ties himself to a few procurers' solutions to the needs of the country. The more resources the TNC invests in a specific country, on the other hand, the more its flexibility to divest is reduced. This tie-up grows gradually as the parties become absorbed into the relationship, and the flexibility of both parties is reduced. The stronger the inter-dependence becomes, the larger the risks are for both parties, since costs for replacing each other increase.

Situations similar to these are often analyzed as bargaining pro-cesses between TNCs and governments. As implied earlier, procure-ment expenses are often already high in the early phases of the GTN – the scanning and preparation phases – because of the contacts that are cultivated with the government to create influence and trust. The cost for preparing documents for the applications are normally consider-able, too. The largest costs involved, however, normally concern business aspects, for instance, preparation of investment proposals or lost profits in case applications are turned down. Since each solution is company-specific, most of the expenses are wasted if no license is received. The degree of linkage specificity is normally high with high switching costs. It is therefore, important for the parties to protect themselves from the dangers in these kinds of networks. This is usu-ally done within the relationship by building up a mutual balance of gradual commitment of resources. Another possibility is to safeguard the involvement by keeping to official rules (the mandate), that is analogous to some kind of third party. The decisive judgements for both parties concern the degree of commitment for each phase of this process leading to a licence being applied for, processed and maintained.

The Competitive Strategy

The competitive strategy is the second part of the procurement strat-egy, and more directly related to competition with other TNCs. As was observed earlier in the book, various types of linkages are avail-able to the TNC to get a competitive edge, for example, creating different favours, giving information about the TNC itself and its products, informing how the company can benefit the country. These linkages are directed at government, but should be packaged so that competitive advantages are achieved, the package favourably differentiating itself from the competitors' offers. The package may consist of information about various benefits to the country, for example hardware in the form of high-quality products and software such as service, transfer of know-how and finance. Favours can also be offered to officials and social contacts used to separate the TNC from its competitors. This package is thus communicated through the linkage strategy, mainly by personal transfers of information and through social influence. The procurer may sometimes be assisted or supported by a third party, such as the home government, embassy or trade associations.

First-mover Advantages

As observed above, a crucial part of the strategy is to find the best mix and sequence of linkages over time with the ultimate aim of finding the right combination of the two main objectives: legitimacy and efficiency. One way is to transform the competitive situation from a situation with many parties to a situation with few parties, the number of actual competitors being gradually reduced. This is accomplished by building and maintaining a network so that the supplier is enclosed at the same time as competitors are locked out. The strategy is interpreted to aim at creating and maintaining first mover advantages over competitors. A first-mover advantage is either achieved through the resource linkage, when the authorities are tied up to information from the procurer, or through the social linkage, when the supplier is socially committed to the TNC. Product and financial tie-ups, when the supplier becomes dependent on the procurer's products and technology, are the other alternatives.

It is a question of finding the right linkage strategy for various stages of the build-up of the relationship. For example, since procurement of certain licenses has such a large software component, the mixture of social and information linkages is crucial, particularly at the initial establishment phases. Since the tie-up is mutual, the procurer is also impacted in the network, which is often a condition for the supplier to accept his commitment. This was established in the study, which does not mean, however, that the network is equally balanced.

A first-mover advantage is also achieved through a competitive offer. The strategy consists of a right combination of the interconnected linkage and competitive strategies. The linkage strategy constrains the transfer of the competitive strategy, but is also influenced by what the TNC can offer, as expressed through the strategic procurement profiles. An advanced technical solution far ahead of the host country's present capability, for instance, requires a more long-term build-up of information and social networks for the transfer of the know-how.

THE LINKING PROCESS

The process to bridge the gap between the organizations studied, mainly to establish the GTN, was seen to have a preparation and processing stage. This is now elaborated into two main stages and four main substages or phases. The establishment stage is followed by the habitual stage, when the relationship has been established, routinized, and habits have been developed. In the latter stage, when the relationship is working according to certain customs, one important task is to follow up the established relationship.

The four substages or phases of the establishment process and the habitual phase are illustrated in Figure 7.2. First there is a 'scanning' phase, where an investment proposal or similar investigation is made to study the feasibility for operating in the host country, to establish a factory for example, or import a new technology. Towards the end of this stage the TNC also looks into how the government views such a project and what are the permits needed. But the actual contacts with the administrative units to find out about the license opportunities start at the preparation phase, which runs until the license application is filed. In the next phase the license is processed. In the follow-up substage, which starts after the license has been approved, officials are contacted to keep the relationship going, while awaiting future applications. The establishment and habitual stages are common for all types of license relations, although the characteristics of each stage are different. Moreover, as discussed above, the importance of the whole establishment stage varies for the main types of licenses. Establishing relationships for complicated licenses take a long time,

Figure 7.2   The linking process

Scanning phase

Preparation phase   *Establishment stage*

Processing phase
- -
                                      Habitual stage

Follow-up phase

and therefore it is fruitful to divide the process into different sub-stages. For simpler licenses, the habitual stage is the important one.

The first two substages of the establishment stage mostly concern information collection. The parties collect information about each other on different aspects of the requirement and its solution. A lot of resources are spent in getting a first-hand knowledge about the parties and competing solutions, with regard to the needs of the country. This information dominated phase is usually terminated when the license application is filed. Negotiations may also be a part of the preparation process, for example, to reach a basic agreement, which is followed by the license application being filed. But negotiations could also occur at the processing phase, if there is no such basic agreement. The outcome of this substage is the licence. In the processing stage, the relationship becomes more and more routinized, and slowly develops into a habitual stage. At the final substage – the follow-up phase – it is important to follow up the established relationship in various ways.

With the parties' increasing knowledge of each other the organization of the network changes. For example, the licensing process becomes more simplified and routinized. Parties know a lot about each other and the competitors. Improved knowledge may make the individual participants re-organize license matters.

The process described above looks different for different types of licenses. Import licenses are a more regular business, for which the habitual stage (see below) is important. For technology licenses, the establishment stage predominates, since in the latter case each license is special and takes a longer time to prepare and process. The length of the habitual stage varies between different licences. In this stage, the parties have come together, thereby excluding other parties. Competitiveness is maintained by a regular course of procedure that constitutes a barrier for the competitors. It is essential not to lose this competitiveness by letting the relationship be set in a fixed mode. It is necessary that flexibility is maintained through adaptations to changes.

STRATEGIC PROCUREMENT PROFILES

A procurement strategy describes a certain action profile of a company, where procurement situations depict the conditions for this action. To be able to act on the basis of these conditions, resources are needed, for which four main strategic procurement profiles have been developed, each describing the specific assets of a company for a certain strategy, such as knowledge, skills or other resources related to both the linkages and organizations of the network. To decide on and implement a strategy in a certain environment, specific types of resources are needed, for example, specific knowledge about certain authorities or a general knowledge about many authorities. These strategic profiles illustrate a company's ability to handle various types of government network linkages for certain types of licenses.

The grouping of the profiles, which is illustrated in Figure 7.3, rests on a distinction between two main types of solutions to license requirements: whether the resources of the TNC are directed at getting licenses according to specific or general requirements, that is, the kind of operation for which a license is needed. In one profile, solutions are made and adapted to individual requirements, where authorities are treated in a more individual way. To be able to find solutions of this kind information is collected about the specific needs of the country and the government. Information is transmitted about possible solutions that are evaluated, possibly negotiated, and licenses applied for. Such a strategic profile, where activities are directed at specific authorities, is called authority specialist. As earlier described, many of the TNCs studied have a lot of contacts with the Directorate General of Technical Development (DGTD) at the Ministry of Industry, thus being specialists on that agency. However, in the second case, when the network is organized to solve common needs of the authorities, activities tend to converge on the license procedure as such, rather than on the authority itself. This strategic profile, where the network is organized around the procedure is called procedure specialist.

Figure 7.3   Strategic procurement profiles

		Authority Specialist
	Direct linkages	
		Procedure Specialist
Procurement		
		Linking-Pin Specialist
	Indirect linkages	
		Intermediary Specialist

A second distinction is based on the configuration of the network, whether relationships are direct between supplier and procurer or indirect via a third party. The profiles of procedure and authority specialists are both oriented towards direct contacts. Where network relationships are indirect, intermediaries are focused on. A strategic profile, directed at an indirect bridging of the gap, and where relations with intermediaries (associations/agents/brokers) are more important than linkages with authorities, is termed intermediary specialist. A profile, on the other hand, that is specialized at being an intermediary, is described as linking-pin specialist. While no linking-pin specialist has been studied in this research project, the other three procurement profiles are analysed in this chapter.

These strategic profiles are refined strategic categories of a certain resource aspect. When the resources of a firm are classified according to this scheme one profile or a mix of profiles are obtained, which can be further classified into dominating, subordinated or non-existent profiles.

Authority Specialist

The main feature of the authority specialist's capacity profile is to get a license directly oriented towards specific needs of the TNC. The activities denoted by this profile are signified by long lead times and high costs in long-term relationships and broad contact nets. Flexibility is important, since the license and the license procedure are adapted to specific needs. The scope of the problem solving capacity varies with how many different kinds of particular needs are catered for. Authority specialist capabilities tend to partly emerge through the continuous contacts with the authority, learning and adapting to changing requirements in order to achieve goals. A deliberate planning of activities built on such capacities is difficult, making continuous contacts very important. Development of contacts is then a key activity. This capacity should be high throughout the company, in liaison as well as in manufacturing and procurement. These capabilities are all important as are their coordination if a profitable strategy is to be achieved.

The resources are confined to specialized networks, where the degree of linkage specificity is high. The costs of switching between authorities and officials are high. Competition is need-positioned and oriented directly towards authorities. Competition takes place between GTNs of specialized linkages.

Procedure Specialist

Companies demanding licenses that are not adapted to individual specific needs are classified as procedure specialists. Procurement activities are concentrated on the procedure, where there is a common need for a rational and consistent handling of licenses. A high technological capacity is normally not needed, since the technical aspects of the products/production are not a prominent feature of such applications. Instead, a first-mover advantage is maintained through the contact net. Development of contacts is also an important activity, in liaison as well as in procurement. The need for flexibility is less than for an authority specialist, the linkage specificity being low to medium-sized, depending upon how the authority interface is organized. As a result, stability is more important than change. Long, stable periods are alternated with shorter period of change. The latter occurs only when government policy is changed. As illustrated by the Indian example, the strong legitimacy positions enjoyed by TNCs makes it very hard to implement policy changes, caused, for example, by the move towards liberalization. But finally, when the pressure has been built up with many proposed policy changes, there is a radical change. Companies thus follow a deliberate strategy. Competition is procedure-positioned and oriented directly towards authorities. Competition takes place between standardized GTNs.

Intermediary Specialist

In some instances license contacts are not handled by the TNC itself directly, either with the administrative or political organizations. Rather an external organization is used, for instance, a trade association or an external liaison officer. In such cases, TNCs are classified as intermediary specialists. There are two main reasons for using intermediaries. One is, if costs for this network should be lower than for building up one's own network with the government or for setting oneself up as an intermediary to become a linking-pin specialist. Relationships with intermediaries are in this case less expensive than direct relationships with the authorities. However, the work involved in getting information about potential intermediaries, and in controlling them, adds to the costs. This is really the case in India, where different intermediaries abound, making the situation extremely complex. There is also the risk of being misled. Network costs are lower for simple licenses because of the more routinized contacts.

The second reason is that certain types of relationships (as for example involving politicians) are better handled by intermediaries. TNCs themselves may not want to get involved in certain relationships, for instance, those established to handle 'kick-backs', which seem to be a common feature of arms deals, as illustrated by the Bofors case.

Appendix 1   Methodology

INTRODUCTION

There were no ready network models that could be used directly to analyze the problems found in this area of inquiry. The main task of our research is thus to develop a suitable network theory. We describe here how this is done. Other essential methodological issues of the project are also covered. In chapter 2 the main result of this endeavour is presented – a network theory that is valid for the three main types of networks studied.

NETWORKS

Networks are found within a societal context. Focused transorganizational networks are connected to their environment through ties with other networks.

> Individual organizations are affected by the structure of relations of the interorganizational systems in which they are embedded, and these systems are in turn affected by the societal systems in which they are located, and these systems are in turn affected by the world system in which they are located. All of these systems are evolving over time, and each is comprised of elements created at differing points in time. (Scott, 1983, p. 174)

A study of networks always presupposes certain limitations. How much of a network needs to be 'laid out' for the analysis of a particular arena, is a major problem. Other questions which arise are: What parts of a network belong together, and which others have the most vital connections with the selected parts? How many links are relevant for the study of such a chain?

Hence, some of the main methodological problems in network studies include:
– Charting the ramifications of a network.
– The description of the degree of complexity of the network.
– Study of the temporal aspect.

– Selection of research tools.
– The problem of duration of contact; the meaning of contact.

A basic contradiction is found in much research on networks, which also pertains to this study. Lack of adequate theoretical frameworks constrain the empirical data collection to manageable proportions at the same time as it is hard to generate a network theory from empirical research, because when viewing the real world from a network metaphor, it becomes immensely complex.

Since the network approach lacks a comprehensive set of theoretical and empirical guidelines, how should researchers proceed with network analysis to reduce this complexity? We assume in this study that networks are organized around more or less enduring structural features of societies, as for example bureaucracies and business enterprises. But problems do remain, particularly with regard to the number of indirect links to be identified, mapped, and analyzed.

MAIN RESEARCH PERSPECTIVE

Our conclusion is that theory and method are inseparable in network research. Methods are not seen as tools that can be used by any researcher for any type of problem. Nor is methodology viewed as the starting point from where boundary-specific theories are developed. While the former approach results in a wide gap between theory and method, the latter limits the possibilities of developing a general theory. Therefore, the network approach, which is a synthesis of theory and method serves as the main methodology for the problems studied in our work. A transorganizational network theory has been developed from this approach with the methods described in this appendix. It might be mentioned that our approach to research is very similar to that suggested by Denzin (1978, p. 6):

> The function of theory – an integrated body of propositions, the derivation of which leads to explanation of some social phenomenon – is to give order and insight to what is, or can be, observed. Methodology represents the principal ways in which sociologists act on their environment; their methods, be they experiments, survey, or life histories, lead to different features of this reality, and it is through their methods that they make their research public and reproducible by others. As the sociologist moves from theories to the selection of methods, the emergence of that vague process called research activity can be seen. In this process the personal preferences of a scientist for one theory or method emerge.

Furthermore, selection of a given problem area (delinquency, or the family) often represents a highly personal decision.

Our research is founded on the belief that it is not possible to have one abstract and universal theory to explain all types of organizational behaviour. A theory which explains social behaviour in industrialized countries, cannot simply be transferred directly to another environment. It is incorrect for instance, to assume that organizations work in the same way in less industrialized countries as in industrialized countries. Cultural differences and varying government policies affect company behaviour. A deficient infrastructure, an underdeveloped basic industry structure, and an unequal distribution of income all act as constraints on company action. Additionally, local activities are restricted by the group's strategy and organization structure. Therefore, subsidiaries are woven into a network of different impacts from various parts of its environment. The entirety is more important than particulars. Phenomena in a peculiar and many-sided environment are best understood through a multi-dimensional study.

Strauss (1987, p. 14) when using previous theory in a new area without checking its relevance stressed:

> it is only applied like a label to one's data. This practice almost totally relieves the researcher of three very important responsibilities: of (1) genuinely checking or qualifying the original data; (2) interacting deeply with his or her own data; and (3) developing new theory on the basis of a true transaction between the previous and newly evolving theory.

The empirical relevance of the theories thus has to be asserted, which does not mean a statistical test of hypotheses derived from theory. A classical deductive, hypothesis testing method is based on the logical-positivist presumption of an objective world consisting of universally valid scientific laws. Organizational behaviour cannot be reduced to such simple laws, since the organizational world is much more complex. A social science theory is broader and lacks the rigour of tightly constructed mathematical models. In the present case it is construed for the special problems encountered in the study of the relationship between TNCs and government agencies and consists of several individual theories that are adjusted to each other within the developed theory. These theories have in their turn been selected from a number of other theories. One main problem is to select and fit theories together in a consistent way, so that individual theories do not contradict each other.

Through this process theories are accepted or refuted in a new situation. This framework can then be utilized as a vehicle for examining other cases and generalized for other situations. This adjustment process is mainly controlled by empirical data, and the theoretical framework becomes empirically motivated. The boundaries of the individual theories and the premises of the theories are studied against the case studies. As in other research in social science, our method is a combination of inductive and deductive methods, a constant interchange between data and theory.

SUBSTANTIVE AND FORMAL THEORY

This work combines substantive and formal theory (Glaser & Strauss, 1967; Glaser, 1978; Strauss, 1987). The theory is mainly substantive, since it is primarily developed for a specific empirical or problem area, that is, implementation of industrial policy through government–TNC relations. But formal theories like interorganizational theory or institutional organization theory are also adapted to this area. Formal theory helps to develop a substantive theory, which in turn helps to extend or reformulate established formal theories. The emphasis is on the cumulative nature of knowledge. Both types of theories then become grounded in data. Since the formal theory is not empirically extended to other areas, the final result is primarily a one-area formal theory, although to some extent it may also be viewed as a preliminary multi-area formal theory, as some already established formal theories are extended to another empirical field studied in this research project. The theory can best be termed a middle-range theory. Its conceptual or theoretical framework is defined by Denzin (1978, p. 49), as under:

> Here descriptive categories are placed within a broad structure of both explicit and assumed propositions ... The framework is still too imprecise to permit the systematic derivation of propositions, but deductions are possible. The empirical verifications in the framework are of varying quality, yet there is a continuous interaction between the framework and empirical observations.

We do not present a theory formalized to a degree where hypotheses can be systematically deduced. We present instead suggestions for hypotheses. These suggestions are called propositions to distinguish them from the hypotheses that are operationalized propositions meant for statistical testing of a theory.

TELEOLOGICAL EXPLANATIONS

Organizational units are assumed to make conscious, intentional decisions to establish linkages. Purposive action is the critical premise on which this research is based. One example is exchange of products to increase profit. Another is to create influence in order to get legitimacy from government through exchange of information, gifts and sentiments. Organizations are thus special-purpose collectivities created to achieve goals, to perform work. It is important to distinguish the teleological explanations that we use here from the more general explanation well described by Myrdal (1968, p. 1851):

> By a teleological approach is meant one in which a purpose, which is not explicitly intended by anyone, is fulfilled while the process of fulfilment is presented as an inevitable sequence of events. Originally, the purpose was explicitly God's purpose unfolding itself in history. But with the growth of rationalism 'nature' replaced God, and later such entities as 'Zeitgeist', 'history' itself, 'progress', and more specific notions such as the 'invisible hand', the 'market', 'the logic of events', appeared as secularized versions of Providence. Common to these various approaches are three features: inevitability, unintended purposiveness, and implicit valuation (though not necessarily that of the writer). The suggestion of inevitability gives the stream of historical forces a stickiness that reduces greatly the scope for maneuver, both in the past, ruling out hypothetical alternatives, and in the present, ruling out planning. The unintended purposiveness introduces terms like 'natural progress' and 'growth', in which valuations are disguised as descriptions, teleology as causality, and reason as nature.

As discussed by Hunt (1983, pp. 101-108) teleological explanations, are hard to distinguish from functionalist explanations where by function is meant 'some generally recognized use or utility of a thing'.

For biologists, primarily, the term function refers to organic processes or vital functions such as reproduction. Similarly, anthropologists, mainly Malinowski, hold that culture and everything it consists of fulfils vital functions.

Function may have another meaning. According to Hunt (ibid, p.102), it 'often signifies the contribution that an item makes or can make toward the maintenance of some stated characteristic or condition in a given system to which the item is assumed to belong. Thus, functional analysis seeks to understand a behaviour pattern or a sociocultural institution by determining the role it plays in keeping the given system in proper working order or maintaining it as a going concern.'

We reserve the term functionalist for such unintended purposes. Intended purposiveness is the kind of teleological explanation sought in this work. In our view, then, organizational processes act through men, motives, organizations, and institutions, not apart from them.

We are not concerned with making causal statements about consequential behaviour, since we have not tried to determine whether an event x led to event y. One sequel is that prediction is not important, since it will be difficult to find laws to extrapolate into the future. Instead, the focus of the research is on explanation. Covariance and the consideration of rival explanatory factors are then still important. Covariance between different factors is looked for and inferred to conscious acts of behaviour. It is impossible in this kind of research to fully control for rival explanatory factors, since experiments or quasi-experiments are not used. Consequential interacting factors are instead inferred by a combined use of qualitative analysis and quantitative analysis, where a main purpose is to exclude rival determinants.

As seen above, systems theory is based on functionalist explanations. In our view, this is one of the main differences between the network approach and a systems approach. A network approach is not constrained to such explanations. Teleological explanations can be used instead as in this research project.

TASK-ORIENTED NETWORKS

When teleological explanations are sought, it is vital to separate more important intentions from less important ones. A distinction is therefore made between instrumental ties, which arise in the course of performing work tasks, and primary ties, which come about to fulfil the employees' personal goals. Such informal primary relations could both enhance and impede the attainment of formal organizational goals.[1]

Personal goals originate in the following ways :

1. They originate from the individual and are for instance related to certain background attributes of individuals, as for example age, sex and education. If linkages are primarily instrumentally oriented, such personal factors should not have a consistent influence on how interviewed persons answer questions about transorganizational relations.

2. They are socially motivated, for example membership through

an institution other than the organization such as family or work group.

3. They are culturally motivated, for example determined by race or caste.

In the first case above individuals represent themselves, in the second case they represent their social group, and in the third case they represent their cultural group.

Questions are included in the questionnaires about the purpose of social networks to check if social and cultural ties cause any bias to the study, since transorganizational networks chiefly determined by such ties are not task-oriented. Primary ties are therefore essentially assumed to be instrumental in this project, being viewed as a means to accomplish a certain task. Thus, individually, socially and culturally motivated bonds could also be important for achieving instrumental objectives. The critical point is that primary ties do not result in a non-instrumental behaviour or suboptimization. Or, that communication and resource networks are mainly used for personal reasons. Rather, they are part of the individual's repertoire to reach his task goals. His belonging to a certain social or cultural group is taken advantage of for instrumental purposes. In this way the conflict between instrumental and primary ties is solved. Friendship, for example, is used in a calculated way. Friendship is defined accordingly, ranging from a task-oriented professional friendship to a personal and deep emotional friendship.

When friendship networks influence organizational processes, reasons sometimes give way to prejudice. Such nets are formed from reasons other than instrumental contacts, for example cultural stereotype or personal factors. This could, however, be seen as a response to the pervasive drive by organizations to limit uncertainty.

Social homogeneity increases ease of communication and improves predictability of behaviour, values which are central to organizational culture. Thus, if differentiating organizational members on the basis of ascribed attributes violates such tenets of rationalism as universalism and achievement, it is nonetheless an (possibly warped) expression of another rationalizing process – the need to eliminate uncertainty from organizational arrangements. (Lincoln & Miller, 1979, p. 197)[2]

THE RESEARCH STRATEGY

Research strategy concerns the methods which are used to solve the problems for a specific area of research. Keeping our perspective to research in mind a comparative case study method is the chosen strategy. Cases are compared and inferences drawn from them through qualitative analysis. A preliminary theoretical framework is developed by doing a few broad case studies. In a second stage this framework is developed further through a re-examination of these cases and the inclusion of several more cases. At this stage, qualitative analysis is complemented by quantitative analysis. At the first stage a method similar to participant observation is used, while the method used in the second stage to further specify the theoretical framework and work out more elaborate propositions resembles the survey method. The case study method allows the researcher to use different methods, for example standardized and nonstandardized interviews of respondents and informants, document analysis and observation. Therefore it is very suitable for triangulation.

Most research about TNCs in developing countries is done at the industry level or industrial sector level. We believe that micro level studies are more suitable for the problems studied in this research project. Our previous studies of TNCs in developing countries also support such an approach. That is particularly true for India, which is a complex country with large cultural differences, political uncertainty, an underdeveloped infrastructure, a complicated bureaucracy and a planned economy. Domestic markets are imperfect and do not work in the same way as in the Western market economies. Thus, the Indian reality is extremely complex and multi-faceted, where it is hard to narrowly isolate specific factors for research. The economic system interacts in an intricate way with the larger society. Moreover, the relations between these systems change gradually and are often unpredictable. This makes it difficult to limit the research to narrowly defined constructs.

A broader and more holistic approach is necessary, which has a direct bearing on the research methodology. Relevant factors for the problem are mapped and related to each other. In principle, this is better accomplished by selecting a few cases and studying many aspects than using a few aspects in the study of a great number of companies. However, this does not mean that we have collected as much data as is possible for a few cases. On the contrary, in theoretically informed research, collection of data is selective. And it becomes more so with the evolvement of the theoretical framework. In the first phase of this study, for instance, more factors were investigated than in the second phase.

The case study method is thus the most suitable method for a study such as this. Networks are viewed as historically and situationally specific phenomena, where only a broadly focused strategy will permit one to sort out the conditions behind the relational configurations observed. Such an approach does not preclude a quantitative analysis of network characteristics, particularly if it is complemented by a descriptive discussion of context, without which the patterns of quantitative data cannot be fully understood (Lincoln & Miller, 1979, p. 182). To understand the pattern of network ties as it exists in and between particular organizations at a particular time, an investigation must gain a familiarity with the network and its participants, that goes beyond the information readily available from questionnaires and interview surveys. Case studies are a necessary part of network research on organizations (ibid., p. 198). This is also valid for trans-organizational networks and their environment.

Thus, within this perspective the case study method becomes the logical research strategy.

A case study is an empirical inquiry that: investigates a contemporary phenomenon within its real-life context; when the boundaries between phenomenon and context are not clearly evident; and in which multiple sources of evidence are used. This definition not only helps us to understand case studies, but also distinguishes them from the other research strategies that have been discussed. An experiment, for instance, deliberately divorces a phenomenon from its context, so that attention can be focused on a few variables (typically, the context is 'controlled' by the laboratory environment). A history, by comparison, does deal with the entangled situation between phenomenon and context, but usually with noncontemporary events. Finally, surveys can try to deal with phenomenon and context, but their ability to investigate the context is extremely limited. The survey designer, for instance, constantly struggles to limit the number of variables to be analyzed (and hence the number of questions that can be asked), to fall safely within the number of respondents that can be surveyed. (Yin, 1984, p. 23)

ABDUCTION

The research process in a case study is defined as a method of abduction:

That is, they do not use a full-fledged deductive-hypothetical scheme in thinking and developing propositions. Nor are they fully inductive, letting the so-called 'facts' speak for themselves. Facts do not speak for themselves. They must be interpreted. Previously developed deductive models seldom conform with the empirical data that are gathered. The method of abduction combines the deductive and inductive models of proposition development and theory construction. (Denzin, 1978, pp. 109-110)

The theoretical framework has been developed through a combined process of abstraction and analytical generalization. Generally, this process of abduction took place as follows. Before making the questionnaires, a preliminary theoretical framework was developed from earlier research (chiefly in India), a study of literature, and preliminary broader case studies of some critical TNCs. There were interviews of key informants in the subsidiaries. The purpose was to get insights into the matter under study, sources of corroboratory evidence, and permission to further study the subsidiaries. The theoretical framework was rather broad, since the purpose was to cover the main activities of the companies towards government. In the beginning, there was no well-structured theory about TNC–government relations, local and regional organization of TNCs in far-off markets, as well as about cultural and government influences on such activities. For these areas, the questions were therefore formulated in a general way in the first case studies.

Certain factors were found to be more common in the empirical material than others. Specific patterns were also observed between these factors to which explanations were sought. A priori knowledge and knowledge acquired in the first phase of the project made it possible to specify the network in the following ways:

– delimit it.
– decide on the relevant types of linkages.
– broadly state structural properties of linkages and nodes.
– define how the delimited network or organizational field is related to its environment.

These findings were refined through a parallel study of literature. The result was now a higher theoretical elaborateness of the areas under research. The pattern established by these field studies was judged to be satisfactory for the problem studied and for making the questionnaires.

THEORETICAL MEMOS

Theoretical memos play an important role in the project both for the gradual development of theories and to give the involved researchers a common theoretical foundation. This latter point is very important in this project, where all researchers make interviews as well as having very different backgrounds regarding theory and culture. In the beginning the memos circulated among the participants only contained preliminary theoretical questions and simple summaries of related theories believed to be relevant. In time they were further refined to finally become the foundation for the theoretical write up of the project, for example working papers, articles and book chapters. In the process certain theories were discarded, others added, and the ones chosen increasingly refined and integrated.

ANALYTICAL GENERALIZATION

Case studies are preferred when analytical generalization is the main purpose of the research. 'In analytical generalization, the investigator is striving to generalize a particular set of results to some broader theory' (Yin, 1984, p. 39).

The normal procedure, as is done in a true experimental design in social sciences as well as in the survey method, is to generalize from samples to a universe, i.e. statistical generalization. Analytical generalization, on the other hand, has only certain characteristics in common with experiments, since generalization is achieved through a replication process, where the relevance of various theories is studied for several cases. There are similarities with the process described as analytical induction by Denzin (1978), but chiefly with theoretical sampling (Glaser & Strauss, 1967; Glaser, 1978; Strauss, 1987).

> Our criteria are those of theoretical purpose and relevance ... The basic criterion governing the selection of comparison groups for discovering theory is their theoretical relevance for furthering the development of emerging categories. (Glaser & Strauss, 1967, pp. 48-49)

The literature on analytical induction and theoretical sampling provide vital insights into how to conduct research.[3] But these processes have not been completely adopted in this study. Analytical induction is directly modelled on experiments and aimed at causal analysis, while theoretical sampling in combination with the constant comparative method of qualitative analysis is mainly an inductive process meant for discovering theory. For example 'the initial decisions in theoretical sampling are based only on a general sociological perspective about a substantive area within a population, not on a preconceived problem or hypothesis' (Glaser, 1978, p. 36). This means that theory is chiefly built up inductively and that deductive reasoning comes in rather late in the process and is used only in the service of the inductive method. This is too strong a condition for the method used in this research project, where adaptation of formal theory to the substantive area is a critical ingredient. The main goal is neither causal analysis nor discovery of theory.

The purpose of analytical generalization is not to statistically validate formal theories, but to study the generality of theoretical concepts for various cases. Cases are selected from a theoretical basis in order to confirm or invalidate primarily substantive theory. One purpose of this research project is to study the suitability of various formal theories in unfamiliar economic environments. In this way statistical generalization is replaced by the flexibility criterion, where the range of utility of various concepts and underlying theories are established for a certain empirical problem area (Brunsson, 1982; Bulmer, 1979). Theoretical flexibility or sensitivity is vital in such studies. Glaser (1978, p. 40) calls this a conceptual elaboration in contrast to logical elaboration found in deductive, hypothesis testing research.

The final theoretical framework emerges as a result of an interaction process with the empirical world. Researchers interested in statistical validation can build their research on the results of this project. From such a perspective the conclusions presented are suggestive rather than definitive. Attempts can be made to formulate hypotheses from the propositions of the developed theoretical framework.

EMBEDDED CASE STUDIES

A comparative case or multiple-case study method is used in the project. Cases have been researched as parts. Subdivisions of the companies, for example various departments or divisions, have been individually studied. Our case study is thus embedded (Yin, 1984, pp. 44-47). The cases are the subsidiaries in India.

An embedded approach is fruitful in this research on TNCs in developing countries, inter alia because of the clear distinction made between relations to other business firms that are primarily governed by efficiency, and relations to government bodies that are primarily governed by legitimacy.

Theoretical Locus

It was thus considered necessary to decide, before the main effort to collect data started, whether empirical network relations between organizations stem from a process relevant for the whole organization or part of it. If the study is holistic and based on total organizational processes, the researcher constrains himself to a certain type of empirical data, that is to say composite data at the level of the organization. Such "global" data cannot be disaggregated for other uses, making it impossible to explain linkages between organizational parts. On the contrary, at this general level sub-unit level processes are conceived of as a source of bias, confounding one's ability to estimate true relations between organizations as wholes. So here network theory should be concerned with matters which hold at this organizational macro level and not below it.

If it is not possible to determine the theoretical locus of the network, as for example whether observed relations between organizations have organizational or individual unit origins, an embedded approach should be used. Task environments could vary with different organizational positions, since organizations are hierarchically stratified with different levels specializing in different organizational functions – technical, managerial, and institutional. Because the frame of reference of members of these various levels varies significantly, one would expect that questions about transorganizational relations would be answered differently, depending on the organizational level of the respondent (Aldrich & Whetten, 1981, p. 400). For these reasons a disaggregated approach is used in this research project. This approach is based on results from the initial study, where informant interviews were made with persons at different organizational levels. This approach will make it possible to separate individual unit and organizational effects. Aggregate measures permit decomposition while global measures do not. (Lincoln & Zeitz, 1980, pp. 392-393, 404-406). Questions will thus be put to individuals representing positions at different levels.

Positioned Action

Consequently, action is mainly determined by the position of an individual in the organization, which is supposed to be independent of his personal goals, values and intentions. From the point of view of the individual, the analytical dimension is structural, which means that the behaviour of people is determined by the position they occupy in an ordered set of positions in the organization. These positions could be formally determined (prescribed) or informally determined (emergent), for example membership of a clique or a coalition. A common behaviour of individuals within an organization is studied, which is caused by their task, position, etc. Once any network is in place the pattern of possible exchanges between actors within the network and with its environment are circumscribed. All actors do not have free access to all other actors. Access is restricted and mediated. For instance, some units or organizations become influential due to their centrality of their position within the network. (Schnelberg, 1986, pp. 20-21). Networks are thus studied at two main levels: trans-organizational and transunital.

Interview questions are based on the chosen theoretical locus of the study. Individuals are interviewed, but they are supposed to represent the organization's network relations and not their own. Usually a few persons at an organization are interviewed about their transorganizational links, and where they are seen as representing either their respective units within the organization, the organization as a whole, or both. There are thus one or several key informants/respondents within an organization. This approach is necessary, because it is believed that one person, for instance at a top position, could be unaware of the extent and quality of interactions of his subordinates with other organizations.[4] This is particularly relevant in our case, since we do not limit ourselves to formal organization but also study the informal aspects of organization. Data from different parts of an organization is thus obtained, which it will be possible to analyze at the organizational level of the parts or aggregated to the level of the whole organization.

SOURCES OF EVIDENCE

Most of the empirical data have been collected through interviews. Thus, behaviour has mainly been indirectly established and has not been directly observed.

In the first phase of the research process, a nonscheduled standardized type of interview was utilized, where a certain type of information was sought from all informants. At first no questions were specified in advance. Rather there were points of common discussion, which were gradually developed into a kind of questionnaire. Through this process a preliminary theoretical framework was developed. Because of an indefinite theory, questions were broad, and none of the preliminary interviews were alike. Broadly, they were a hybrid of interview and conversation about specific issues. During the entire initial phase, the phrasing of the questions and their order were fixed to fit the characteristics of each case. The project leader from Sweden was responsible for this initial phase, since his task was to develop most of the theoretical framework. As a consequence he also made almost all interviews, utilizing established contacts with subsidiaries studied in an earlier research project. Another researcher from Sweden made a few complementary interviews, which were recorded on tape. The prime purpose was to make them comparable to the other main interviews. So it was possible for the project leader to indirectly 'participate' in and also check those other interviews.

In the second phase of the research process, the scheduled standardized interview was utilized, where the wording and order of the questions were the same for all respondents. Multiple choices were also preformulated for the majority of the questions. From the various types of data collected in the first stage of the case study research, four main questionnaires were made for the interviews. The theoretical framework was developed to make this possible. The first questionnaire covers basic data on the Indian company in the form of 19 questions. The second one contains 30 questions about the relationships between subsidiaries in India and important group companies in Europe, mainly the parent and some of the product companies. In the main questionnaire 45 questions are put about the relationships between the subsidiaries and the Indian government. These three questionnaires were to be answered by the subsidiaries in India. There is also a fourth questionnaire for the government's relations with the subsidiaries and the groups. It mirrors the subsidiary–government questionnaire. More or less the same questions are put to the 'other side' about these relationships. The constructs, which are operationalized through the questions, are stated in lists of operational concepts. In accordance with the idea behind these questionnaires we tried to standardize the interview situation as much as possible.

A basic idea behind the research is that interviews are looked upon as 'talk' and its social organization. The interaction between the interviewer and the interviewee becomes critical, particularly in a relationship-oriented country like India. This is a potential source of invalidity. First, it is very difficult to conduct interviews in organizations in India, if there are no established relationships. For most of the companies they were already in place when the project started due to the earlier research activities of the team in India. Relationships with the remaining TNCs were established through different channels. For the government units the earlier established contacts were not very useful in this new situation. Unfortunately they were proven to be too old and of little current use. And new contacts were shown to be very difficult to be established even for the researchers based at Indian Council for Research on International Economic Relations (ICRIER) in Delhi. This has made it difficult to collect enough data from the government part of the studied network.

Second, when designing the research we were aware of the dangers involved in this interaction method, particularly for the second phase. One solution was to standardize the interviews and interview situation as much as possible. But then it was very vital to foresee most of the dangers of such a method, for example differences in meaning caused by language, or variation in rules and symbols between groups, the problem of fabrication by the respondents, or influences from the tensions normally prevailing in the encounter between interviewer and the person interviewed. And also to select interviewers who are able to reduce such problems as far as possible. By having the same background as the respondents, for instance, the possibilities to observe and understand their behaviour is increased considerably. For this reason, all the standardized interviews were made by the Indian members of the research team. The majority were made by one researcher from ICRIER, who has extensive experience of interviewing subsidiaries of TNCs in India including many of the firms participating in the research project.

The environment has also been partly researched by interviewing. But a broader number of multiple sources of evidence have been used for this part of the study. Informal discussions and conversations with different persons inside and outside the case companies were very important in order to know, for example how culture works in practice in business and government and in contacts between them. Observations were also critical for our understanding. To understand the conditions under which firms operate in India, observations and the researchers' experience of different aspects of the environment have been invaluable. Such observations constitute complementary information, which is also true for the company documents, chiefly annual reports, organization charts and various information and commercial material which were collected.

A major reason for conducting this research as a joint effort between Swedish and Indian researchers was to solve such critical problems discussed above. In addition, the Swedish representatives have a long experience of doing research in India.

Due to the embedded approach to the cases, key positions were selected at different levels and functions (divisions) at each subsidiary and government agency. At the subsidiaries mainly three positions were selected: the Managing Director or President, the 'Liaison Manager' (the person in charge of the government contacts), the 'Liaison Officer' (the person handling the contacts directly on the spot in Delhi).

VALIDITY AND RELIABILITY

Basically validity concerns whether a developed theoretical framework is a relevant representation of reality. It concerns how empirical data and theory are connected. Through the first part of the research process described above, we hope to have abstracted from the empirical data, certain factors to describe the kind of behaviour in India of interest to us. How these factors are related to each other (patterns) should also correspond to actual behaviour (for example in average). Rival factors explaining this behaviour have been minimized. In that case, the theoretical framework consists of the stable factors and patterns that best explain this behaviour.

A great effort has been made to get a good construct validity (a goodness of fit for the concepts). The first stage of the research process – the broad case studies – produced sensitizing concepts and an underlying tentative theoretical framework. The questions in the questionnaires were formulated from this basis by an elaborate process, where tentative questions were circulated several times among the participating researchers in and in-between meetings. Each main construct has also been operationalized through more than one question. Internal validity (a goodness of fit in patterns and explanations) is acceptable through the long and careful process of fitting theory and empirical data to each other, described above. As has been demonstrated, we have tried to exclude rival explanations by a control of distortions caused by the process of research itself. It was standardized as far as possible, for example, the interview situations, and the research instruments used. A good internal validity also presupposes a good internal logical consistency of the framework. A prime purpose of the research process is to create a high external validity. This is achieved through an elaborate process of analytical generalization, where a combination of qualitative analysis and quantitative analysis is used to analyze the many and varied cases. The external validity started to be established in the first field study, through the recurrent replication of new theoretical findings over the selected preliminary cases. An inspection of the collected data during the first field studies in India and afterwards confirmed the validity.

Our results are not statistically valid and can only be partly generalized. First, our findings are probably of limited validity for first time entrants in the Indian market. No such TNC was studied. New entrants are exposed to a different set of rules than those already active in the Indian market. Second, the results are of limited relevance for domestic firms, which are guided by a different set of rules. Third, our research does not include non-equity investments (pure technology sales or other contractual arrangements), since they also are guided by a different set of rules.

Lastly, the research project was chiefly undertaken to generate theory and not to validate theory, and a comparative case study method was used to that end. Therefore findings are limited to indications and general patterns. However, based on our general knowledge of India and TNCs operating in the country, we strongly believe that our findings are valid for numerous other TNCs operating in India. The laws and the ministerial organizations are the same for all TNCs.

Reliability, defined according to Yin (1984, p. 36), is considered to be acceptable. It is hard to grade in a study like this. But the data collection procedures can most certainly be repeated on the same cases with the same results. The main reason for standardizing interviews and interview sessions was to achieve a good internal validity by having a fair reliability. This was considered mandatory for a good result in an international project that involves researchers from diverse backgrounds. Of course this does not automatically result in high validity. On the contrary, the rigidity of standardized interviews can lead to low validity, where it would have been better to use a non-standardized interview. But on the other hand, unstructured methods like these are very difficult to use and only recommended for researchers who are well experienced in their use. To be on the safe side, it is better to employ more structured forms.

The essence of reliability is thus that the theoretical framework established by the study should reflect the true stable factors and relations of the research situation. By standardizing the main part of the research process, we wanted to avoid too strong an influence from temporary conditions of the researcher (fatigue, anger), the research situation (weather, disturbances, stress) or the research instrument (wrong formulations). A more standardized and structured operational research procedure is also easier to repeat.

THE CASES

A main problem in our kind of research is to define the scope of the studied substantive area. In its broadest terms, this study concerns governments and their relations with TNCs when implementing industrial policy. India, an extreme case in this respect, is the subject of study. Here, the most relevant implementation events for the policies towards TNCs were selected, notably industrial licensing, technology and foreign investment licensing, together with import licensing. Within these limits a multiple-case study method was selected. The reasons for this were discussed above. The number of cases is a product of several considerations. On one hand, there is a certain initial theoretical specification of the research area, specifying certain boundaries, factors and connections for study. From this background many case studies can be included, particularly since one important objective of the research is to get as general a theory as possible under the circumstances stated above. On the other hand, the uncertainty surrounding the application of the theories in less industrialized countries, requires a broad approach. In addition, resources and access opportunities limit the number of cases that can be selected. To start with, an approximate number of cases can be determined from such general grounds, although not the exact number, which is possible only as the research progresses.

The aim of our study was to cover as broadly as possible certain types of TNCs. We sought certain similarities among them, for example that they should have a long experience of the area and belong to large TNCs active over most of the globe. Experience and variation in industrial activity were supposed to be characteristic of companies having manufacturing units in the area. Therefore such cases have mainly been studied.

But dissimilarities between the company cases were also necessary. Our main criterion for selecting subsidiaries was the hypothesized variation in how government policies influence the conduct and performance of the TNCs. This would vary with certain characteristics of the companies. Information on these background factors were collected through questionnaire 1 and 2.

- The size of the total TNC and its operations in India.
- Year of establishment in India. Older firms have both been exposed to policies and have a longer experience of them than newly established firms.

– Relation to group.
– Group structure.
– Type of business. A broad coverage of various engineering industries in India is necessary.
– Degree of involvement. Whether the TNC is involved in a majority or minority owned company? This would have a decisive effect
  on the policy exposure.
– Coverage in terms of country of origin. TNCs from various home
  countries could react differently to industrial policies. Companies
  from two West European countries have therefore been compared.
– Involvement with government.

A more practical issue that was considered was the willingness of
TNCs to cooperate in the project and allow us to conduct interviews
with the decision makers.

Thirteen cases have been studied. Six TNCs originate from Sweden
and seven from Germany. At least one person at each subsidiary has
answered most of the questions in Questionnaires 1, 2 and 3. For
seven TNCs there are two respondents for each subsidiary. This
means that there are a total of 20 respondents for the second phase of
the project, which we consider a good result. This has only been possible through the careful planning and execution of the interviews. As
seen above, it is not an easy task to motivate the respondents to
answer such a large number of questions, of which some are of a
quite sensitive nature. We were not entirely successful in getting
answers from the government officials about their relations with the
subsidiaries. The TNCs studied are, nevertheless, merely a fraction of
the total number of TNCs operating in India (which runs into around
300). The six Swedish TNCs represent over two thirds of the Swedish
FDI in India, and the German TNCs represent about half.

According to conditions stipulated for the interviews, the informants remain anonymous.

SUMMARY AND CONCLUSIONS

Because of the complexities involved in network research, method
and theory are inseparable. A dual utilization of theory and method is
achieved through comparative case studies. This research is founded
on the belief that it is not possible to have one very abstract and general theory to explain transorganizational behaviour. A theory,

mainly developed to explain organizational behaviour in industrialized countries, cannot be transferred directly to another environment. The empirical relevance of the theories have to be asserted in a new situation. Phenomena in a peculiar and many-sided environment are best understood through a multi-dimensional study.

This work combines substantive and formal theory. The cumulative nature of knowledge is emphasized, where formal theory helps to develop substantive theory, which in turn, through an empirical process, helps to extend or generate modified formal theories. Both types of theories then become grounded in data. The final result is primarily a one-area formal theory; a middle-range theory, that is classified as a conceptual or theoretical framework.

Teleological explanations are found to be more relevant than causal and functionalist explanations to understand the actions which have taken place within the substantive area of research. To separate the essential from less essential intentions a distinction is made between instrumental and primary ties.

Cases are compared and inferences drawn from them through a combination of qualitative and quantitative analysis. A preliminary theoretical framework is developed by conducting a few broad case studies. In the second stage, this framework is developed further through a re-examination of these cases and the inclusion of several more cases. At the first stage a method similar to participant observation is utilized, while the method used in the second stage is more akin to the survey method. This combined research process of abstraction and generalization is called abduction. Compared to theoretical sampling it is a more deductive process. Compared to analytical induction, it is based on teleological explanations instead of causal explanations. It also resembles these two processes through its use of analytical generalization instead of statistical generalization.

The multi-case method used is classified as embedded. A decomposed view is taken of organizations, which makes it possible to separate individual unit effects from those of the organization as a whole. Consequently, action is chiefly determined by the position of an individual in the organization, being independent of his personal goals, values and intentions. Questions are therefore put to individuals representing positions at different levels.

Most of the empirical data have been collected through interviewing, and where behaviour has mainly been indirectly established. In the first phase of the research process a nonscheduled standardized type of interview was utilized. Because of an indefinite theory questions were broad and different. Generally they can be character-ized as a hybrid of interview and conversation about specific issues. During the whole of this initial phase the phrasing of the questions and their order was changed to fit the characteristics of each case. In the second phase of the research process the scheduled standardized interview was utilized, where the wording and order of the questions were the same for all respondents. Multiple choices were also pre-formulated for the majority of the questions. From the various types of data collected during the first research stage, four main question-naires were made for the interviews.

A basic idea behind the research is that interviews were regarded as "talks". The interaction between the interviewer and the interviewee is critical, particularly in a relationship-oriented country like India. The research was designed to reduce this potential source of invalidity as much as possible, particularly for the second phase of the project, inter alia by standardizing the interviews and interview situation as much as possible. The environment has also partly been researched by interviewing and the use of a broader number of multiple sources of evidence.

A large effort has been made to get a good construct validity. The first stage of the research process – the broad case studies – produced preliminary concepts and an underlying tentative theoretical frame-work. These were precised further in the second stage, where each main construct was operationalized through more than one question. Internal validity is achieved through the long and careful process of fitting theory and empirical data to each other. The external validity has been improved gradually through the recurrent replication of new theoretical findings over the selected cases. A main reason for stan-dardizing the interviews and interview sessions was to achieve a good internal validity by having a fair reliability, which was considered mandatory for a good result in an international research project involving researchers from diverse backgrounds.

Thirteen TNCs from two West European countries are studied. They were selected because of their similarities for certain aspects, e.g. type of group, industry, and experience of the area, and for their dissimilarities concerning those characteristics that imply a variation in how government policies influence the conduct and performance of the TNCs.

NOTES

1.   This division of ties is taken from Lincoln & Miller (1979, p. 182). But the categories are redefined to better suit the purpose of this study.
2.   The three aspects mentioned above could be developed in a separate study oriented towards individuals, social networks, and culture. In a study of the categorical order, for instance, the behaviour of people is not determined by their position in an organization, a group or by their personal links with other people, but by social stereotypes (Mitchell, 1973).
3.   As described by Denzin (1978, p. 195) analytical generalization seems to offer the same advantages as analytical induction.
4.   Compare with Hall *et al* (1977, p. 462).

Appendix 2 Liberalization of the Indian Economy – a Post Script

Our earlier analysis in the book is based on the highly regulated Indian economy. However, since July 1991, there has been a drastic change in economic policies of India. There has been deregulation and liberalization in the fields of industry, foreign investment, trade, the exchange rate regime and finance that could result in a change in the strategy or networking of the transnational corporations as well. However, since it is still too early to know how TNCs' strategies towards government will be influenced, this appendix is about the policy changes and some preliminary reactions of TNCs to these changes.

Thus, in this chapter, we briefly review the new economic policies mainly Foreign Investment policies of the Indian Government and the reactions of the bureaucracy, Indian industry and the political parties to the new policies. Although it is not an in-depth analysis as in the other Chapters of the book, but it gives an indication of the situation that exists today.

LIBERALIZATION SCENARIO SINCE 1991

Since July 1991, there have been fundamental changes in industrial policies in India. There is a positive shift in the mood of the Indian business community and an acceptance even among the conservatives. The new economic policies have emerged out of national consensus. This guarantees their irreversibility.

Significantly, the progress made has been without any of the economic fallouts which usually accompany major structural reform. Inflation is well under control, large scale retrenchments have been avoided, industrial activity is picking up, exports are surging and foreign exchange reserves are at a record high. Consecutive union budgets have over the last three years progressively introduced bold and far reaching measures to consolidate and extend the reforms. The reforms in the trade and payments regime have encouraged exports; fears that the economy would be swamped by imports have not been borne out. Despite the collapse of trade with the former Soviet Union, exports have shown remarkable buoyancy.

Increased attention to competitiveness and productivity has been encouraged by dismantling of systems which required licenses to establish new industrial units or even to undertake substantial expansion. The list of industries reserved for the public sector has been drastically reduced from 17 to 6. Several initiatives are under way to modernize and simplify the banking system. This process is still on. We will briefly mention the important changes which are of interest to business and foreign investors.

The average import tariff has been reduced from 135% to 50% and the aim is to reduce it even further to 25% by 1996. Ownership legislation has been rewritten, the rupee is now fully convertible on current account, MRTP act has been relaxed, allowing firms to diversify; commercial banking has been opened up to the private sector. Public sector banks have been recapitalized, and the new credit policy has given much more flexibility to the banks by lowering reserve ratio requirement and by killing off the maximum permissible bank finance provisions. Interest rates are still high at 15%.

On the industry front, the Board of Industrial and Financial Reconstruction is now beginning to tackle the problem of loss-making public sector units, although full-scale privatization still seems a long way off.

The changes in Foreign Direct Investment policies are more glaring among others; what the Finance Minister calls a 180 degree turn on foreign investment. Fundamental changes in the rules governing FDI have taken place over the last two and half years.

FDI Policies

After forty five years of reluctance, India is now actively wooing foreign investment. Automatic approval is granted for FDI up to an equity level of 51% in a large majority of manufacturing industries. Repatriation of profits is permitted subject to a streamlined approval procedure for all approved investments except a few specified consumer goods industries where dividends can be repatriated only out of net foreign exchange earnings. Technology transfer agreements following certain guidelines are automatically approved under the new liberalized policy for FDI. Foreign investment can come in either in the form of money or capital goods. Hiring of foreign technicians no longer requires prior clearance.

Industries open to FDI
Except six specified industries (arms and ammunition, atomic energy, coal, mineral oils, minerals for use in production of atomic energy, and railways) which are reserved for state owned enterprises, FDI is permitted in almost all other manufacturing industries. The policy regarding FDI in service industries is generally less clearly defined, though FDI is also automatically permitted in trading companies engaged primarily in export activities and in tourism-related activities such as hotels.

Foreign equity
FDI up to 51% is given automatic approval in 34 priority sectors provided foreign equity covers the cost of imported capital goods. Higher foreign equity in these areas and the share of foreign equity allowed in other sectors is still decided on a case-by-case basis. Moreover, when the ceiling of 40% was raised to 51%, many promoter (foreign) companies were allowed preferential allotments to take their holding to 51% at hugely discounted rates, a privilege which has upset many a domestic industrialists.

One hundred percent foreign ownership is allowed in 100% export-oriented units. Full foreign ownership is also allowed in certain high priority areas (power generation and distribution, hydro carbon/oil/natural gas exploration etc.). Large foreign investment proposals are considered in totality, free from pre-determined procedures and parameters and may be allowed up to one hundred percent foreign ownership depending on the merits of individual proposals. Full foreign ownership is also allowed for Non-Resident Indians (NRIs) and Overseas Corporate Bodies (OCBs) in all the high priority areas, and approval for this can be automatic provided certain conditions such as dividend balancing are fulfilled.

Other restrictions on FDI
Earlier, foreign companies (i.e. those incorporated and registered abroad) have generally been permitted to open a branch or liaison

office only in a few specified service industries such as banking, shipping, airlines etc. or in export-oriented ventures. However, a more liberal policy is now followed in allowing branches/offices of foreign companies to undertake various activities in India (subject to RBI approval), including acting as buying/selling agents in India of foreign companies, undertaking export and import trading activities and promoting technical and financial collaborations between Indian and foreign companies. The branch form is however not generally favoured for carrying on manufacturing operations within India. A liaison office, on the other hand, must confine its work to liaison and it is not allowed to carry out any commercial activity, and the entire expenditure of the office must be met by inward remittances in foreign exchange from the overseas parent.

A limited number of industries require an industrial license (for environmental, strategic or social concerns) while others require such a license only if they are located in the proximity of a large city. This licensing requirement applies equally to domestic and foreign investment. Also, there are over 800 products that are reserved for the small scale sector and large undertakings are ordinarily permitted limited equity participation (up to 24%)in these.

Legislation for FDI
Foreign Exchange Regulations Act (FERA)

India has no specific legislation governing FDI other than the Foreign Exchange Regulations Act (FERA) which regulates transactions involving foreign exchange as well as certain activities of FERA companies i.e. those with more than 40% foreign shareholding. In the new policy, the distinction between FERA and non-FERA companies has been abolished. There is no longer any discrimination between companies with more than 40% foreign shareholding and other companies. This is true even if the foreign shareholding is 100%. However, for carrying on any activity relating to agriculture or plantations, or for investing in any undertaking engaged in such activities, FERA companies require RBI approval.

However, as mentioned earlier, foreign companies incorporated outside India are still required to obtain Reserve Bank permission for acting as agents in India of any company in trading or commercial transactions.

Repatriation

India permits repatriation of profits subject to a streamlined approval procedure, after payment of the applicable taxes for all approved investments other than in 22 consumer goods industries.[1] The remittance is to be made through an authorised dealer who will obtain clearance from the RBI for the payment.[2] In the 22 consumer goods industries, repatriation of profits needs to be covered by net foreign exchange earnings monitored over a period of seven years from the commencement of production. Balancing will not be required beyond this period. Reserve Bank approval is also required for repatriation of profits of branches of companies. Repatriation of capital is also allowed, subject to RBI approval. In order to speed up this process, the RBI has announced guidelines for disinvestment. For example, if the disinvestment of shares is effected through the stock exchange or a registered banker or broker, RBI approval of the disinvestment is near "automatic".

Intellectual property rights

Intellectual Property Rights (IPRs) in India are covered by comprehensive legislation relating to trade marks, patents, copyright and industrial designs. India is a member of the World Intellectual Property Organization and the Universal Copyright Convention, but is not a signatory to the Paris Convention or the Patent Cooperation Treaty.

It is argued in some quarters that the Indian Patents Act of 1970 constitutes a deterrent to FDI. The Act, while not discriminating between Indian and foreign nationals, does not allow for product patents in the case of substances intended for use in food, medicines or drugs, or for substances produced by chemical processes (such as alloys, semi-conductors, and inter-metallic compounds). In these cases, only process patents are granted, and the products can be legally copied if a different method of manufacture is employed. The duration of the patent is 5-7 years in the case of process patents for food, medicines and drugs, and 14 years for any other invention. However, in the survey of TNCs in India and the USA, rules regarding IPRs in India did not come up as an issue that deterred FDI. For example, of the total number of foreign collaborations approved between 1981-90, 11.7% were in the chemicals sector (including drugs and pharmaceutical), where the Indian patent regime is most rigid.

The signing of the Dunkel Draft, will result in a drastic change in Indian IPR regulations. However, its results are not visible as yet.

Approval Process
Foreign investment

The demise of permit raj has speeded up the investment process for domestic and foreign investors alike. The approving agency under the automatic approval scheme is the Reserve Bank of India. All foreign investment not falling under the automatic scheme is approved by the Foreign Investment Promotion Board (FIPB) in consultation with the concerned administrative ministry.

Automatic approval is granted for FDI up to 51% in the 34 identified high priority areas, provided foreign equity fully covers the cost of imported capital goods.[3] Approval is normally granted within 15 days.

There has been a remarkable decline in the time taken for approval. For example, M/s Gabriel applied for two technology collaborations. They received the approval for one in eight days and the other in eleven days, both by post. A Japanese company received approval in six days. Before liberalization, approval could take as much as two years.

For the non-automatic process, proposals are considered on a case-by-case basis by the FIPB. In this case, the Government tries to give clearance within 45 days. According to one estimate, the average time taken today for FIPB approval is 38 days.[4]

Technology collaboration

Automatic permission is granted by the Reserve Bank of India for foreign technology agreements in the 34 priority industries which provide for a lump sum payment up to Rs. 10 million and/or 5% royalty on domestic sales and 8% on exports, subject to a maximum total payment of 8% of sales over a 10 year period from the date of agreement or 7 years from commencement of production. Approval is also automatic even in industries outside the priority list, provided the same criteria as above are fulfilled. The approval in this case is accorded by the FIPB. For rates of royalty/lump sum payments higher than those described above, specific approval is required from the FIPB.

Some foreign collaborators feel that the prescribed royalty rates are too rigid, and are often unremunerative in the case of transfer of highly R&D-intensive technology. Higher royalty rates are seldom approved by the government.

Working Environment for Foreign-Invested Companies
Taxation

Foreign branches are taxed at a flat rate of 65% on branch incomes. A closely-held Indian company is taxed at 57.5% and widely held Indian company at 51.75% (including surcharge of 15% on the basic rate of 50% and 45% respectively).

Income of TNCs by way of dividends, interest, royalty and other technical know-how fee in India is subject to the following withholding tax rates :

	Dividend	Interest	Royalty/Tech. fee
Non-Treaty country	20%	20%	30%
Treaty country	10-25%	10-25%	10-30%

India has tax treaties for avoidance of double taxation of income with 37 countries. An Indian company is taxed on its world-wide income. A foreign company is taxed only on income that is received in India. Double taxation of foreign income is avoided by means of foreign tax credits.

Incentives

There are no exclusive incentives for foreign investment. Most manufacturing enterprises are allowed a 30% deduction in computing taxable profits for the first 10 years from the commencement of production. There is also full tax exemption for all export profits. 100% export oriented units and firms in Export Processing Zones are eligible for full tax exemption for a block of five years during the first eight years.

Financing

Transnational companies are now treated at a par with domestic companies in the matter of borrowing funds or raising deposits in India.

Duties

All new manufacturing investments or those where substantial expansion is occurring are eligible for concessional import duty on capital goods at 35%. Further concessions are available in sectors like electronics, textiles, leather etc. The duties on capital goods are only 15%

if an export obligation of 4 times the CIF value of imported equipment, to be fulfilled over a period of 5 years, is undertaken. These exports should be generated from the capital goods imported under the scheme.

Monopolies and Restrictive Trade Practices
The Monopolies and Restrictive Trade Practices (MRTP) Act has been significantly diluted under the new industrial policy. The law now aims at controlling only restrictive trade practices instead of the size of an enterprise. This is a major gain for FERA firms, most of whom, because of their size, required MRTP clearance in order to expand, relocate, diversify and so on.

Multilateral Investment Guarantee Agency
India does not provide any formal investment guarantee to foreign investors as yet. However, it has signed the MIGA convention, but this not yet been ratified. Very recently, the Finance Minister in Washington is reported to have said that India has ratified the MIGA Convention, and looks forward to participating in it as a full member.[5]

Exit Policy
'Exit Policy' is the most talked about issue in India these days. It is argued that since India does not have a meaningful exit policy, a potential investor is deterred since it reduces the flexibility of his over all operations.[6]

However, in our interviews with various TNCs operating in India, exit policy did not figure as an issue. Recent examples show that the workforce can be reduced, in spite of all the procedural hurdles. Indian Oxygen (in which British Oxygen has a 51% stake) has been able to down-size its workforce from 6000 to 2000 without any industrial unrest. Similarly, the Indian Tobacco Company has also reduced its workforce without any problems. The National Textile Corporation succeeded in laying off 40,000 workers as part of its rationalization drive, using state funds granted under the National Renewal Fund.

The possible reasons as to why exit policy did not figure as a prominent disincentive to foreign investment could be because: (a) It has been less of a problem to shed workers at a price above the legal minimum (15 days per year worked), as done by the Indian Tobacco Company; (b) foreign companies who have invested in India usually have a long-term perspective since India's potential market size would be very attractive for any investor. In other words, TNCs usually come to stay. They are therefore willing to and capable of absorbing losses if that is necessary in the short run. Pepsi, for example, has been running losses for the last 3 years. Yet, they are consolidating their investment in India and are confident that in the long run they will recoup their losses.

The above arguments pertain more to existing investors. It is conceivable that for potential investors, who are exploring alternative investment sites, the lack of an exit policy may prove to be a negative factor. But in field interviews in the USA with potential TNC investors the exit policy issue was not brought up by the firms, and they considered other factors such as infrastructure and red tape as more serious obstacles.

OPERATIONAL PROBLEMS AFFECTING FOREIGN INVESTMENT

Once a foreign investment proposal is approved, the company enters Indian ground where it is treated more or less on par with any Indian firm. It has therefore to grapple with the same operational problems that an Indian company faces.

The major problem in actual operations is that the policies and new attitudes are not filtering down fast enough to the functional level. 'Regulations are being abolished but it is difficult to get rid of regulators' was the succinct comment of one of the managers of a transnational company. Since liberalization is an on-going process and the policies are not always clear, administrators find it easy to interpret a policy announcement in any way they want to. Moreover, policy changes are announced so frequently that it is very difficult for investors to keep pace with or seek clarification on the changes.

Since the projects are actually implemented in the states, that is where the operational hurdles are faced. Apparently, there is little change in the attitude of bureaucracy at the state level, except in the case of some states. The view is that since approval at the center had become almost automatic, it had generated many new projects. As against this, there is scarcity of infrastructure like power, transport, telecommunication etc. in the states. The increased demand for these limited facilities has made state bureaucracy very powerful and increased their incentives for corruption. Even at the government level, states have sufficient powers to obstruct or delay the process; they are responsible for irrigation, water and power distribution, transport and sales tax. It is principally opposition from the states which is thwarting a unified value added tax. The central government is responsible for tax on production, but states have the right to raise taxes on sales as well as entry taxes. The states also bear the responsibility for the rules which make infrastructure companies somewhat reluctant to invest, despite their right to 100% equity in the power sector. It is the states for example which are loth to abandon subsidies on power supplies for farmers; a situation which means that commercial rates cannot be charged; moreover, power companies are hesitant because distribution is in the hands of the state governments that is, with the electricity boards.

In view of the rapidly changing economic scenario, a survey was conducted in India, the US and Germany to determine the perceptions of foreign investors about the Indian policy reforms pertaining to FDI. The purpose of the survey was to find out their motives, problems and suggestions to enhance FDI in India, which we will now briefly mention.

THE PERCEPTION ON LIBERALIZATION – SURVEY RESULTS

The economic reforms and liberalization of FDI policies were very much appreciated. It was mentioned that the liberalization process is moving in the right direction but they were sceptical about the continuation of this process. The reason for the uncertainty about continuation of the liberalization process is the weak government at the center. Although 'there is no threat to the political system, any change in government or elections will break the flow of the economic process'.

Another major complaint is that reforms are confined to the center only; they have not trickled down to the grass roots level where the action is. After getting an approval or registration at the center, the investors ultimately have to go to the site to implement the project. Then one has to acquire land, water, electricity etc; in short some 17 approvals are required before one can think of constructing the building for the plant. Excessive bureaucratic controls, red-tapism, adhocism still exist at the state level which delays the project implementation and its feasibility. A case in point is a firm which has been running on generators for the last one and a half years because of some trouble with the electricity department. This is a big trans-national company with branches all over the world. Such instances leave a bad impression on potential foreign investors. To remove or reduce the bureaucracy or red-tapism at the state level, government should issue comprehensive approval at the centre itself. This is possible if states have their representatives at the centre with the authority to issue all required approvals in one go. This will also create competition among states to attract FDI by giving fast approvals and better terms.

Another issue which bothers foreign investors is the labour relations/exit policy. There is no exit policy which makes investment in India more risky. Investors do not want to get trapped by starting a new venture. India needs labour intensive foreign investment to generate employment but without an exit policy, investors, especially small and medium firms abroad, are scared to go in for labour intensive ventures.

Most of the foreign investors have complained about India's tax rates, tax laws and their implementation. The corporate tax is higher than in other countries in Asia and tax laws are very complicated. There were also suggestions to further reduce interest rates and import tariffs. The government has already taken some steps towards these issues. Apart from the Patent Act, FERA regulations and infrastructure were also mentioned as problem areas which need reforms.

Remaining Barriers to Foreign Direct Investment

The lack of legal security is regarded as a continuing restraint both from the Foreign and the Indian positions. The Indian side made a special note that the bureaucracy does not keep up with political decisions, that decisions made at the top are too slow in trickling down, and that a high degree of corruption is to be found at all levels. The system of jurisprudence is viewed as too weak. The legal insecurity is fostered by frequent and abrupt changes in the law, with the promulgation of retroactive laws creating additional problems. Finally, a particular problem is that the enacted liberalization presently only applies to the Central government level, whereas the individual states of the union frequently apply other regulations.

It is interesting to note that large firms both in India and abroad give a somewhat less pessimistic assessment of the political situation and administrative inefficiency than the average. This difference is doubtless due to the fact that large firms are less affected by political turbulence and are in a better position to get their way with the administration than for smaller businesses. A differentiation according to industrial branches revealed no significant differences in assessing the political–administrative problems.

On the economic and labour-policy constraints more than half of the firms in the survey see labour impositions, foreign and domestic trade difficulties and foreign currency restrictions as important constraints that still exist.

With respect to labour policy – the key word being 'exit policy' – it is astonishing that survey participants with 50 to 70% did not respond even more negatively. Apart from the problem of not being able to order dismissals despite the necessity of rationalization, the survey participants especially criticized the fact that there are not laws with the help of which inefficiency can be reduced and the abuse of workers' rights can be curbed. The foreign firms strongly recommend that a controlled exit policy be introduced as soon as possible – being at the same time aware, of course, that the Indian government would like to address this problem but does not know how to cushion the negative social effects.

There is general criticism that India presently has a very complex tariff structure that business cannot fully comprehend. The import licensing system has certainly been liberalized to a great extent, but the negative list published by the government still contains about one third of all tariff provisions and leads to trade restrictions especially for road vehicles, electronic products and a number of chemicals and pharmaceuticals.

In addition, the Indian government still controls a major portion of foreign trade via state-owned firms and trade monopolies. A further restriction is that a domestic preference rate of up to 25% and in some cases even up to 40% is still being retained in public-sector procurement; this excludes foreign competition to a great extent.

With regard to domestic trade, a subject of special criticism is the antiquated system of the local octroi tax which very often leads to delays in deliveries and should thus be replaced by a more rational type of local taxation.

It is perhaps surprising that despite a substantial step towards full convertibility of the rupee nearly half of the firms still cite foreign currency restrictions as a barrier. The foreign firms especially, expressed the wish that the still-required individual foreign currency permits be eliminated for transfers from savings by foreigners and also for dividend transfers of portfolio investments; this should be replaced by a liberal, quasi-automatic procedure. Also criticized was the fact that the disinvestment regulation in cases of liquidation or sale of shares of a private limited company, in contrast to foreign participation in a public-sector enterprise, have still not been liberalized. Here the wish was expressed that all regulations that stand in the way of free selling of shares be removed.

Evidently of little importance for industry as a whole is government influence in determining the consumer price of a product. Only the pharmaceutical industry expressed a different opinion here, referring to the still-unchanged drug price regulation which today, as a result of the cost hikes of the past, has reduced the profits of Indian pharmaceutical companies to a minimum and which of course reduces new foreign investment in this area. A change of these price control regulations is evidently in preparation, and the industry is thus urging a quick introduction of this new legislation.

Environmental regulations and the still-existing restrictions of foreign investors' fields of activity are hardly viewed as barriers by firms, whereas these factors are regarded as restrictions by one third and one half of the Indian joint ventures respectively. In their view, the reservations of certain areas to small-scale industry still results in much 'forbidden territory' at the expense of efficiency. The foreign firms also wanted to see the number of industrial areas subject to licensing further reduced. Their proposals were that in contrast to current rulings, coal mining and mining in general, sugar production, wood processing and furniture manufacturing be freed from the licensing obligation. They also suggested that the eight industrial areas still reserved for the state be opened to the private sector; the only exceptions should be firms devoted to atomic energy and military purposes.

With regard to the question on barriers of an enterprise and economical nature, both Indian and foreign firms gave a nearly identical assessment of problems of a purely enterprise nature, such as personnel, labour productivity, supplies of intermediate products and spare parts. A comparatively small problem with 20 to 30% of the responding companies is the availability of qualified technical and commercial personnel.

However, nearly two thirds of the firms complained about low labour productivity and the often insufficient supplies of necessary intermediate products and spare parts – an aspect that is attributable to the already mentioned and still existing restrictions on foreign trade.

A highly negative response of between 50% and 75% was given to the inadequate supplies of external services, such as energy, water, transport, telecommunications and financing. Here it was obvious that a much more critical appraisal was given by the joint ventures already operating in India than by the parent companies – a fact that is certainly attributable to the daily experience and confrontation with the various infrastructural bottlenecks. The Indian government is of course aware of this problem, and many liberalization measures and tax incentives are specially aimed at removing some of these infra-structural bottlenecks through private initiative. Other areas, how-ever, such as the transport infrastructure and water supplies, are mat-ters for the state. But regardless of whether the state or the private sector are responsible, infrastructural improvements will only be noticeable in the medium or long term. A number of suggestions were made to make the areas of power generation and telecommuni-cations more attractive for foreign investors.

A specially problem complex is the taxation system which was addressed by the firms without having been specifically asked by the questionnaire. The Indian side pointed out the inadequacy of the taxa-tion system for a modern economy and the too high tax level. In order to make new firms more competitive in the first years of their existence, proposals have also been made for a five-year exemption of new investment from sales tax followed by a period of reduced tax rates.

Clear differences existed in the efficiency assessment of the finan-cial services available in India. In Germany nearly 30% of the firms indicated restrictions of this nature, but in the survey in India the share was nearly twice as high. Both sides criticized in particular, the high interest rates demanded by the banks, which in many cases offset the advantages of low wages. Also listed as detrimental were imprac-tical banking rules, insufficient support, the rebuffing demeanor of the banks in granting loans and the low efficiency of the state-run banks. A basic demand was the liberalization of the capital market, which the government also wants but has evidently not yet effectively implemented.

In the following sections, we will now discuss the views of some of the principal interest groups, namely businessmen and political par-ties, about the economic reforms taking place in India.

INDUSTRY AND LIBERALIZATION – 'THE BOMBAY CLUB'

A select group of India's top businessmen met in Bombay, ostensibly to review the country's economic reforms. The major complaint of industrialists is that reforms have proceeded haphazardly and they have not been given a level playing field compared to foreign companies. Their major objections are that the government should have begun with internal reform and then invited TNCs. Bad infrastructure, inadequate level of operating capital, high rates of taxation and a wasteful public sector have dulled domestic competition.

- Indian promoters cannot thwart takeovers as banks do not give funds against their holdings. Companies are not allowed to buy back shares, and foreign companies can take a majority stake at low prices.
- Import tariffs have been reduced without commensurate reduction in excise duties and sales tax. The result is dumping of goods in some areas. The Commerce Ministry takes six months to act on complaints.
- Foreign companies can obtain credit at 5-6 per cent abroad while Indian pay at 15 per cent or more.
- Foreign investment attracts 10 per cent lower capital gains tax: 30 per cent for short and 10 per cent for long term. Indian get 40 and 20.
- There is a lot of fragmentation in each market segment. Companies are not allowed to consolidate or close down a manufacturing plant leading to inefficient function of the unit.

Some of these objections seem valid and deserve consideration.

But as in any major change there are initial problems. It takes time to settle down. As far as their view that internal changes should come first is concerned, the government argues that it has brought about changes against the looming foreign exchange crisis and that there was no time to carry out internal reforms. India had reached a point where no one would have lent two dollars for 10 minutes. With regard to the unfair import duties and dumping of goods, there has been hardly any instance where industry has been hit by cheaper imports and moreover it takes time to identify and take decision against goods dumped. As far as the availability of cheap credit for foreign companies abroad is concerned, Indian companies have been allowed to raise capital abroad. Foreign companies who bring in money also have to bear exchange risk. For unfair incentives on lower capital gains tax, if India wants to attract FDI, these incentives seems necessary because of high domestic tax rates and that other countries give better incentives. The revenue consideration prevents similar treatment to domestic companies. Lastly an exit policy is in the making, but large scale closures will fuel political and labour unrest.

POLITICS AND LIBERALIZATION

The process to get political legitimacy for the new reforms is very complex. Swadeshi (Be Indian Buy Indian)! It had a magic appeal. Indian protest against foreign rulers found a symbol in the boycott of imported goods before independence. Today, in its second incarnation, the fervour is dampened and the magic seems to be lost. Swadeshi is now more a symbol of political parties, industrialists and academics to suit their protest against the opening up of the economy. The political parties like the Bhartiya Janata Party (BJP) and Communist Party of India (Marxist) have been protesting for a long time. The BJP which had liberalization on its agenda, has suddenly turned around after the success of Congress's liberalization package. CPI (M) has always been against opening of the economy to foreign investors.

The recent economic reforms are not smooth sailing for the government. Facing the reality of a bankrupt economy, ramshackle infrastructure and a highly sheltered and controlled industry that just cannot face the pressures of globalization, has made sections of people jittery. Even in the ruling party there was a growing undercurrent of resistance to these reforms – a phenomenon that could have gained momentum, had there been a short term fall out of these reforms. However, the gains from these reforms over the last three years have subdued but not eliminated this resentment. This dissention in the ruling party has resulted in the reviving of the 'socialist forum' within the party, alleging the straying of the party from 'the sacred path' of building a 'socialistic society' – a path laid down by Jawaharlal Nehru. To address this concern, the government included pages in the industrial policy statement directed not so much at the Indian public, but at its own party cadres which tried to convince the sceptics within the Congress (I) that reforms were supposedly based on Nehru's own thinking.

The inner-party conflicts on economic philosophy and economic policy permeates all of India's political parties today. On many occasions the ideology of the politicians somersaults with time and opportunity. For example, the same Chandra Shekhar who had publicly campaigned against Ajit Singh's attempt to liberalise India's industrial policy, became a liberaliser himself on assuming the past of the Prime Minister. Similarly V.P. Singh as a Finance Minister who initiated the liberalization process in Rajiv Gandhi's regime, stalled the process when he became the Prime Minister himself. This was because he was taking support from the Communist Party for his government.

The so-called disciplined Bhartiya Janata Party (BJP) has at least three types of economic thinking within. There are those in the BJP like Viren Shah, Jaswant Singh and M.L. Sondhi who have publicly taken a modernizing market position and are not fearful of globalizing India's economy. Then, there are those like K.R. Malkani, who have deep socialistic roots going back to the days of a Marxist commune in Punjab. This group which tends to be more worried about market failure and inequality, do not see much good in privatising the public sector and are suspicious of opening up the economy to foreign investments. And then, there is the growing influence of integral humanism of Deendayal Upadhaya on the younger cadres of RSS backgrounds – a force led by Govindacharya who are campaigning for the Swadeshi Movement.

The CPI (M) is going all out to defeat the present economic policies. Their method is strikes in banks, against exit policy and against privatisation of public sector units. While Janata Dal is yet to formalise its position on liberalization, its stand so far is restricted to opposing entry of TNCs like Cargill, Pepsi and Coke.

The most protectionist party is the RSS-BJP combine. The BJP is preparing lists of what constitutes Swadeshi products and educating people on why they should not buy foreign goods. That erstwhile 'Swadeshi' companies like Hindustan Lever and TOMCO have now moved to the foreign list complicates matters. The implementation of their plans looks impossible because of so many complicated and conflicting views.

The implication of these contradictions within India's political parties is that if the going gets tough with short run inflation and some uncertainties on the labour front, the vested interests who have benefited from the license-control-quota raj may combine with the socialistic faction within the ruling party to create hurdles in the liberalization process.

CONCLUDING REMARKS

The attitude towards foreign capital in India has traditionally been one of suspicion, an inheritance from her colonial past. This has, however, not always been reflected in the government's policies on foreign investment. These have been changing from time to time. Hence the need to look at these in a historical perspective.

The policies and measures taken prior to July 1991, reveal the government's apprehensions about foreign investment for e.g. FERA, MRTP Act etc. But these were characterized by a number of loopholes and were not very effective in implementation. It is also obvious that the government believed in the necessity of foreign investment for the country's economic development.

After an initial enthusiastic response to the economic reforms, industrialists are now raising various objections, witness the Bombay Club, which is raising strong objections on grounds of being exposed to unfair competition from foreign firms. But except for some sections, on the whole the business community welcomes these reforms.

Political parties like the BJP and the CPI(M) have been protesting against the reforms for a long time. The BJP which had liberalization on its agenda is now talking about 'Swadeshi' and a level playing field for Indian firms. Even within the ruling party, there are dissenting voices.

Despite these hurdles, India has managed to transform its image as an investment target and money is pouring in. This would not have happened without the timely reforms in July 1991. The government took advantage of a favourable political situation, which was caused by very serious economic problems. The attitudes of major interest groups changes, which made it easier for government to justify its liberalization policy and also implement it. This conclusion is in accordance with the analysis made in Chapter 5 of the situation before 1991, when such a situation was not at hand (see also Jansson & Sharma, 1993). From the changes that have taken place since 1991, it seems reasonable to assume that the government–TNC network focused on the central government bureaucracy will gradually be refocused on the state government bureaucracy. But the many uncertainties still prevailing in the implementation of the liberalization policy would most certainly caution the TNCs against dismantling the well-established relationships with the central government bureaucracy. One may also assume that the recent changes have made technical legitimacy increasingly more important and institutional legitimacy less important for the TNCs.

The new reforms benefit India. The country no longer needs IMF aid, and it is paying off the 1991 loan ahead of schedule. Exports have grown at 21% in U.S. dollar terms in the present fiscal year. The rupee has been made convertible in trade and invisibles. Tariffs have been cut drastically. This is only a beginning and if the reforms really fructify, India can become a major player in the global economic scene.

NOTES

1. These are: manufacture of food and food products, manufacture of dairy products, grain mill products, manufacture of bakery products, manufacture and refining of sugar (vacuum pan sugar factories), production of common salt, manufacture of hydrogenated oil (vanaspati), tea processing, coffee, manufacture of beverages, tobacco and tobacco-products, distilling, rectifying and blending of spirits, wine industries, malt liquors and malt, production of country liquors and toddy, soft drinks and carbonated water industry, manufacture of cigars, cigarettes, cheroot & cigarette tobacco, manufacture of wood and wood products, furniture and fixtures, manufacture of leather and leather and fur products, tanning, curing, finishing, embossing and japanning of leather, manufacture of footwear (excluding repair) except vulcanized or moulded rubber or plastic wear, manufacture of footwear made primarily of vulcanized or moulded products, prophylactics (rubber contraceptive), motor cars, entertainment electronics (VCRs, Color TVs, CD Players, Tape recorders), white goods (domestic refrigerators, domestic dishwashing machines, programmable domestic washing machines, microwave ovens, airconditioners).
2. Prior to April 1993, only FERA companies were required to obtain RBI approval for repatriation. Since April the procedure, albeit streamlined, has been made equally applicable to FERA as well as non-FERA companies.
3. The listing of industries was made more transparent via a Press Note issued on June 24, 1992, which detailed all the sectors as well as subsectors under the Harmonized System of Classification.
4. According to one senior official just retired from Government.
5. Observer of Business and Politics, September 30, 1993.
6. What people usually have in mind are the barriers to reducing the work force. The recent Goswami Committee Report on Industrial Restructuring mentions that it is not the labour force but state governments which create obstacles in the way of private sector restructuring.

Bibliography

Anderson, B. and Carlos, M.L. (1976), 'What is a Social Network Theory?' in T. Burns and W. Buckley (eds.) *Power and Control. Social Structures and Their Transformation,* Beverly Hills: Sage, pp. 27-51.

Alexander, S. and Ruderman, M. (1987), 'The Role of Procedural Justice and Distributive Justice in Organizational Behaviour', *Social Justice Research,* 1, pp. 177-198.

Aldrich, H.E. (1979), *Organizations and Environment,* Englewood Cliffs, N.J.: Prentice Hall.

Aldrich, H. and Whetten, D.A., (1981), 'Organization-sets, Action-sets, and Networks: Making the Most of Simplicity', in P. Nyström and W.H. Starbuck (eds.), *Handbook of Organizational Design,* Vol. 1, New York: Oxford University Press, chap. 17.

Ansoff, H.I. (1965), 'The Firm of the Future', *Harvard Business Review,* September-October.

Austin, J.E. (1990), *Managing in Developing Countries. Strategic Analysis and Operating Techniques,* New York: The Free Press.

Bales, H.E. (1990), 'International Investment Policy: A View From the Private Sector', in C.D. Wallace (ed.), *Foreign Direct Investment in the 1990s,* Dordrecht: Martinus Nijhoff Publishers, pp. 61-84.

Banerji, R. (1975), *Export of Manufactures from India,* Tubingen: J.C.B. Mohr.

Barnet, R.J. and Muller, R.E. (1974), *Global Reach: The Power of the Multinational Corporations,* New York: Simon and Schuster.

Barney, J.B. and Ouchi, W.G. (1986), *Organizational Economics. Towards a New Paradigm for Understanding and Studying Organizations,* San Francisco: Jossey-Bass.

Bartlett, C. (1986), 'Building and Managing the Transnational: The New Organizational Challenge', in M. Porter (ed.), *Competition in Global Industries,* Boston, Mass: Harvard Business School Press, pp. 367-401.

Bartlett, C. and Ghoshal, S. (1989), *Managing Across Borders: The Transnational Solution,* Boston, Mass: The Free Press.

Bartlett, C.A., Doz Y. and Hedlund, G. (eds.) (1989), *Managing the*

233

Global Firm, London/New York: Routledge.

Benson, J.K. (1975), 'The Interorganizational Network as a Political Economy', *Administrative Science Quarterly*, 20, pp. 229-249.

Behrman, J. and Grosse, R. (1991), *TNCs and Host Governments.*

Bhagavan, M. (1987), 'A Critique of India's Economic Policies and Strategies', *Monthly Review*, July-August, pp. 56-79.

Bhagavan, M. (1988), 'India's Industrial and Technological Policies into the Late 1980s', *Journal of Contemporary Asia.*

Birgersson, B.O. and Westerståhl, J. (1978), *Den svenska folkstyrelsen,* Stockholm: Publica.

Blau, P. (1964), *Exchange and Power in Social Life,* New York: Wiley.

Business India.

Boddewyn, J.J. (1988), 'Political Aspects of MNE Theory', *Journal of International Business Studies*, 19, No. 3, pp. 341-363.

Brewer, T.L. (1992), 'An Issue-Area Approach to the Analysis of MNE-Government Relations', *Journal of International Business Studies,* 23, No. 2, pp. 295-309.

Brunsson, N. and Jönsson, S. (1979), *Beslut och handling,* Stockholm: Liber.

Brunsson, N. (1986), 'Organizing for Inconsistencies: On Organizational Conflict, Depression, and Hypocrisy as Substitutes for Action', *Scandinavian Journal of Management Studies*, May, pp. 165-185.

Brunsson, N. (1987), 'Industrial Policy as Implementation or Legitimation', in R. Wolf (ed.), *Organizing Industrial Development,* Berlin: De Gruyter, pp. 137-156.

Brunsson, N. (1989), *The Organization of Hypocrisy*, Chichester: Wiley.

Carzo, R. and Yanouzas, J.N. (1969), 'Effects of Flat and Tall Organizational Structure', *Administrative Science Quarterly*, pp. 178-191.

Cavusgil, T. (1980), 'On the Internationalization Process of Firms', *European Research*, 8, No. 6, pp. 273- 281.

Caves, R.E. (1982), *Multinational Enterprise and Economic Analysis*, Cambridge, Mass: Cambridge University Press.

Chandler, A. (1962), *Strategy and Structure. Chapters in the History of the Industrial Enterprise*, Cambridge, Mass: MIT Press.

Cipriani, R. (1987), 'The Sociology of Legitimation: An Introduction', *Current Sociology*, 35, No. 2, pp. 1-20.

Cook, K.S. and Emerson, R.M. (1984), 'Exchange Networks and the

Analysis of Complex Organizations', *Research in the Sociology of Organizations*, 3, pp. 1-30.

Crozier, M. (1964), The Bureacratic Phenomena, Chicago: University of Chicago Press.

Denzin, N.K. (1978), *The Research Act*.

Dagens Industry, 1992, 30 Sept. 1992, p. 8.

Daft, R. and Lengel, R. (1984), 'Organizational Information Requirements, Media Richness, and Structural Design', *Management Science*, 6, pp. 367-422.

Doz, Y. (1986), 'Government Policies and Global Industries' in M. Porter (ed.), *Competition in Global Industries*, Boston, Mass: Harvard Business School Press, pp. 225-266.

Doz, Y. and Prahalad, C. (1981), 'How MNCs Cope with Government Intervention', *Harvard Business Review*, pp. 149-157.

Dunning, J.H. (1988), *Explaining International Production*, London: Unwin and Hyman.

Dunning, J.H. (1988b), *Course Curriculum. Transnational Corporations and Economic Development*, 2nd ed., New York: UNCTC.

Economist (1991), 'India Survey', 4th May, pp. 1-18, and various versions.

Encarnation, D.J. and Vachani, S. (1985), 'Foreign Ownership: When Hosts Change the Rules', *Harvard Business Review*, September-October, pp. 152-160.

Encarnation, D.J. and Wells, L.T. (1986), 'Competitive Strategies in Global Industries: A View from Host Governments', in M. Porter (ed.), *Competition in Global Industries*, Boston, Mass: Harvard Business School Press, pp. 277-290.

Ellis, N.C. (1990), 'Foreign Direct Investment and Capital Flows to Third World Nations: U.S. Policy Considerations', in C.D. Wallace (ed.), Foreign Direct Investment in the 1990s, Dordrecht: Martinus Nijhoff Publishers.

Far Eastern Economic Review (1992), 12 Nov. and various issues.

Financial Times (1986), May 12. and various issues.

Forsgren, M. and Pahlberg, C. (1991), 'Managing International Networks', *IMP Conference Paper*, Department of Business Studies, Uppsala University.

Forsgren, M. and Holm, U. (1991), 'Multi-Centre Structure and Location of Divisional Management in Swedish International Firms' in H. Westergaard (ed.), *An Enlarged Europe in the Global Economy*, Proceedings of the 17th Annual Conference, December 15-17, Copenhagen, pp. 187-205.

Fox, A. (1974), *Beyond Contract: Work, Power, and Trust Relations*, London: Faber & Faber.

Franko, L.G. (1976), *The European Multinationals. A Renewed Challenge to American and British Big Business,* London: Harper & Row.

Frankena, M. (1972), 'Restrictions on Exports by Foreign Investors. The Case of India', *Journal of World Trade Law*, pp. 572-592.

Ghoshal, S. and Bartlett, C.A. (1990), 'The Multinational Corporation as an Interorganizational Network', *Academy of Management Review*, 15, No. 4, pp. 603-625.

Glaser, B.G. (1978), *Theoretical Sensitivity*, San Francisco: Sociology Press.

Glaser, B.G. and Strauss, A.L. (1967), *The Discovery of Grounded Theory. Strategies for Qualitative Research*, Chicago: Aldine.

Galbraith, J.R and Nathanson, D.A. (1978), *Strategy Implementation: The Role of Structure and Process*, St. Paul, Minn.: West.

Gladwin, T.N. and Walter, I. (1980), *Multinationals Under Fire: Lessons From Conflict Management*, New York: Wiley.

Government of India (1956), *Second Five Year Plan*, New Delhi.

Granovetter, M. (1973), 'The Strength of Weak Ties', *American Journal of Sociology*, 78, pp. 1360-1380.

Granovetter, M. (1982), 'The Strength of Weak Ties. A Network Theory Revisited', in P.V. Marsden and N. Lin (eds.), *Social Structure and Network Analysis*, Beverly Hills: Sage, pp. 105-130.

Grosse, R. and Aramburú, D. (1989), 'A Bargaining View of Government/MNE Relations: The Latin American Case', *International Business and Banking Discussion Paper Series 89-1*, University of Miami, Fla.

Gupta, A.K. and Govindarajan, V. (1991), 'Knowledge Flows and the Structure of Control Within Multinational Corporations', *Academy of Management Review*, 16, No. 4, pp. 768-792.

Hall, R.H. *et al.* (1977), 'Patterns of Interorganizational Relationships', *Administrative Science Quarterly*, 22, pp. 457-471.

Hedlund, G. (1986), 'The Hypermodern MNC – A Heterarchy?', *Human Resource Management*, 25, 1, pp. 9-35.

Hedlund, G. and Åhman, P. (1984), *Managing Relationships with Foreign Subsidiaries. Organization and Control in Swedish MNCs,* Stockholm: Sveriges Mekanförbund.

Hofstede, G.H. (1980), Culture's Consequences, Beverly Hills: Sage.

Hymer, S. (1976), *The International Operations of National Firms*, Cambridge, Mass: MIT Press.

IMF Survey, in *The Economist,* 1992, July 20.

India Today (1991), Addressing the Real Issues, 31st May, pp. 66-69.

Jacbsson, B. (1989), Konsten att reagera, Stockholm: Calssons.

Jansson, H. (1982), *Interfirm Linkages in a Developing Economy. The Case of Swedish Firms in India.* Acta Universitatis Upsaliensies, Studia Oeconomiae Negotiorum 14, Almqvist and Wiksell, Uppsala

Jansson, H. (1986), 'Purchasing Strategies of Transnational Corporations in Import Substitution Countries', in T. Cavusgil (ed.), *Advances in International Marketing,* Volume 1, Greenwich, Conn: JAI Press.

Jansson, H. (1994a), *Transnational Corporations in Southeast Asia. An Institutional Approach to Industrial Organization,* New Horizons in International Business, P. Buckley (ed.), Aldershot: Edward Elgar.

Jansson, H. (1994b), *Industrial Products. A Guide to the International Marketing Economics Model,* Binghamton, New York: Haworth Press.

Jansson, H. and Sharma, D.D. (1993), 'Industrial Policy Liberalization and TNCS: The Indian Experience', *Scandinavian Journal of Management,* 9, pp.129-143.

Johanson, J. and Vahlne, J-E. (1977), 'The Internationalization of the Firm – A Model of Knowledge Development and Increasing Market Commitment', *Journal of International Business Studies,* Spring-Summer, pp. 23-32.

Johanson, J. and Wiedersheim-Paul, F. (1975), 'The Internationalization of the Firm – Four Swedish Cases', *Journal of Management Studies,* 12, pp. 305-322.

Johnson, C. (1984), 'The Industrial Policy Debate Reexamined', *California Management Review,* 27, No. 1, pp. 71-89.

Johnson, C. (1985), 'The Institutional Foundations of Japanese Industrial Policy', *California Management Review,* 27, No. 4, pp. 59-69.

Kakar, S. (1971), 'Authority Patterns and Subordinate Behaviour in Indian Organizations', *Administrative Science Quarterly,* 16, No. 3, pp. 298-307.

Karlsson, A. (1991), *Om Strategi och legitimitet,* Lund: Lund University Press (dissertation).

Kindleberger, C.P. (1969), *American Business Abroad,* New Haven: Yale University Press.

Kline, John M. (1985), *International Codes and Multinational Business,* Greenwood, pp. 76-85.

Knoke, D. and Kuklinski, J.H. (1982), 'Network Analysis', *Quantitative Applications in the Social Sciences:* 28, Beverly Hills: Sage.

Lall, S. (1978), 'Transnationals, Domestic Enterprises, and Industrial Structure in Host LDCs', *Oxford Economic Papers*, pp. 219-248.

Larsson, T. (1986), 'Att vara riksdagsledamot', in *Folkets främsta företrädare*, Stockholm, SOU, 1986:27.

Lecraw, D. and Morrison, A.J. (1991), 'Transnational Corporation – Host Country Relations: A Framework for Analysis', Essays in *International Business*, No. 9, The University of South Carolina.

Maurer, J.G. (1971), *Readings in Organization Theory: Open Systems Approaches,* New York: Random House.

McNeil, I.R. (1974), 'The Many Futures of Contracts', *Southern California Law Review*, 47, No. 3, pp. 691-816.

Mahini, A. (1988), *Making Decisions in Multinational Corporations*, New York:

Mahini, A. and Wells, L.T. (1986), 'Government Relations in the Global Firm', in M. Porter (ed.), *Competition in Global Industries*, Boston, Mass: Harvard Business School Press, pp. 291-312.

Martinez, J.I. and Jarillo, J.C. (1991), 'Coordination Demands of International Strategies', *Journal of International Business Studies*, 22, No. 3, pp. 429-444.

Meyer, J.W. and Rowan, B. (1977), 'Institutionalized Environments: Formal Structure as Myth and Ceremony', *American Journal of Sociology*, 83, no. 2, pp. 340-363.

Meyer, J.W. and Scott, W.R. (1983), *Organizational Environments. Ritual and Rationality*, Beverly Hills: Sage.

Miller, K.D. (1992), 'A Framework for Integrated Risk Management in International Business', *Journal of International Business Studies*, 23, pp. 311-332.

Mintzberg, H. (1978), 'Patterns in Strategy Formation', *Management Science*, 24, No. 9, pp. 934-948.

Mintzberg, H. (1987), 'Crafting Strategy', *Harvard Business Review*, No. 4, pp. 66-75.

Mintzberg, H. and Waters, J.A. (1985), 'Of Strategies, Deliberate and Emergent', *Strategic Management Journal,* 6, pp. 257-272.

Myrdal, G. (1968), *Asian Drama – An Inquiry into the Poverty of Nations*, Vol. I-III, New York: Twentieth Century Fund.

Negandhi, A and Palia, A.P. (1988), 'The Changing Multinational Corporation-Nation State's Relationship: The Case of IBM in India', *Asia Pacific Journal of Management*, 6, No. 1, pp. 15-38.

Oliver, C. (1990), 'Determinants of Interorganizational Relationships:

Integration and Future Directions', *Academy of Management Review*, 15, No. 2, pp. 241-265.

Olsen, J.P. (1983), *Organized Democracy, Political Institutions in a Welfare State: The Case of Norway*, Bergen: Universitetsforlaget.

Orton, J.D. and Weick, K.E. (1990), 'Loosely Coupled Systems: A Reconceptualization', *Academy of Management Review*, 15, No. 2, pp. 203-223.

Paulson, S.K. (1985), 'A Paradigm for the Analysis of International Networks', *Social Networks*, 7, pp. 105- 126.

Penrose, E.T. (1966), *The Theory of the Growth of the Firm*, Oxford: Blackwell.

Perrow, C. (1984), *Normal Accidents: Living With High Risk Technologies*, New York: Basic Books.

Perrow, C. (1986), *Complex Organizations. A Critical Essay*, New York: Random House.

Pinelo, A.J. (1973), *The Multinational Corporation as a Force in Latin-American Politics: A Case Study of International Petroleum Company in Peru*, New York: Praeger.

Pfeffer, J. (1978), *Organizational Design*, Arlington Heights, Ill.: AHM.

Pfeffer, J. (1981), *Power in Organizations,* Marshfield, MA: Pitman.

Pfeffer, J. and Salancik, G.R. (1978), *The External Control of Organizations – A Resource Dependence Perspective*, New York: Harper & Row.

Porter, M. (1986), 'Competition in Global Industries: A Conceptual Framework', in M. Porter (ed.), *Competition in Global Industries*, Boston, Mass: Harvard Business School Press, pp. 15-60.

Poynter, T.A. (1982), 'Government Interaction in Less Developed Countries: The Experience of Multinational Companies', *Journal of International Business*, vol. XIII, No. 4, pp. 9-29.

Poynter, T.A. (1986), 'Managing Government Intervention: A Strategy for Defending the Subsidiary', *Columbia Journal of World Business*, Winter, pp. 55-65.

Poynter, T.A. (1985), 'Strategic Responses to Government Intervention in Developing Countries', in T.L. Brewer (ed.), *Political Risk in International Business: New Directions for Research, Management and Public Policy*, New York: Praeger.

Prahalad, C.K. and Doz, Y. (1987), *The Multinational Mission. Balancing Local Demands and Global Vision*, New York: The Free Press.

Pye, L.W. (1985), *Asian Power and Politics. The Cultural*

Dimensions of Authority, Cambridge: Belknap Press.

Robock, S.H. and Simmonds, K. (1989), *International Business and Multinational Enterprises*, Homewood, Ill.: Irwin.

Sarathy, R. and Samuel, R. (1987), 'Corporate Response to Industrial Policy', *International Marketing Review*, Summer, pp. 33-46

Schnelberg, M. (1986), 'Interorganizational Networks and the Problem of Governance', *Draft*.

Scott, R.M. (1983), 'The Organization of Environments: Network, Cultural, and Historical Elements', in J.W. Meyer and W.R Scott, *Organizational Environments. Ritual and Rationality*, Beverly Hills: Sage, pp. 155- 178.

Scott, W.R. (1981), *Organizations. Rational, Natural, and Open Systems*, Prentice-Hall, Englewood Cliffs, N.J.

Scott, W.R. (1987), 'The Adolescence of Institutional Theory', *Administrative Science Quarterly*, 32, pp. 493-511.

Scott, W.R. and Meyer, J.W. (1983), 'The Organization of Societal Sectors' in J.W. Meyer and W.R. Scott, *Organizational Environments. Ritual and Rationality*, Beverly Hills: Sage, pp. 129-153.

Selznick, P. (1948), 'Foundations of a Theory of Organizations', *American Sociological Review*, 13, pp. 25-35.

Selznick, P. (1965), *Leadership in Administration*, New York: Harper & Row.

Sharma, D.D. and Jansson, H. (1993), 'In Quest of Legitimacy Government–TNC Network Relationships', paper presented at the Annual EIBA Conference, Copenhagen, December.

Singh, J., Tucker, D.J. and House, R.J. (1986), 'Organizational Legitimacy and the Liability of Newness', *Administrative Science Quarterly*, 12, pp. 447-470.

Staw, B.M. and Ross, J. (1980),'Commitment in an Experimenting Society: An Experiment on the Attribution of Leadership from Administrative Scenario', *Journal of Applied Psychology*, 65, pp. 249-260.

Stopford, J.M. and Wells, L.T. (1972), *Managing the Multinational Enterprise*, New York: Basic Books.

Stopford, J. and Strange, S. (1991), *Rival States, Rival Firms*, London: Cambridge University Press.

Steiner, G.A. and Steiner, J.F. (1988), *Business Government and Society*, New York: Random House.

Stokman, F.N., Ziegler, R. and Scott, J. (1985), *Networks of Corporate Power*, Glasgow.

Strauss, A.L. (1987), *Qualitative Analysis for Social Scientists*,

Cambridge, Mass.: Cambridge University Press.

Tichy, N. and Fombrun, C. (1979), 'Network Analysis in Organizational Settings', *Human Relations*, 32, No. 11, pp. 923-965.

Thibaut, J. and Walker, L. (1978), 'A Theory of Procedure', *California Law Review*, 66, pp. 541-566.

Thompson, J.D. (1967), *Organizations in Action*, New York: McGraw Hill.

Thompson, J.D. and Tuden, A. (1959), 'Strategies, Structures, and Processes of Organizational Decisions', in J.D. Thompson *et al.* (eds), *Comparative Studies in Administration*, Pittsburgh: University of Pittsburgh, pp. 195-216.

Thompson, J. and McEwen, W. (1958), 'Organizational Goals and Environment: Goal Setting as an Interaction Process', *American Sociological Rewiew*, 23, pp. 23-31.

UNCTAD (1971), *Restrictive Business Practices*, Document No. TD/122, Geneva.

US Department of Commerce (1988), 'Direct Investment Update', *Staff Report*, Investment Research Division, International Trade Administration, Washington.

Vernon, R. (1971), *Sovereignty at Bay,* London: Longman.

Wallace, C.D. (ed.) (1990), *Foreign Direct Investment in the 1990s*, Dordrecht, The Netherlands: Martinus Nijhoff Publishers, pp. 61-84.

Weber, M. (1947), *The Theory of the Social and Economic Organization*, New York: Oxford University Press.

Weick, K. (1969), *The Social Psychology of Organizing*, Reading, Mass: Addision Wesley.

Weinberger, M.W. (1988), 'The Political Education of Bob Malott, CEO', *Harvard Business Review*, May-June, pp. 74-81.

Wilkes, S. and Wright, M. (eds.) (1987), *Comparative Government–Industry Relations: Western Europe, United States and Japan*, Oxford:

Williamson, O.E. (1985), *The Economic Institutions of Capitalism. Firms, Markets, Relational Contracting*, New York: The Free Press.

Yin, R.K. (1989), *Case Study Research: Design and Methods*, Beverly Hills: Sage.

Yoffie, D.V. (1988), 'How An Industry Builds Political Advantage', *Harvard Business Review*, May-June, pp. 82-91.

Zucker, L.G. (1983), 'Organizations as Institutions', in S.B. Bacharach (ed), *Perspectives in Organizational Sociology: Theory and Research*, 2, Greenwich, Conn: JAI Press.

Index

strategic management, 15
strategic profile, 184-85
structured mode, 15
structured network, 155
subsidiaries of TNCs, 3
subsidiary level contacts, 89
supplier network, 179
survey results, 74, 130
Swedish industry study, 3
Swedish parliament, 114
Swedish respondents, 75
Swedish TNCs, 74

taxi service, 86
technical legitimacy, 6l, 79, 81
Thailand, 77
Thompson, J.D. 57
Thompson, J.D. & Tuden, A. 114
Tichy, N. & Fombrun, C. 53
tie-up strategy, 179
tightly coupled network, 154-55
TNCs, 3, 9, 40, 92, 100, 178
TNC–government interaction, 8, 15,
    44, 76, 107
TNC–government network, 12, 39,
    46, 50, 109, 149
TNC nationality, 74-5, 103
TNC perspective, 22
transaction cost theory, 31, 79
transorganization network, 32, 48,
    123, 146
types of control, 146-48, 157
types of linkages, 39, 45

Wallace, C.D. 20
way of legitimacy, 119
Weberian bureaucracy, 62
Weick, K.E. 73, 96, 119
Wilkes, T.S. & Wright, M. 22
Williamson, O.E. 53
World Bank, 5

Vernon, R. 13-14, 43
Vietnam, 2

Zero-sum game, 14